THE

EVERYTHING®

PERSONAL FINANCE IN YOUR 20s AND 30s BOOK, 3RD EDITION

Dear Reader,

Today, young Americans are facing extremely tough financial times. Unemployment rates are stubbornly high, the cost of gasoline, food, shelter, medical care, and insurance continues to climb, and saving for the future has become exceedingly difficult. It is more important than ever to become financially educated so that you don't get sucked into the vortex of debt, paying way too long and way too much for things you don't even need.

In this book, it is my intention to give you the appropriate financial guidance in words you can understand so you feel empowered to navigate successfully through your financial future. Nothing happens without a plan, and it is my sincere hope that you can use the concepts in this book as a blueprint for your own success. Good luck!

Howard Davidoff

Welcome to the EVERYTHING® Series!

These handy, accessible books give you all you need to tackle a difficult project, gain a new hobby, comprehend a fascinating topic, prepare for an exam, or even brush up on something you learned back in school but have since forgotten.

You can choose to read an Everything® book from cover to cover or just pick out the information you want from our four useful boxes: e-questions, e-facts, e-alerts, and e-ssentials.

We give you everything you need to know on the subject, but throw in a lot of fun stuff along the way, too.

We now have more than 400 Everything® books in print, spanning such wide-ranging categories as weddings, pregnancy, cooking, music instruction, foreign language, crafts, pets, New Age, and so much more. When you're done reading them all, you can finally say you know Everything®!

QUESTION

Answers to common questions

FACT

Important snippets of information

ALERT

Urgent warnings

ESSENTIAL

Quick handy tips

PUBLISHER Karen Cooper

MANAGING EDITOR, EVERYTHING® SERIES Lisa Laing

COPY CHIEF Casey Ebert

ASSISTANT PRODUCTION EDITOR Melanie Cordova

ACQUISITIONS EDITOR Kate Powers

ASSOCIATE DEVELOPMENT EDITOR Eileen Mullan

SENIOR DEVELOPMENT EDITOR Brett Palana-Shanahan

EDITORIAL ASSISTANT Matthew Kane

EVERYTHING® SERIES COVER DESIGNER Erin Alexander

LAYOUT DESIGNERS Erin Dawson, Michelle Roy Kelly, Elisabeth Lariviere

Visit the entire Everything® series at *www.everything.com*

THE
EVERYTHING®
PERSONAL FINANCE
IN YOUR 20s AND 30s BOOK
3RD EDITION

Eliminate your debt, manage your money, and build
for an exciting financial future

Howard Davidoff, JD, CPA, LLM

Avon, Massachusetts

An Everything® Series Book.
Everything® and everything.com® are registered trademarks of F+W Media, Inc.

Published by Adams Media, a division of F+W Media, Inc.
57 Littlefield Street, Avon, MA 02322 U.S.A.
www.adamsmedia.com

ISBN 10: 1-4405-4256-2
ISBN 13: 978-1-4405-4256-5
eISBN 10: 1-4405-4272-4
eISBN 13: 978-1-4405-4272-5

Printed in the United States of America.

10 9 8 7 6 5 4 3 2 1

Library of Congress Cataloging-in-Publication Data
Davidoff, Howard.
 The everything personal finance in your 20s and 30s book / Howard Davidoff. – 3rd ed.
   p. cm. – (The Everything series)
 Rev. ed. of: The everything personal finance in your 20s & 30s book : erase your debt, personalize
 your budget, and plan now to secure your future / Debby Fowles. 2nd ed.
 Includes bibliographical references and index.
 ISBN 978-1-4405-4256-5 (pbk. : alk. paper) – ISBN 1-4405-4256-2 (pbk. : alk. paper) – ISBN 978-1-4405-
 4272-5 (ebook:) – ISBN 1-4405-4272-4 (ebook)
 1. Generation X–United States–Finance, Personal. 2. Young adults–United States–Finance, Personal. 3.
 Finance, Personal–United States. 4. Investments–United States. I. Fowles, Debby. Everything personal
 finance in your 20s & 30s book. II. Title. III. Title: Everything personal finance in your twenties and
 thirties book.
 HG181.F713 2012
 332.0240084'20973–dc23

                    2012014763

This book is available at quantity discounts for bulk purchases.
For information, please call 1-800-289-0963.

Contents

Acknowledgments

I would like to thank my children, Evan, Allison, and Max, for providing me with the inspiration to help future generations become more fiscally fit, and Michele for her love and support.

Top 10 Personal Finance Tips

1. Make the effort to educate yourself about personal finance. Read financial magazines and good financial books and use well-known, reputable sites on the Internet.

2. Budget! Operating without a budget is like driving a car without a steering wheel. You don't have control over where you are headed.

3. Save the pennies, and the dollars will save themselves. Lots of small amounts add up to big savings.

4. Pay cash. If you can't afford to pay cash, maybe you can't afford to buy.

5. Always think about opportunity costs. You may not be paying for something directly, but giving up the opportunity to make money is a real cost.

6. If possible, take savings out of your paycheck before you see it. After a while you'll get used to planning your spending on the lower amount, while your savings grow.

7. Be a smart shopper. Don't buy cheap items that won't last and don't pay for bells and whistles that you don't need and won't use.

8. Know how to recognize the warning signs of too much debt, and if you see yourself headed for trouble, act quickly, before you ruin your credit record.

9. Don't go without some type of medical insurance, even if you can only afford a policy with a very high deductible. If you become ill or are injured in an accident, the medical bills could ruin you financially.

10. Remember, most millionaires are just average people who practiced sound financial principles like those in this book. You could be one of them.

Introduction

BACK IN THE EARLY part of this century, young Americans were growing up in a world where the only message they received about money was how to spend it and acquire as many material items in as short amount of time as possible.

Though the advertising media initiated this message, it was also confirmed by the spending and saving patterns of the baby boomer generation—a generation that grew up with parents who served as a counterweight to the advertising media. The baby boomers were told that if you really wanted something, you should save up for it, and that only a fool would go into debt because of unnecessary spending. Sure you might take out a mortgage to buy a home or an automobile if you needed one to get to work, but that was it. The old furniture would do until you saved up to replace it, vacations were just a drive away, and entertainment consisted of visiting with friends and family. In order to get the things they wanted when they were young, the baby boomer generation worked for them.

Then they grew up and adopted the attitude that they deserved to acquire material goods now and worry about paying for them tomorrow. All of a sudden, the world of money changed. Easy credit became available, and saving was a sucker's game. Succeeding generations, people who are now in their twenties and thirties like you, entered into a world of buy now and pay (if you can) later.

This book is an attempt to inject a little "fiscal sanity" back into the equation, and to give you an alternative point of view to the mainstream notion that you should pay everybody else before yourself. This book will show how to use debt in a way that makes sense, and how to curtail frivolous spending caused by impulse purchases made by clicking a mouse, using your cell phone, or watching an infomercial. You will be introduced to the concepts of budgeting, compounding growth and income, making credit cards work for you rather than the credit card issuers, acquiring transportation and living space, and understanding the financial consequences of marriage and living together. This book will also give an overview of the biggest obstacles you will face on the road to accumulating meaningful wealth such as inflation and taxation, and will address retirement planning, estate planning, as well as insurance options.

As a person in your twenties or thirties, time is your greatest ally. The earlier you establish a long-range financial plan, the better off you will be. Acquire good financial habits now and you will reap the rewards for decades to come!

CHAPTER 1

Setting Goals: Your Financial Road Map

All successful organizations have short- and long-term goals and a written plan for reaching them. If you want to be financially successful, so should you. The first steps are to determine your financial status today and then decide what you want to achieve for your future and how you're going to accomplish it.

Why Financial Goals Are Important

You wouldn't start out on a long trip into unfamiliar territory without a road map, yet many people go through life without a concrete plan for their financial future. In fact, most people spend more time planning a single vacation than they spend on financial planning. The road you take to financial freedom can lead directly to your destination or to a dead end. Specific financial goals and written plans for meeting them help you focus your efforts on the end result.

ESSENTIAL

Starting in your twenties is a huge advantage. If you invest $5,000 at the age of twenty, and it earns 7 percent interest per year, at retirement (age seventy) it will total over $147,000. The same amount invested at the age of forty would total less than $29,000.

Goals are like the wheels on your car; they keep you moving in the direction you want to go, and you won't get very far without them. If you haven't already started planning for your future, now's the time to begin, no matter what your age.

Saving and investing in your twenties will give you the most powerful financial tool available: time. In fact, the smartest thing you can do in your twenties is save and invest. Ultimately, you'll have to save and invest a lot less money at a time and will still come out far ahead of the person who starts a decade or two later. As the saying goes, "Most people don't plan to fail, they just fail to plan." Without planning, even the best of intentions lead nowhere. Start mapping out your route now. Your entire future depends on it.

Calculating Net Worth: Your Financial Snapshot

As with any road map, before you can determine how to get from here to there, you need to know where "here" is. Where do you stand financially? Answering this critical question is the job of the net worth statement.

Your net worth is the difference between all the things of value that you own and all the debts you owe—or in financial terms, your assets minus your liabilities. Your net worth statement is a list of each of these items and their current value or balance.

Why You Need a Net Worth Statement

The net worth statement gives you a snapshot of your financial condition at this moment in time. You need this information in order to effectively set the financial goals that you'll be working toward, assess your progress along the way, and make adjustments, using the important clues gleaned from updating your net worth statement on a regular basis. It will also come in handy when applying for a mortgage, credit card, or car loan.

Sometimes people avoid making a list of their debts because they're afraid they won't like what they find or they believe they already have a good "gut feel" for their overall financial picture. However, burying your head in the sand like the proverbial ostrich won't get you far, and gut feelings can be way off the mark. Not having a handle on your financial condition can seriously hurt you in a time of crisis, such as a job loss or disability, and it's difficult, if not impossible, to plan for the future if you don't know where you are today.

How to Prepare a Net Worth Statement

Start by listing all the things of value that you own, even if you owe money on them, such as your house and car. Use their full market value as of today. The balances of the loans related to these assets will be included in the liabilities section, so your equity in the assets you list won't be overstated. For bonds, stock options, and retirement accounts, use the current value, not the value at maturity or the value on the date you're fully vested. You should receive statements showing the current value of your accounts from your employer for retirement accounts and from your broker for bonds. The human resources department where you work can help you determine the current value of your company stock options if you're lucky enough to have them.

List only those life insurance policies that have a cash value. Most life insurance policies are provided by employers and are term policies good only for the time you're employed by that company. These are not considered assets. If you've purchased cash-value life insurance from an agent and you're unsure of the current cash value, she should be able to help you determine the amount you would get if you cashed it in today. Use that amount for your net worth statement.

For cars and other vehicles, use the Kelley Blue Book value, which is the estimated price the car would sell for if sold privately to another consumer or to a car dealer. You can look up Kelley Blue Book values at the library or online at *www.kbb.com*. For all other assets, use your best estimate of the fair market value.

▼ ASSETS

Cash Equivalents	Investments	Retirement Funds	Real Estate
Bank and money market accounts	Stocks, bonds, mutual funds	401(k)/pension funds	House
CDs	Savings bonds	IRAs	Land
Cash on hand	Stock options	Small-business plans	Rental property
Personal property	**Household goods**	**Money owed you**	**Other assets**
Vehicles	Furnishings	Rents due you	Life insurance
Campers and RVs	Jewelry and furs	Rental deposits	Privately owned business
Boats	Electronic equipment	Utility deposits	

Now you've listed everything you own that has a monetary value, but the total is not a true representation of your financial worth. It doesn't take into account the money you may owe banks or finance companies before you really own some of your assets—such as your house or car, for example. It also doesn't yet take into account the money that you owe to other creditors. These are called your liabilities.

▼ LIABILITIES

Loans	Credit Card Balances	Taxes Owed	Other Debts
Mortgages	Visa/MasterCard	Real estate taxes	Unpaid bills due
Home equity loans	Discover	Unpaid income taxes	Alimony
Vehicle loans	American Express	Quarterly estimated taxes	Child support
401(k) loans	Department store credit		Miscellaneous
Student loans	Gas credit cards		

QUESTION

What is "fair market value"?
The price a willing, rational, and knowledgeable buyer would pay. Fair market value may be more or less than you paid for the item and is the most meaningful measure of its current worth.

When you've listed everything you can think of, total the assets, and then total the liabilities. Now, subtract your liabilities from your assets. If the number is positive (assets are greater than liabilities), you have a positive net worth. Congratulations! Now you can start working on building that net worth. If the number is negative (liabilities are greater than assets), you have a negative net worth, but don't let it discourage you. Now that you know exactly where you stand, you can map out your route to a positive net worth.

Decide What You Want to Achieve

Setting goals is as simple as deciding what you want and mapping out a plan for getting it. Many people focus on paying their monthly bills at the expense of their short- and long-term goals. Monthly bills have a way of expanding to use all your available money, making planning for the future a moot point. If you live beyond your means by using credit, or if you live paycheck to paycheck with nothing left over to save or invest, you'll never get ahead.

Go for the Goal

Think seriously about what you want to achieve. Do you envision retiring while you're still young enough to enjoy travel or an active lifestyle? Would you like to buy your first home or move up to a larger home in a better neighborhood? In the shorter term, maybe a new car or a boat is on your wish list. If your short-term liabilities (due in a year or less) are greater than your current assets (cash and cash equivalents), paying down credit card debt may be your first priority. What's important to you?

Don't choose goals just because they sound like what you should want. The question is, do you want them badly enough to give up the instant gratification of spending all your money now for the future enjoyment of having what is really meaningful to you later?

Put It in Writing

Whatever your goal, simply dreaming about it won't make it happen. A goal should be written down and reviewed often. Written goals give you something to work toward and make your efforts to save more meaningful.

Figuring out how to achieve your goals is just as important as stating them. Include a description of the goal, the time frame for achieving it, the amount of money needed, the amount already saved, and your plan for achieving the goal (for example, putting aside $100 a month, working ten hours of overtime a week, cutting entertainment costs in half, or getting a second job). Having a deadline for achieving your goal creates a sense of urgency that makes it easier to stay focused.

When writing down your goals, do it in enough detail to give yourself a visual each time you read it. If you're saving to buy a house, don't just write down "buy our own house." Write so you can almost see it: "I want to buy a cozy cape-style home with a water view on two or more wooded acres on the coast of Maine." Each time you think of this goal, picture this cozy home in your mind. The more vividly you can imagine what your goal will look like, feel like, and smell like, the better chance you have of achieving it.

Break It Down

At first, what you may have are long-term goals (goals you expect to meet in five years or more). You can break these goals down into short-term goals (one year or less), making it easier to stay focused on the future and giving you a sense of accomplishment and satisfaction along the way. In some cases, you may also want to identify a medium-term goal (one to three years). Remember to make the goals specific. Ask yourself how you'll know when you've reached each of your goals. If you can come up with a concrete, measurable answer, you're on the right track.

After you've written down as many goals as you can think of, choose two or three short-term and two or three long-term goals to work on this year. Let's say you choose building a retirement fund as one of your most important long-term goals. To break it down into short-term goals, set a monthly goal to contribute a set dollar amount to your employer's 401(k) or other retirement plan.

ESSENTIAL

Make goals specific. Instead of saying "I want to save for retirement," say "I want to contribute $100 monthly to my 401(k)." Instead of saying "I want to have less debt," say "I want to pay $100 extra a month toward my credit card with the highest interest rate."

Most people struggle with the question of whether to use available funds to pay off long-term debt, such as paying down the balance on a mortgage, or to use the money for short-term goals, such as building an emergency fund. The answer is to find a balance between the two. This takes thoughtful consideration of your short- and long-term goals, careful planning, and making adjustments in your plans as your goals and your financial situation change.

Evaluating Your Progress

You've prepared a net worth statement, thought about what you want to achieve in life, identified some goals, and broken them down into short- and long-term goals. Now you need to determine how you'll evaluate your progress.

You probably have a sense of whether you're making progress on your goals from month to month, but take the time to sit down at least monthly after you've updated your budget for the month and review how you're doing. Long-term goals can be reviewed less frequently than short-term goals because your time frame for achieving them is longer, but more frequent reviews allow you to spot problems earlier and take corrective action if you're falling short of where you want to be.

Tips for Recalculating and Reviewing

You should recalculate your net worth statement at least annually, but more frequently is even better. For most people, it only takes a few minutes to update the information once you've generated your first statement.

Go over your updated net worth statement, and if you're married, talk with your spouse about how much you've accomplished and where you've fallen short. If you're single you'll have to do this on your own, unless you want to involve a close friend or family member. If you're not making satisfactory progress on a particular goal, reevaluate your approach and discuss what would help you get on track. If you're making steady progress, seeing it in black and white can be motivating and rewarding. Give yourself credit for what you've achieved so far.

From time to time you may find that your goals have changed, and that's okay. A good financial plan is flexible and changes with your needs. If you lose interest in a goal, don't consider it a failure. There's no reward in working for something you don't really want. Make the necessary changes in your goals and move on.

Sometimes it can be a tremendous help to engage the assistance of others. Talk to friends and acquaintances who have achieved a goal similar to one you're working on. You can gain from their experience and insight, and seeing their success can help keep you motivated.

If you find yourself falling short of your goals because you just don't feel motivated enough to stick with your plan, try making a list of all the benefits of succeeding in your goal, and review them often. Don't underestimate the power of your subconscious to help you stay motivated. Put positive thoughts in your mind about your goals and they'll be easier to attain.

Educating Yourself about Money Matters

Unfortunately, people don't always learn the basics of personal finance from their parents, and the current education system doesn't adequately teach them, either. In fact, the Jump$tart Coalition for Personal Financial Literacy, whose mission is to improve the financial literacy of young adults, says that the average high school graduate lacks fundamental money management skills and a basic understanding of earning, spending, and saving money. It's no wonder that most people make financial mistakes in their twenties and thirties that they pay for over the next decade or longer. You can avoid these mistakes by educating yourself about basic money matters and practicing good money management.

Where to Go for Help

Where do you start? Books like this one are one source. Check your local bookstore or surf an online bookstore such as Amazon, searching for keywords like "personal finance" or "money management."

Magazines are another source. The bookstands are filled with financial magazines such as *SmartMoney*, *Bloomberg's Personal Finance*, *Money*, and *Kiplinger's Personal Finance*. Some of them are definitely for people who are avid investors or interested in business financial news, but thumb through a few and see if any of them seem readable and interesting without being overwhelming or terribly boring. If you find one, consider subscribing to it.

ALERT

The less financially savvy you are, the more vulnerable you are to being taken advantage of or falling victim to financial scams. Not everything you read is true, so it's important to use reputable sources of information and practice some healthy skepticism if something sounds too good to be true.

The Internet is a source of nearly limitless information. Try to stick with well-known sites rather than the folksy "this is how I did it" personal sites. Although the latter can have useful information, these sites can steer you in the wrong direction with some questionable advice or information. On the other hand, the personal sites about frugal living, downsizing, and cutting costs can be great for giving you ideas on how to do the same. (See Appendix B for a list of recommended websites.)

It's All in the Attitude

Personal finance doesn't deserve the bad rap of being boring or complicated that it sometimes gets, so don't feel a sense of dread about it or be intimidated by the fact that it involves numbers or terms you don't understand. Develop a positive attitude and consider your time and effort as an investment. You can learn everything you need to know, and you'll find it empowering as you learn to take control of your money and your future. With this control, you can enjoy more freedom, expanded options, and a higher standard of living. How boring is that?

CHAPTER 2

Guilt-Free Budgeting

Part of meeting your goals is being able to create a budget and stick to it. Budgeting consists of setting up spending categories, tracking your expenditures, monitoring your progress, making adjustments, plugging spending leaks, and staying motivated. Your chances of being financially successful without budgeting are slim. It takes time and effort, but the rewards are tremendous.

It's All about Attitude

Budget. For some, the word conjures up images of sacrifice, penny-pinching, and doing without. At least 50 percent of budgeting is mental, so if the word makes you shudder, work on replacing this negative image with a positive one. If you've failed at budgeting in the past, ask yourself whether your budget was simply a review of how you spent your money after it was already gone, rather than a plan for spending and saving. The former is ineffective and frustrating. The latter is freeing and rewarding.

Why Budget?

A budget is really a spending plan. You may struggle with an unrealistic plan to save thousands of dollars when what you really need to do is spend more wisely. Creating a spending plan is the first and most basic step you can take toward putting your money to work for you.

Many people who spend more money than they make don't even realize they're spending too much until they're deeply in debt. Credit cards and loans are often the culprit, but spending without knowing how much money you have available can create the same problem. Decide in advance how to put your money to use instead of letting it happen accidentally. When you spend without a spending plan, you're not in control of your money; your money is in control of you.

The Benefits of Budgeting

Budgeting and tracking your expenses show you where your money goes and how seemingly inconsequential daily or weekly expenditures can add up over time. By tracking all of your expenditures, you can make conscious decisions about how to spend or invest your money instead of dribbling it away a dollar or two at a time. This can be the difference between never having enough money and being able to afford the things that are really important to you, such as saving for a down payment on a house, buying a new car, paying off credit card debt, planning for retirement, or saving for that trip to Cancun.

Having a working budget can greatly reduce the stress in your life that revolves around money issues. You'll know what you can or can't afford. You'll feel confident that you'll be able to pay your bills when they're due, or you'll have advance warning that there's going to be a problem, giving you time to plan alternatives.

FACT

> *The Millionaire Next Door* by Thomas J. Stanley and William D. Danko shows that simple lifestyles, not big incomes, turn average people into millionaires. Many Americans buy a more expensive house than they can comfortably afford, drive the latest cars, spend large sums on their wardrobes, buy all the latest electronic gadgets, and live from paycheck to paycheck.

What Makes a Good Budget?

A good spending plan is flexible and realistic. It's a road map that offers alternative routes to your destination, depending on your personal road conditions. It should be dynamic, changing to fit your needs. If you have no kids, you wouldn't use the same budget as someone who does; if you live in rented housing, you wouldn't use the same budget as someone who owns his home. Life changes, and so should your budget.

The complexity level of a good budgeting system should match the level of your time and interest. Some people love recording the details. If you're not one of them, choose a simpler approach so it's not too much of a chore. The objective is to come up with a system you can live with for a long time.

Customizing Your Budget

It's a good idea to put together a worksheet to get started in setting up your budget. You'll get some help for doing it here, but make sure the categories you use fit your personal lifestyle. Use the basic common categories that apply to everyone, such as housing, utilities, insurance, and food, but customize the other categories to fit your situation.

Your categories should be detailed enough to provide you with useful information, but not so detailed that you become bogged down in trivia.

First, list all your sources of income:

- Wages from your job(s)
- Bonuses
- Child support or alimony
- Rental income
- Interest income
- Dividend income
- Capital gains income
- Other income

Next, list the expense categories you want to track. Start out with a little more detail rather than a little less. You can always combine categories later if you find expenditures in one category are so small that they don't warrant being tracked separately.

Some sample expense categories include:

- Savings
- Mortgage or rent
- Utilities
- Auto expense
- Other transportation
- Credit card payments
- Student loan payments
- Other loan payments
- Home maintenance
- Child care
- Child support or alimony
- Insurance
- Out-of-pocket medical expenses
- Computer expenses
- Entertainment/ recreation
- Eating out/ groceries
- Clothing and shoes
- Gifts and donations
- Hobbies
- Interest expense
- Household/personal care products
- Federal, state, and local income tax
- Social security tax
- Property tax
- Retirement contributions
- Investments
- Pet expenses

Don't forget things that come up throughout the year but are not monthly expenses, such as subscriptions, holiday gifts, clothing, birthday gifts, insurance, maintenance agreements, adult education classes or seminars, car repairs, medical expenses, and so forth.

Think about your own personal habits (smoking, drinking, buying lunch at work) or hobbies you engage in (woodworking, skiing, boating, golfing, gardening) to identify other spending categories. Some of your spending habits might make you uncomfortable when confronted in black and white. That's okay. Identifying them doesn't change the facts; it just brings them to light so you can make a conscious decision about your spending. The purpose of budgeting is not to make you feel guilty about how you've spent your money in the past.

ALERT

The first rule of personal finance is to pay yourself first. Make savings an expense category, with a set amount that you pay to yourself monthly when you pay your bills. Don't plan your savings around what's left over when you've paid everything else. Chances are there won't be anything there.

How Much Money Do You Have Available?

To curtail overspending, you need to set realistic spending goals in each category. First, figure out how much money you have available, and where that money goes now. To get started, collect as many of your pay stubs, bills, credit card statements, and receipts as possible for the last three months and complete the income section of your budget. Calculate your average monthly gross pay (before taxes) by adding the gross pay from a month's worth of pay stubs. If your pay varies substantially from one pay period to the next, try to calculate a realistic monthly average, but don't include uncertain amounts such as year-end bonuses or overtime until you're actually paid for them. Estimate monthly averages for the other income categories as well.

Where Is Your Money Going?

In addition to bills, credit card statements, and receipts, your check-book register will be important in completing the expense portion of the worksheet. Go through these documents and jot down your expenditures in each of the categories you've set up, then total the numbers in each category and transfer them to the worksheet. For the items you identified that aren't paid every month, calculate the yearly cost and divide it by twelve to get the monthly cost. Each month, set aside the monthly amount in a savings account so it's available when the bill becomes due.

To really get a fix on where your money goes, you'll need to keep track of your cash expenditures, too. Save receipts to record later, or jot the expenditure down on a notepad as you use cash. The more often you use an automated teller machine (ATM), the more important it is to write down your cash expenditures, because this is where many people lose control of where their money goes. Tracking your cash expenditures is one of the more tedious aspects of budgeting, but it's where you have the most potential for budget leaks.

Tracking Small Expenditures

You may think you know where your money goes, but most people are more than a little surprised when they really start tracking their expenses. Small cash expenditures can add up to significant sums of money by month's end. That daily cup of coffee is probably costing you almost $600 per year. Three six-packs of beer a week add up to at least $600 per year. If you smoke two packs of cigarettes a day, it's probably costing you over $280 a month, $3,360 per year, or $33,600 in ten years—and that's if you discount the impact of inflation!

ESSENTIAL

An important part of budgeting is coming up with concrete ways to cut costs. Setting a spending limit with no thought about how to reduce expenses will be an exercise in frustration as you review your failures monthly. Come up with innovative ways to put money in your own pocket.

Finding Ways to Reduce Spending

After a month or two of tracking your actual spending, you'll begin to see a pattern, and will be better able to identify where you can comfortably make adjustments to start saving money. Consider this a process of self-discovery. You can start with an in-depth look at your largest spending categories if you prefer, but don't overlook the smaller categories. Sometimes these are the easiest to make cuts in because the spending may be more discretionary, and small amounts can add up quickly.

Set Spending Goals by Category

Once you feel comfortable that you know where your money is going and you've identified some ways to cut costs in a number of categories, establish a monthly spending target for each category. Do your fixed expenses first, such as your mortgage and car payment. Look at each of your remaining budget categories and set a spending target, taking into consideration what you know about your own spending habits and where you can cut back without causing a hardship.

FACT

If you invested $280 every month instead of spending it on cigarettes, beer, or other common habits, and it earned a modest 5 percent return starting when you were thirty years old, by the time you reached retirement age you would have over $319,000! Think of what you could do with that money.

Calculating Your Net Income

When you've set a tentative target for each category, subtotal the income and expense categories and subtract the total expenses from the total income to arrive at your net income. This will be the amount of money you have left over for building an emergency fund, making additional payments on your credit cards, and working on your other financial goals, assuming you've recorded all of your income and expenditures accurately. If the number is negative, your expenses are greater than your income. Don't be discouraged. Your situation can no doubt be greatly improved by tweaking your spending habits. If you have a positive net income, be sure to transfer most of it to a savings or investment account at the end of each month. Extra cash left in a regular checking account has a way of getting spent.

Monitor Your Progress Monthly

As soon as possible after the end of each month, update your budget with your expenditures for the month. You can do this manually—by going through your checkbook, statements, and receipts—but consider using personal-finance software and perhaps online banking.

Making Adjustments

If you find you've exceeded your budget for the month, don't despair. Use it as a learning experience to improve your budgeting for the future. Your budget will get more refined every month and you'll get better and better at managing your money and working toward your goals. If you find after a month or two that tracking your expenses is too much work, consider combining some categories, such as miscellaneous household expenses or utilities, to reduce the record keeping, rather than giving up.

As you readjust the categories, look for areas where you can save small amounts of money. Remember, the idea is not to deprive yourself, but to funnel as much of your money as possible toward the goals that are most important to you. As your personal situation changes, reflect those changes in your budget. Examples of changes that should prompt an overhaul of your budget include the following factors:

- Change in marital status
- Change in family size
- A new job
- Salary increase (or decrease)
- A new home
- Disability
- A major purchase that requires monthly payments

Plug Any Spending Leaks

Most spending leaks are the result of impulse buying and frittering away cash in small amounts, which add up by month's end. Impulse spending, or buying things you don't realize you need until you see them, is often the result of powerful advertising messages that are so appealing that you buy things you don't need and often end up not using. Why let advertisers influence your decision-making?

Plan all purchases and don't buy anything that wasn't part of your plan. If there's something you feel you really must have, think about it for at least two days and if you still feel compelled to buy it, do a little comparison shopping first so you don't overpay. Then plan on how you're going to cover the cost by reducing another expense in your budget for the month.

The Small Leaks

Grocery shopping is one area ripe for cost cutting. Do you buy a lot of prepared foods instead of doing the cooking yourself? There's a trade-off between the cost and the convenience of prepared foods when you're too busy to cook. Snacks are another expensive item, especially if you buy the serving-size packages to include in the kids' school lunches. Consider buying bulk and using baggies. Buy generic brands. Use coupons.

ESSENTIAL

Shop for long-distance telephone deals twice a year. Long-distance companies are constantly changing their plans, and you could save a chunk of change if you make a lot of long-distance calls. Be sure to read the fine print and ask specific questions.

Do the workers at the fast-food restaurants in town know you by name? If eating out is a lifestyle instead of a treat, consider cutting back on fast food and enjoying a monthly dinner out with your spouse or a friend. You'll feel like you've treated yourself, and you'll probably end up spending less money than if you regularly buy fast food.

What's the deductible on your auto insurance? It should be at least $250, and if you have a good driving record, $500 is even better. The certain cost of paying higher insurance for a lower deductible weighed against the likelihood of having an accident may not be to your advantage. If the car is more than eight years old, consider dropping collision coverage altogether, and just keep liability coverage on that vehicle. The cost of collision coverage on a car that is worth only a few thousand dollars is out of proportion to the benefit you receive, especially if you have a good driving record.

These are just a few ideas to get you thinking about how you can cut costs. As you go through each item in your budget and on your net worth statement, question everything and look at things from a different perspective. You may save more by coming up with a number of ideas for small savings than you will by trying to reduce the large expenses.

The Bigger Picture

Once you've reviewed your spending and identified some small spending leaks that you can plug fairly painlessly, start looking for the larger leaks. Review items such as your mortgage, car payments, taxes, and insurance policies. The most painful cuts will be those related to your personal habits and hobbies, but these areas often yield the biggest savings.

Personal-Finance Software

If you're willing to invest the time, a personal-finance software program can bring your money management to a whole new level, but you don't need to do more than the basics if you don't have the time or interest. Unless you have very few expenses and they're relatively simple, a good software program will make the job of tracking everything easier and less time-consuming. If you don't want to use a computer, that's okay too. It's entirely possible to budget successfully with paper and pencil.

FACT

Many banks now offer free or low-fee online banking and free personal-finance software. You simply log in to your account and view your transactions and checks. You can even download this information into your personal-finance software, then indicate an expense category for each transaction and click a button for a report.

How Can Software Make Budgeting Easier?

With personal-finance software, you can balance your checkbook, pay bills, create budgets, and do a basic comparison of budget versus actual expenses by category. You can also enter more detailed information such as investments, assets, liabilities, and so on, and print personal financial statements showing your net income and net worth.

Start out with the simplest steps. Detailed tracking of investments with personal-finance software can be time-consuming and complex—not for the faint of heart. You can get the same results in your reports by setting up an account in the software for each investment and changing the balances each month to reflect the balance on the statement you receive from your brokerage, bank, or mutual fund.

Shop Around

Some of the most popular personal-finance software programs for automating your checkbook and tracking your expenses are Quicken, Mint, and Moneydance. These are available for purchase online or at big office supply stores such as Staples.

ESSENTIAL

To purchase Quicken, visit *www.intuit.com*; for Mint, go to *www.mint.com*; for Moneydance, hit *www.moneydance.com*. All three software packages are also available for purchase at *www.amazon.com*. The basic version of each software package costs between $30 and $40 after rebates.

A program like Quicken has many features you'll probably never use, but it is also a great program for the average person who just wants to do online banking, automatically reconcile their bank statement, track expenses, budget, prepare for tax time, and print reports. The budget versus actual report alone is worth the investment. Moneydance is a simpler program that is not as well-known, but it provides the same basic features without all the fancy bells and whistles.

Stay Motivated

Your budget won't work unless you stick with it. One of the keys to staying motivated is to keep the budgeting process from being too complex or time-consuming. Make budgeting a family activity and involve each family member in some way. Reward yourself for reaching saving and spending goals and making progress on paying down debt.

One of the most rewarding things about budgeting is seeing results every month. This is easy if you use personal-finance software, because once you enter your expenditures and income for the month, a click of the mouse produces reports that show budgeted versus actual expenses by category, your new and improved net worth, balances in savings and investment accounts, and more. You can even print or view colorful graphs and pie charts for a vivid picture of how you're doing.

Remind yourself of the importance of your real goals. The budget is just a tool that increases your awareness of where your money goes and provides guidelines for spending so your money goes toward the things that are most meaningful to you.

CHAPTER 3

The Secrets to Saving Money

Without a savings plan, your chances of saving enough money to meet long-term financial goals are very slim. Like financial success, saving money doesn't happen by accident. It requires smart buying, cutting costs, planning, and understanding a few basic financial concepts, such as the magic of compounding, the rule of 72, the time value of money, and the danger of inflation.

The Magic of Compounding

Compounding is the main reason it's so important to start saving in your early twenties. People who wait until their forties to start saving will have to save much more than those who began in their twenties. What's worse, the late starters will never be able to catch up with those who started in their twenties without saving and investing drastically higher amounts than would have been necessary had they saved at a younger age.

There are two basic methods of calculating interest: simple interest and compound interest. Simple interest accrues only on your initial investment. Compounding means that as you earn interest on your investment, the interest is added to your original investment, and as a result you earn interest on your interest as well. The difference may not seem like much, but the effect that compounding can have over a long period of time is astounding, especially with larger initial investments and higher rates of return.

ESSENTIAL

To illustrate how compounding works, assume you invest $1,000 at 10 percent interest compounded annually. At the end of the first year, you'll have earned $100, for a total of $1,100. At the end of year two, the interest is calculated on $1,100, so you'll earn $110, for a balance of $1,210.

Frequency of Compounding

Interest usually compounds annually, monthly, or daily. The more frequently compounding takes place, the faster your money will grow. As the balance grows larger, the difference between simple interest and compound interest becomes greater. Let's say you put $5,000 in an account that earns 10 percent interest. Here's what your investment would be worth at the end of ten years if you didn't add another penny to it:

- Compounded annually: $12,968
- Compounded monthly: $13,535
- Compounded daily: $13,589

To illustrate the effect of a longer period of time on compounding, consider Bill, who contributed $2,000 at 6 percent interest to an IRA beginning at the age of twenty-two and continued doing so each year until he was thirty-nine. By the time he was sixty-five, his $18,000 investment had grown to over $579,000. His friend Jim made a $2,000 contribution every year for thirty-five years, for a total of $70,000, but because he started at the age of thirty-one, his nest egg only totaled $470,000. Even though he contributed much more than Bill ($70,000 versus Bill's $18,000) he ended up with 23 percent less money.

The Rule of 72

The rule of 72 is a nifty mathematical computation you can use to estimate how long it will take a certain sum of money to double at a certain interest rate (assuming the interest is compounded annually), or to determine how long it will take a debt to double.

The Calculation Is Simple

To calculate how quickly your investment will double, divide 72 by the interest rate or expected rate of return. The result is the number of years it will take your money to double at that interest rate, assuming you reinvest your earnings. So if your money is invested at 8 percent interest, you make the following quick calculation: $72 \div 8 = 9$. This means it will take approximately nine years.

You can also use the rule of 72 to estimate what rate of return you'd need to earn in order for your money to double in a certain number of years, for example, ten years: $72 \div 10 = 7.2$, so you'd need to earn 7.2 percent annually for your money to double in ten years.

How Many Times Will Your Money Double?

The power of the rule of 72 doesn't stop there. It illustrates how important differences in interest rates are, because the lower the interest rate, the longer it takes to double your money, and the real key to growing your money is to double it as many times as possible. Look at this example of $100 doubling eight times:

$100	$3,200
$200	$6,400
$400	$12,800
$800	$25,600
$1,600	

As you can see, the real growth comes after the money has doubled several times. By using the rule of 72, you can calculate how much you'll have by a certain time and you can compare the long-term effects of interest rates on various investments that you own.

Double Savings, Don't Double Debt

You can use the rule of 72 to see how long it will take your credit card or other debt to double, too. If you have a $5,000 credit card balance with an interest rate of 10 percent, your debt will double in 7.2 years. If the interest rate is 19 percent, your debt will double in 3.8 years. You can see why it's so hard to pay off your credit card debt, especially if the interest rate is high. If you're only paying the minimum payment each month, it doesn't take long for your balance to double.

The Danger of Inflation

Inflation is the effect of rising prices on your buying power. Inflation is often left out of the equation when calculating how much money you'll have available at some point down the road, but it can make serious inroads into the buying power of your money. In the United States, the average inflation rate since 1994 has been approximately 2.5 percent, but in the early 1980s, the country experienced double-digit inflation. Since 1980, the price of goods and services has increased 80 percent, so an item that cost $100 in 1980 costs $180 in 2002. Since much of financial planning is done for years into the future, it's important to consider the impact of inflation when determining how much money you'll need in retirement, for example.

You can use the rule of 72 to estimate the real buying power of a sum of money at some point in the future, taking inflation into consideration. If the inflation rate is 4 percent, prices will double in eighteen years (72 ÷ 4 = 18), so if you plan to retire in eighteen years and you need $3,000 a month in today's money, you'd need $6,000 a month to retain the same buying power you have today.

ALERT

The $30,000 salary you earn this year will be worth only $28,800 next year if inflation is 4 percent. If you're fortunate, you'll get a salary increase annually that at least keeps pace with the rate of inflation; otherwise you fall further behind each year.

The Time Value of Money

The time value of money is a basic financial concept based on the assumption that a dollar received today is worth more than a dollar received at some future date because a dollar received today can be invested and earn interest. If someone agreed to pay you $1,000 ten years from now, or some lesser amount today, you could calculate the amount you'd need to receive today to equal the value of $1,000 in ten years. You do this by discounting the amount using current interest rates. If the current interest rate is 6 percent, you might be willing to accept $558 today rather than waiting ten years for your $1,000 because you're confident that if you invest the $558 at 6 percent it will grow to $1,000 in ten years.

FACT

Opportunity costs are the benefits you lose by not choosing the best alternative for the use of your money. If you pay $100 in credit card interest each month, you've lost not just $100, but also the added value you could have received if you had invested that $100.

There's more to the concept of the time value of money, but the most important thing for you to remember is that receiving $1 today is better than receiving $1 tomorrow, and the entire amount in a lump sum is better than installment payments (assuming there's no interest involved). If you're paid in installments, you lose the opportunity to invest the lump sum for a longer period of time.

Building an Emergency Fund

Everyone should have an emergency fund, but you probably won't know how much your fund should be unless you know what your basic monthly expenses are. Financial advisors suggest having enough savings in an easily accessible account to cover your living expenses for three to six months. Having this financial safety net will give you peace of mind about how you'll meet your most basic financial obligations in the event of illness, job loss, or unplanned expenses such as major house or car repairs, or medical costs not covered by insurance. If you're uncertain about your job and the job market, an emergency fund is especially important.

When you have a budget in place, you can easily calculate how much money you'd need to cover your basic, no-frills living expenses if you had a sudden loss of income. Write down your goal for your emergency fund and decide on an amount to contribute to it each month, using the "pay yourself first" rule. If possible, keep the fund in a separate account, such as a money market account, so you're less tempted to dip into it. Since emergency funds might be needed without notice, they should be kept in liquid accounts that are easy to cash in quickly.

The Fun of Frugality

Don't be discouraged if you currently have no extra money to put away. By developing a realistic budget, setting spending and savings goals, and sticking to them, you can create money for savings.

Decide on a percentage of your income to designate as savings. Financial planners suggest 10 percent, but if 8 or 5 percent is all you can handle at this time, start with that. Don't make the mistake of thinking that if you can't save a large amount of money all at once, it's not worthwhile to try. This couldn't be further from the truth. If you saved $25 a month at 6 percent interest, in five years you'd have $1,744. If you saved $100 a month at 6 percent interest, in five years you'd have $6,977; in ten years, you'd have $16,388.

Strategies for Pumping Up Your Savings

Set up a separate savings account. If you mingle your day-to-day funds with your savings, it's almost inevitable that you'll end up using some or all of the savings, and you may never repay them. There's also a mental component. Seeing your savings balance grow from month to month and your financial goals becoming more of a reality is highly motivating.

If you have direct deposit at work and your employer allows you to split your deposit between multiple accounts, consider having a set amount deducted from your paycheck each pay period and deposited in your savings account. It's much easier to save when the money doesn't have to take a detour to your checking account before reaching your savings account. If you don't have this option at work, write yourself a check every month before you pay your bills, or set up an automatic draft into your savings account. Most Internet bank accounts will do this for free—they'll even pull money from a different bank. After a while, as you adjust your budget and spending, you won't even miss the money you're putting into savings.

ALERT

If you feel forced to dip into your savings in an emergency, consider it a loan. If you can't pay it all back at once, set up a repayment plan and pay yourself as though it were a regular bill. Otherwise you may never replenish your savings.

Use windfalls to pump up your savings instead of spending them. Bonuses, tax refunds, rebates, overtime pay, income from hobbies or yard sales, cash gifts from family, lottery winnings, and other sporadic cash receipts can make faster advances toward your goals without requiring additional spending cutbacks. When you receive a salary increase, put all or part of it into savings each pay period and continue living on your previous salary. When you pay off a loan, continue putting the payment amount aside each month, but pay it into your savings account instead of to the bank or finance company. Because you're already in the habit of doing without that money, you won't even miss it.

Don't Be a Victim of Advertising

With a spending plan, you don't need to deprive yourself of things you really need, but you should question whether you really do need them. Experts recommend these strategies:

- Don't use shopping as a form of recreation.
- Don't shop on impulse.
- For items you really do need, look for sales and special offers.
- Shop at outlet or discount stores and websites.
- Before buying appliances, electronics, computer equipment, and other expensive items, research them in *Consumer Reports* or other magazines that do consumer reviews.
- Do some of your shopping at a warehouse club, if there's one near you.

ESSENTIAL

You can find product reviews and cost comparisons on the Internet—just be sure the source is reliable and impartial. One good site is *www .consumerworld.org*, with product reviews, price comparisons, airfare and travel deals, and lots of other consumer resources.

Avoid the Holiday Hangover

If you're like most people, you tend to go overboard on holiday spending, but you can avoid overspending on gifts by setting spending limits. Using your budget, figure out how much you can realistically afford to spend on gifts without going into debt. Make a list of all the people you'd like to buy gifts for, including the small gifts for babysitters, teachers, newspaper carriers, and so on. Set a limit for each person on your list, then add up all the amounts and make sure they don't exceed your overall spending limit. Try to allow a cushion for unexpected items or price fluctuations.

FACT

The Internet is a rich source of advice on being frugal, a word that sometimes has a bad connotation but that simply means economy in the use of resources. It's amazing how many different ways there are to cut costs and save money. Do a little Internet surfing and you'll find hundreds of ideas that have worked for others. Being frugal can be fun!

Finding the Fat

You may think there's no fat in your budget, but nearly everyone can find some if they look hard enough. Consider it a challenge to find ways to cut your expenses, or make a game of it. If you smoke, why not quit? Smoking is one of the most expensive habits you can have; many couples spend as much on cigarettes as they would on a new car payment each month.

Speaking of car payments, ask yourself if you really need the gas-guzzling SUV you drive. You could save considerable money on gas, repairs and maintenance, and insurance, not to mention your monthly car payment, if you bought a less expensive, more fuel-efficient vehicle. You might even get some tax benefits.

Consider buying used instead of new. Check the classifieds for things such as exercise equipment, vehicles, musical instruments, electronics, and more. You can often get great bargains on items that may be as good as new.

Saving for Large Purchases

There are a number of benefits to saving for a big purchase rather than buying it on credit. First of all, you have plenty of time to change your mind about whether it's something you really need or want. Have you noticed how many backyards have unused swimming pools or hot tubs? If you run right out and charge the item to your credit card or take out a loan, you'll be stuck paying for the item for a long time. Paying cash also gives you the satisfaction of really owning the item, and you'll pay much less for it because you won't be paying interest.

Luxury Items and Loss of Value

There are often significant costs beyond the purchase price associated with luxury items such as boats, RVs, or certain cars. Be sure to evaluate all of these costs before making a buying decision, or you may find out after you've already made the purchase that although you can afford to buy the item, you can't afford to own it.

Take the purchase of a boat as an example. A new eighteen- to twenty-one-foot powerboat will probably cost between $15,000 and $20,000. You run all the numbers and decide that the payments fit into your budget. You commit to the sale and drive home with the goods, but during the next year you find you're sinking larger-than-planned quantities of money into owning the boat, starting with the day you register it. Besides registration fees for the boat and trailer, there's gas and oil, maintenance, repairs, insurance, safety courses, inspections, winter storage, personal-property taxes, dock and mooring fees, not to mention depreciation. These costs can add up to a substantial amount, so make sure you get estimates before you buy and make sure you can afford the costs of ownership.

ALERT

Home appliances, electronics, cars, and other items are reviewed in *Consumer Reports* magazine, which accepts no advertising or sponsorships. Subscribe to their website (*www.consumerreports.com*) for about $26 per year.

The same principles apply to buying an RV, expensive car, furniture, appliances, or any luxury item. Buying cheaply made furniture or appliances may cost you more in the long run because you have to replace them more often. Try to buy quality products without overpaying unnecessarily for features you won't use or for a brand name that doesn't necessarily mean better quality. It makes sense to pay more for an item if that brand or model has a better record or costs less to maintain. Do your research, talk to others who have bought a similar item, talk to experts in the field, and read. Then try to balance cost and reward.

CHAPTER 4

Banking Basics

You probably have a checking account and maybe a savings account, but chances are you don't give much thought to the impact banking has on your finances. Being knowledgeable about how banks work can save you money. You might be surprised just how much your banking arrangements and habits are costing you.

Choosing a Bank or Credit Union

When it comes to choosing a bank, consider both convenience and cost. Some charge flat monthly fees; others charge a fee for each check written and each deposit made. Some charge if you go below the minimum balance, use a live teller, use another bank's ATM, make an account balance inquiry, have your canceled checks returned to you each month, or close your account. Most charge for bouncing checks, placing a stop payment on a check, and using your overdraft protection.

ALERT

Reconcile your checkbook monthly and review your credit card statements for errors. Scam artists are finding new ways to target these two areas and if you're not alert, you could get taken for a ride.

Review your banking habits, identify the services that are most important to you, compare fees for those services between several different banks, and then choose the bank that fits your needs for the best price. If you use an ATM to withdraw cash from your account on a weekly basis, for example, you wouldn't want to choose a bank that charges a hefty fee for ATM transactions. You may decide to use a traditional brick-and-mortar bank in your neighborhood or an Internet bank in cyberspace.

In today's world, you've got a few options when it comes to banking. One such option is to pick a credit union over a traditional bank. Banks are owned by investors; credit unions are owned and controlled by customers, who are members. Credit unions are nonprofit organizations and return surplus earnings to members by lowering interest rates on loans, increasing interest rates on deposits, or offering free or low-cost services.

The most basic requirement for any bank or credit union you choose is that it must be insured and fully backed by the U.S. government. This ensures that your account will be protected for up to $250,000 per account in a participating financial institution. The government agency that insures banks is known as the Federal Deposit Insurance Corporation, or FDIC. Accounts in trust for a named beneficiary are treated as separate accounts from individual accounts without a named beneficiary. Additionally, joint accounts are treated as separate from any accounts held by each individual owner in his or her own name and have $500,000 of protection ($250,000 × 2). Retirement accounts such as IRAs are also treated separately for purposes of the $250,000 FDIC protection. For example, a married couple could have the following accounts FDIC protected *at the same bank:*

1. $250,000 in husband's name
2. $250,000 in wife's name
3. $500,000 in a joint account between husband and wife
4. $250,000 in husband's name in trust for wife, and
5. $250,000 in wife's name in trust for husband

That would protect a total of $1,500,000 in one financial institution! And you can still fund IRAs with FDIC protection as well. For credit unions, the National Credit Union Association (NCUA) provides the same type of coverage.

QUESTION

How do I make sure a bank is FDIC-insured?
Go to the FDIC website at *www.fdic.gov*, click on "Find Your Bank" and enter the official name and state of the bank. For credit unions, visit *www.ncua.gov*.

Online Banking

Online banking allows you to manage your money via the Internet—when and where you want. You can view all your banking transactions, move money, view and print your canceled checks, and pay bills online. You can also arrange to have your bank e-mail you when checks clear or your balance goes under a predetermined minimum. As time goes on, online banking continues to evolve. You used to just look at your accounts and download information. Then online savings accounts hit the scene with extremely attractive interest rates. Next, banks moved to checking and loans online. Things can only get better and better from here.

The main attraction to online banking is convenience. You can view your accounts and download information to your computer. Many people have enjoyed using online banks to balance their checkbooks as opposed to doing things the old-fashioned way. In addition, you can have an online bill-pay service write and mail checks for you—or just zap the money to your service providers electronically.

Online Offerings

Another attraction of online banking is competitive pricing. The first Internet bank accounts were savings accounts paying much more than brick-and-mortar banks paid. Some accounts even offer checks, ATM cards, and bill-pay with these high-yield accounts. Banks continue to offer more every year.

Most large banks offer secure online banking free. You can view your accounts, transfer money, and download data in most cases. Online bill-pay is often free as well, although some banks charge a modest fee (perhaps $6 per month) or require you to keep a meaningful balance in your account for free bill-pay services. Some smaller banks offer limited functions only, such as the ability to view your balance and history online.

Even if you don't bank online, you may still use technology to make life easy. For example, you can use automatic debits to have payment for one or more of your bills automatically deducted from your checking account each month. To do so, ask your service provider(s) and they'll let you know how it's done. In addition, you might have your paycheck sent directly to your bank account. This direct deposit makes the money available to you sooner, and saves you a few steps.

Staying Safe

Banking online is actually safer than traditional methods of banking. In fact, the U.S. government has been urging social security recipients to get their payments via direct deposit. There are fewer errors when you use technology, and there is less fraud. An electronic system makes it harder for scammers to intercept documents and forge forms. In addition, every transaction can be tracked in detail.

Staying safe online just requires a little common sense. Anything that looks fishy probably is; however, you can keep yourself from becoming a victim by keeping an eye out for the most common scams. The most common online scam is phishing. This happens when you receive an e-mail from a "bank" asking you to update your account information. They'll direct you to a website, which will ask you for your personal information, bank account numbers, usernames, and passwords. Of course, the site is not really run by any bank. It's simply a way to gather information from people who fall for the scam. Simply put, ignore these e-mails.

ALERT

Some folks say they don't bank online due to security concerns. The fact is that their account information is already online—they've just never logged in. That doesn't stop somebody else from logging in, though. Better to control the account yourself!

You can delete any mail that comes from a bank that you don't remember opening an account with. If you happen to have an account with the bank referenced in an e-mail, don't just click on a link in the message. Instead, you should call the bank directly, using a number that you know is valid (don't use a phone number provided in the e-mail). If there really is a problem, they'll be able to help you on the phone.

Other attacks involve stealing your information from your computer. Software programs may track your communication or your keystrokes, and send that information off to a scammer. To protect yourself from this type of scam, keep your computer secure. Use antivirus and firewall software, and keep other software (browsers, operating system, etc.) up-to-date. For the most part, you can avoid problems by avoiding shady websites and never opening e-mail attachments from people you don't trust.

Finally, keep a close watch on your bank accounts and keep a tight lid on your banking information. Simply telling somebody your account number can expose you to problems, so don't divulge your banking information over the phone or via the web unless you know whom you're dealing with. If you suspect that somebody else is using your account, call your bank immediately.

With the Help of Software

The most popular software programs for taking advantage of online banking are Quicken and Mint. Both are robust personal-finance programs that allow you to download your banking transactions and help to manage your finances, budget, balance your checkbook, pay bills electronically, prepare and file your taxes, track investments, and build a financial plan for your future.

Banking Costs

Sometimes you can gain as much by cutting seemingly insignificant costs that add up over time as you can by earning additional income. Banking costs are a good example. Banks charge so many different types of fees, some of them hidden, that you may not realize what your real costs are.

With minimum balance requirements, ATM fees, overdraft charges, and other fees, even your basic checking and savings accounts might be costing you more than they should. When your money could be earning more somewhere else, you're paying opportunity costs. You may not be paying any fees directly, but you've lost an opportunity to make money elsewhere. For example, the balance that you maintain in your checking account to avoid a monthly fee could be earning more than the monthly fee if invested in a money market account or certificate of deposit (CD).

FACT

Check printing is another area where it's easy to save a little money. Why pay the $25 to $50 or more that your bank charges for printing 200 checks when you can use a discounter and pay between $6 and $8?

Service Versus Cost

Be aware of your banking costs and make intelligent trade-offs to get the services you use for the lowest overall cost. If keeping a minimum balance in your checking account costs you $5 a month in opportunity costs but saves you $7 in fees, it makes sense to go with that option. If you have savings and checking accounts at the same bank, keep only as much money in the checking account as you need to pay bills that are due immediately. Let the rest of your funds go to work for you by earning interest in your savings account. When interest rates are very low, the earnings may be minimal, but when rates are higher, the savings can be substantial over time.

Minimizing Fees

Banks make billions of dollars annually on various fees, and the amounts are growing each year. You probably accept bank fees without question, but why pay more than you have to when it's relatively easy to minimize fees?

Banks use several methods to calculate your average daily balance and interest. If you usually keep a significant balance in an interest-bearing bank account, it's to your advantage to keep it in a bank that uses the average daily balance method for calculating your minimum balance and interest. This reduces the chances of incurring fees if you dip below the minimum balance during the month (as long as your average daily balance for the entire month is not below the minimum). You also earn interest on all your money.

When you borrow money, the costs are stated in terms of interest rates, so it seems fairly easy to choose the best deal, but it's not always as simple as it appears. A lower interest rate will not necessarily save you money if fees and other charges are added in. Be sure to read the small print.

Overdraft Protection

Overdraft protection is a checking account feature that allows you to write checks for more than the balance in your account. It provides a safety net to protect you from accidentally overdrawing your account. Some banks allow you to cover overdrafts automatically from your savings account, money market account, or credit card.

The most common method of covering overdrafts involves establishing a line of credit, which typically has an interest rate that can be as much as two times higher than the going rates on credit cards or loans. The cost to you could be substantial if you don't repay it right away. There can also be a fee each time funds are drawn from another source to cover your overdraft.

If your overdraft protection is linked to your credit card, the bank issues a cash advance to cover your overdraft and charges it to your credit card. You pay a cash advance fee of 2 to 3 percent plus the fee your bank charges for the transaction, plus whatever interest you incur before you pay the cash advance back.

Overdraft fees are one of the costliest banking mistakes you can make, and you should avoid them like the plague. Even if you don't balance your checkbook, at least compare your check register to your bank statement to make sure you've recorded all checks and ATM withdrawals and that the bank has properly credited you with all deposits. This will help prevent bouncing checks.

Typical fees for insufficient funds range from $20 to $35. Often when you bounce one check, at least one more check will bounce before you're aware of the problem, and before you know it you can rack up over $100 in bounced-check fees.

Automated Teller Machines

ATM fees are huge money generators for banks. Originally, ATMs were intended to reduce banks' expenses by automating tasks that previously involved a live teller. Now many banks charge fees for the use of ATMs.

There are several different types of ATM fees. Some banks charge you a fee just to have the use of an ATM card. Others charge ATM access fees, which are weekly, monthly, or yearly fees in addition to the regular account fees. When you use an ATM that is not owned by your bank, you'll incur a surcharge, which is a fee in addition to fees charged by your own bank, a practice called double-dipping.

Out-of-Network Fees

Using an ATM that is not in your bank's network is a costly convenience. Here's how it works: You withdraw $20 from an ATM that doesn't belong to your bank and incur a $1.50 fee. Your bank then adds an out-of-network surcharge of $3.00. You've just paid service fees totaling 22.5 percent of your withdrawal amount to the two banks to access $20 of your own money.

Banks may also charge a fee, commonly $1.50 to $2.00, if you use an ATM to get a cash advance on your credit card. In addition, the credit card company will probably charge a fee for the cash advance, usually around 3 percent of the total advanced, with a minimum fee of $5.00. To make things worse, cash advances on credit cards may have a higher interest rate and be paid off last.

ALERT

Beware of skimming devices posing as ATMs. They record electronically stored information from the magnetic stripe of your card or your personal identification number (PIN) as you enter it. The thieves then skim money from your bank account. Stick to bank ATMs instead of those in malls, airports, and other public places.

The ATM can be an expensive way to check your balance or recent transactions, at $1.00 or $1.50 a pop at some banks. The receipt you get when you make another type of ATM transaction, such as withdrawing cash or making a deposit, often shows your account balance, so why pay extra?

Minimizing ATM Fees

You probably don't keep track of what you pay in ATM fees over the course of a year, but you can see how these fees can add up quickly, so it could be a substantial amount. Simply being aware of how you use the ATM can help you plan ahead so you can avoid some of the costs. Here are a few other ideas for avoiding fees:

- Establish an account at a bank with a large ATM network so you don't get stuck using out-of-network ATMs.
- Plan cash withdrawals when you can access your own bank's ATMs, or look for ATMs that don't impose a surcharge (usually indicated on the ATM).
- Withdraw large amounts of cash less often rather than smaller amounts more often.
- If your bank doesn't charge to use a live teller, use a teller instead of the ATM.

- Use personal checks instead of paying cash.
- Double up transactions, such as using your ATM card to get cash back when you make a purchase at a point-of-sale cash register.
- When traveling, use traveler's checks, personal checks, or credit cards.
- Avoid higher-cost ATMs found in convenience stores, hotels, casinos, restaurants, and airports.

Debit Cards

Many banks allow you to make purchases with your ATM card. The money is taken from your account electronically. These cards are called debit cards, or check cards. You can only take out as much as you have in the account, or in your overdraft-protection account.

Two Types of Debit Card

There are two types of debit cards. The first is referred to as an online debit card, which removes money immediately from your account when you use your PIN. The second type, called a deferred debit card, bears a MasterCard or Visa logo and you can use it anywhere that accepts Visa and MasterCard. Deferred credit cards require you to sign a sales receipt and the amount is removed from your account a few days later.

Some banks combine both functions on one card, so when you're ready to pay using these cards, you have the option of hitting debit or credit on the keypad. Don't be confused by the Visa or MasterCard logo on these cards. They are *not* credit cards. Both types remove money directly from your checking account.

Debit Card Safety

Debit cards that require a PIN are safer than those that require only a signature. If your card is lost or stolen, anyone can sign your name, but a thief can't use your PIN-based debit card unless he has your PIN. If you have a card that allows both types of transactions, a thief could use your card even without your PIN.

Don't leave your receipts behind when you use your debit card or throw them away without shredding them. Thieves who "dumpster-dive" may find your receipt and use the personal information on it to rip you off. Never write your PIN on your debit card or share your PIN with somebody else, and don't use a PIN that is too obvious, such as your phone number or birth date.

If you notice a transaction on your statement that isn't legitimate, report it immediately. If you report it within sixty days, your liability is capped at $500, but if you wait more than sixty days, you're liable for everything the thief removes from your checking account and your overdraft account, if you have one.

ESSENTIAL

Some banks charge a monthly fee for the debit card. Other banks charge a fee for each transaction. There may also be a requirement to keep a minimum amount in your checking account at all times.

Visa and MasterCard have voluntarily extended the same protection to customers using deferred debit cards as they offer to credit card customers: Your liability is capped at $50 if you report the card missing within two days. However, this feature doesn't have the law to enforce it, so it could change at any time.

Under the Fair Credit Billing Act, if you aren't happy with the quality of an item you purchased with a credit card, you can withhold payment for that item. This same protection is not true of a debit card. It's a good idea not to use your debit card for big items or services, for online purchases, catalog purchases, or other purchases where you don't walk away immediately with the goods.

Finally, be aware that debit card purchases can lock up your checking account funds. You may end up bouncing checks even if you have sufficient funds in your account. When you choose credit and sign for a transaction, the vendor may authorize a sufficient amount for most purchases ($100, for example) and bill the actual amount later. For example, if you pay at the pump for gas, the gas station often "reserves" $100 of your account balance, so they know you can pay for the gas you're about to get. It may be a few days before they get around to releasing the unused funds.

Balance Your Checkbook

Balancing your checkbook is a method of verifying that your records (your checkbook register entries) match the bank's records, as shown on your monthly bank statement. The method of accomplishing this task has changed with the use of online banking and personal-finance software, but the pencil and paper method still works. The best time to balance your checkbook is within a few days of receiving your monthly bank statement so there are fewer transactions to wade through. You have sixty days to inform the bank of any errors on your statement (and banks *do* make errors). If you don't balance your checkbook monthly, how will you find an error if it does occur?

How to Balance Your Checkbook

First, determine if there are any checks that haven't cleared the bank yet by sorting your canceled checks in check number order or by using the listing of cleared checks that's printed in a separate section of your bank statement. In your checkbook register, check off each item that cleared the bank, making sure the amount you recorded in your check register agrees with the amount shown on your bank statement. Watch for transposed numbers in your check register—for example, $97 instead of $79. Make sure that each deposit shown on your bank statement is recorded in your check register, including direct deposits. Next, go through your deposit slips and paycheck stubs and make sure that all the deposits you made are included on the bank statement. As you verify each deposit, check it off in your check register.

Go through your ATM and debit card receipts and check off each transaction on the bank statement and in your check register. If you're not sure what the transaction is, call your bank immediately. Check your bank statement for fees you may have incurred on your account and interest you may have earned on your balance. Complete the balancing form.

Best Places to Stash Your Cash

What do you do with money that you want to be able to access quickly when needed, such as your emergency fund? If you put it in a CD, you may incur penalties if you have to withdraw it early. If you mingle it with your checking account, you're more likely to dip into it. Your savings account may not earn a very good interest rate. Under your mattress or in your cookie jar are really not viable options. So where is the best place to stash your cash?

Checking and Savings Accounts

Savings often end up sitting in the checking account just because it's the easiest option. It's not a good idea, though. Savings should be segregated from your day-to-day spending money for several reasons, including the fact that it's much too easy to dip into your savings if they're mingled with your checking account. You'll also earn better interest in a nonchecking account.

Savings accounts, like checking accounts, are safe if the bank is FDIC-insured, and usually pay higher interest rates than checking accounts. Savings accounts are a good place to park some of your savings, but only as much as you would need in an emergency. Because savings-account interest rates may not keep up with the rate of inflation, you actually lose money in the long run.

Internet Bank Accounts

If you want to try for a higher yield, you might look at Internet bank accounts. One of the most attractive features of these accounts is the high interest rate they pay on deposits, plus they may have no minimum balance requirements. Keep in mind that it can be difficult to get cash out of these accounts; it may take a few days to electronically move money from your Internet bank account to your brick-and-mortar account. However, you may be able to get your cash via a check on the account or an ATM/debit card.

Money Market Deposit Accounts

Money market deposit accounts, offered by most banks, are also FDIC-insured. They usually require a minimum balance of $1,000 or more, but they pay slightly higher interest rates than traditional savings accounts.

Certificates of Deposit

CDs are actually loans you make to the bank for an agreed-upon term in return for a guaranteed interest rate on your principal. Some have adjustable rates tied to an index such as Standard & Poor's 500 stock index. Most banks charge a penalty if you withdraw all or part of your CD funds before the maturity date.

Like other bank accounts, CDs carry insurance up to $100,000 as long as the bank is FDIC-insured. The $100,000 refers to the total of your accounts with that particular bank, so if you have more than $100,000 in one bank, you're not fully protected. CD terms range from one month to five years or more. The longer the term, the higher the interest rate and the greater the risk that your money will be locked up at a lower rate when interest rates rise.

ALERT

Be especially careful when investing in broker-issued CDs. These guarantee the return of your principal at maturity, but maturity may be twenty years from the purchase date. If you cash the CD in before the maturity date, you may lose not only interest, but a large chunk of your principal as well.

Banks and brokers also offer callable CDs with rates that may seem too good to pass up, but be sure to read the fine print and ask plenty of questions before investing in a callable CD. Be sure you know the difference between the maturity date and the callable date. Usually the issuer has the right to call the CD at any time after one year, but this doesn't mean it matures in one year. It may be a twenty-year CD, which means you can't cash it in without a penalty for twenty years, but the bank can call the CD at any time.

If interest rates have risen since the CD was issued, the bank will keep the CD in force because the rate will be below the current market rates. If interest rates have fallen, the bank will call the CD so it doesn't have to pay you above-market rates. This leaves you with money to invest at low rates when you may have thought you were locked in at a higher rate for a longer period. An excellent website to compare all types of bank rates is *www. bankrate.com*.

CHAPTER 5

Credit Cards 101

There's no question about it: credit cards are a wonderful convenience that can make your life easier. However, if you overuse them, they're also the biggest deterrent to reaching your financial goals. To avoid this you need to have an understanding of how credit cards really work and how they can work in your favor.

The Good, the Bad, and the Ugly

With credit cards, you don't have to carry cash or your checkbook around with you. You can make purchases over the telephone or the Internet. You can reserve cars and hotel rooms, or have recurring expenses automatically billed to your card. You can buy things you need that you once would have had to wait years to obtain while you saved your money. You can also take advantage of a grace period that would allow you to pay for your purchases up to six weeks after the transaction without any interest and be eligible for all kinds of rewards from free air flights and vacations to cash back and discounts on merchandise. A credit card will allow you to establish credit so when it's time to buy a house or a new car you qualify for the mortgage or car loan.

But the same cards that provide great convenience may become the means by which you are enslaved to debt, as charges you make become grossly inflated by high interest rates. As your debt grows out of control, it may even outlast the purchases that created the debt in the first place.

The Appeal of Credit

The message of credit cards is one of instant gratification—you can have it all now. Credit cards can make it seem as if you're not spending real money. But once you get too deeply in debt it could take you years, or even decades, to get out. In the meantime, your real dreams will be on hold.

What's Out There

There are several types of plastic cards that are loosely referred to as credit cards, but they don't all work alike. *Major credit cards* include Visa, MasterCard, Discover, and Optima. These card companies allow you to make purchases up to a preset credit limit ranging from $500 to $10,000 or more, depending on your income and credit history. You can pay the balance in full each month, the minimum required by the card company (typically around 4 percent of the balance), or any amount in between.

Travel and entertainment cards, including American Express, Diners Club, and Carte Blanche, require you to pay the entire balance due each month. They have no preset credit limits but if you are late with your payment, you may be charged interest or have the use of your card blocked until you catch up.

QUESTION

What are gold and platinum cards?
These are cards that include extra perks such as collision coverage when you rent a car, extended warranties on certain items, travel insurance, discounts, and other benefits. They sound appealing, but consider what exactly you get for the privilege of paying a much higher annual fee. Sometimes the "gold" card is just a plain old card painted gold.

House cards allow you to charge purchases at a particular chain of retailers, such as department stores and gas stations, and make monthly payments, including interest charges. Many retailers do offer certain advantages to their cardholders such as additional discounts on their merchandise and exclusive shopping opportunities, particularly around the holidays. *Smart cards*, the latest in plastic cards, look like credit cards but contain a computer chip with a preset dollar amount built in. Instead of charging to the card, you spend the value at places that accept smart cards, or chip cards.

ESSENTIAL

The Internet is a great tool for finding the best credit card. Visit *www .bankrate.com* for an up-to-date list of the best credit card deals in the country. You can also search the web for "credit card calculators," which will help you understand how different payment strategies will affect your finances.

The Cost of Credit

There are several types of costs associated with credit cards. The annual fee is a flat dollar amount the issuer charges each year for the use of the card. Many, but not all, issuers charge annual fees. Finance charges are calculated based on the interest rate your card issuer charges and are the main cost of using credit. These rates vary significantly from one card to another, so you can save a lot of money by shopping around for a card with a lower interest rate.

Other fees that you might incur on your credit card include application fees, processing fees, charges for exceeding your credit limit, late-payment fees, balance-transfer fees, credit life insurance, and fees on cash advances.

Grace Periods

The grace period, commonly twenty-five days, is the time between the date you're billed and the date your payment is due. If you pay your entire balance within the grace period, you may not incur any interest charges. If you carry a balance, there's often no grace period on new purchases, so interest starts accruing from the date of purchase. Some issuers charge interest from the day you make the purchase, even if you pay your balance in full, so in effect there is no grace period. When you add the fact that charges made at the start of the monthly billing cycle already give you a one-month deferral on payment, this grace period may result in a six week, interest-free deferral on payment. The Credit CARD Act of 2009 mandates that the grace period, if offered, shall be for a minimum of twenty-one days.

Choosing What's Best for You

Before you choose a credit card, think about how you intend to use it. Do you plan to pay off the balance every month or carry a balance from one month to the next? If you pay the balance every month, the annual fee and other charges may be more important than the annual percentage rate (APR), so you should look for a no-fee or low-fee card. Even if the issuer charges an annual fee, you may be able to get it waived by calling and asking the company to remove it. If you carry a balance and pay for your purchases over time, the APR and the method of computing your balance are most important, so you'll want to look for the lowest interest rate and the best grace period.

Beware of teaser rates, which sound tempting because the introductory rate is much lower than the going rate on most cards. The downside is that if you have a balance on the card when the introductory rate ends, you could be in worse shape than you were with a higher rate, depending on how high the rate spikes at the end of the introductory offer. It is also imperative that you make all minimum payments during the introductory period in a timely manner or the rate will revert instantly to that higher rate.

ALERT

Interest rates on cards that award frequent flier miles for certain purchases are usually several percentage points higher than regular credit cards, so don't carry a balance on them. If you pay even one day late, you're hit with finance charges and you may lose any miles earned that month.

In general, if you have a good credit history and you're paying more than 7 or 8 percent above the current prime interest rate on your Visa or Master-Card, you're paying too much. If you can obtain a lower-interest credit card, you can usually use cash advances to pay off the balance on your other credit cards and transfer this debt to the lower-rate card. Be sure to read the fine print, though. The interest rate on cash advances and transferred balances is usually much higher than the standard interest rate, so be sure you can pay off the cash advance before the introductory offer runs out.

If You Have Damaged Credit

Sometimes people make unwise choices or take on more credit than they can handle and end up with a bad credit history. Sometimes they acquire bad credit through divorce, loss of a spouse, or bankruptcy. If you have bad credit, or have no credit history, chances are you can still get a credit card, but it will cost you more, and the terms won't be as favorable as they are for those with good credit or a history of making timely payments. You may only be able to get a $500 credit limit, and you'll probably pay an exorbitant interest rate. Use the card wisely and make your payments on time, and eventually you'll qualify for better terms.

Research the best credit card deals, and apply to only one at a time. Applications for credit show up on your credit report and can make potential credit card issuers nervous, because they think you may be taking on more credit than you can handle. If you get turned down for a major credit card, try a department store card or gas card. These are often easier to get and making your payments on time for one of these cards can build a credit history that will help you qualify at some point for a major credit card.

Secured Cards

If all else fails, consider a secured card. You put your own money into a savings account and that amount, or some portion of it, becomes the security for your credit line. If you don't pay your bills, the card issuer will use the money from your savings account to cover your debt. It may be difficult to come up with the amount to deposit, but you can build a credit history using this method. Many people find that after twelve to eighteen months of making timely payments on a secured card, they can "graduate" to a regular credit card.

ESSENTIAL

Since your goal with a secured card is to establish or re-establish good credit, make sure that the company issuing the card reports to a credit bureau. Otherwise, the card can't help you build or repair your credit history.

Secured cards are a favorite with unscrupulous marketers and you're a potential target because you can't easily obtain credit. Secured cards typically carry a higher interest rate and higher fees than regular credit cards. Ask whether there are application or processing fees, which can total hundreds of dollars. The latest trend in secured cards is no application fees, so do your homework and save yourself some money.

Cosigned Credit Cards

If all else fails, you may be able to find someone to cosign on a credit card for you. Remember this: if you do take this route and you don't make your payments, you can ruin the credit of the cosigner, who would have to pay off your debt. You wouldn't want to do this to someone who was willing to go out on a limb for you.

ALERT

Don't fall for advice given by some credit-repair services or credit doctors telling you to obtain an employer identification number (EIN) and apply for credit using that instead of your social security number, so your credit history doesn't pop up when a credit check is performed. This evasion is a felony.

Questionable Credit Card Offers

If you have poor credit, you're more susceptible to questionable credit offers, so stay on your toes. Don't fall for offers of easy credit, ads that require you to call a 1-900 number (you'll pay a fee for the call and may never see the credit card), or offers to repair your credit. You have the legal right to correct any errors in your credit report by directly contacting the credit-reporting bureaus; don't pay someone to do this for you. Some credit-repair companies make false claims about their ability to clean up your credit. Only the creditor or the credit-reporting bureau can remove a debt from your record, and the only way to clean up your credit history is by making payments on time for several years and paying off your debts.

Using Credit Cards Wisely

Credit cards can be a great tool when used wisely. Unfortunately, many people get in over their heads when they're just out of school and may never recover from the financial decisions they make unless they get serious about getting out of debt.

Staying Out of Trouble

A large percentage of credit card debt is incurred around the holidays. If you use your credit cards to do holiday shopping, you may not pay off the charges until months later. Using credit cards often leads to impulse spending and overspending, and those items that seemed like such bargains end up costing you 10 to 20 percent more than you thought, due to credit card interest. If you can't afford to pay cash, can you really afford to buy the gift?

Instead, try saving small amounts of money throughout the year in a special holiday gift fund.

Some people use their credit card for nearly all of their expenses and pay off the balance in full at the end of the month. This gives them one document that includes most of their expenditures for the month and can help in budgeting and keeping track of where their money goes. If you don't have the money or the discipline to pay off your balance every month, you should avoid using a credit card for things such as clothing, food, gas, dining out, and similar expenses.

Review your credit card statement carefully each month, and if you see anything that doesn't look right, such as purchases you didn't make, or incorrect payments or credits, call the number on your statement for billing questions. If a phone call doesn't clear up the problem, you have sixty days to notify the credit card company in writing. It has thirty days to respond and ninety days to resolve the error. In the meantime, you're not required to pay the disputed amount, and you won't incur any finance charges on the disputed amount while the credit card company investigates.

Cash Advances

Cash advances on a credit card come with a price tag—very high interest rates and fees. This feature is for the true emergency, not for buying nonessentials such as eating out, paying your regular bills, or entertainment or vacations. Grace periods don't apply to cash advances, so you pay interest from the day you get the cash. There's also usually a transaction fee of anywhere between 2 and 3 percent of the cash advance total. To add insult to injury, the interest rate on cash advances is significantly higher than the rate on purchases. All in all, your cash advance can end up costing you a bundle of money.

FACT

Visa cardholders take out a staggering $100 billion a year in cash advances. At an average up-front fee of 3 percent, cash advances are generating $3 billion a year to Visa in this type of fee alone.

Pay It Off!

It may sound obvious, but one of the most important things to realize about credit cards is that the credit card company's goal is to make money from your account. When they establish a low minimum monthly payment, they're not trying to do you a favor; they're trying to maximize their profits. When you pay the minimum payment, it's good for them, but not for you.

ESSENTIAL

By paying credit card interest of $50 a month you've lost the opportunity to invest that money: invested at 8 percent, $50 a month would total over $6,500 in eight years, the time it would take you to pay off a $2,500 balance if you make only the minimum payment.

Until recently, the minimum monthly payment for most credit card companies was around 2 percent of the balance, including interest. If you made a purchase of $2,500 at an annual interest rate of 18 percent, it would take you almost eight years to pay off the balance by making the minimum monthly payment. Initially, 2 percent of your balance would be a minimum payment of $50, with around 75 percent, or $37.50, going toward interest and only 25 percent, or $12.50, reducing the amount you borrowed. You can see why it would take so many years to pay off your balance.

By the time you paid off the $2,500, you'd end up paying interest of $2,156 in addition to the $2,500 principal you borrowed. Your $2,500 item will have cost you $4,656. How can you ever get ahead financially if you're paying such exorbitant prices? Around 2005, banks came under increasing pressure from regulators to increase the minimum payment. Some companies moved faster than others, but most moved quickly to raise minimum payments to 4 percent from 2 percent. While this helps you eliminate debt more quickly, it doesn't solve the problem for you.

If you can't afford to pay more than the minimum payment, can you really afford whatever it was you charged to the card in the first place? Instead of paying the credit card company each month, you could put the money in a savings account until you have enough to pay cash for the item.

Protecting Yourself Against Losses

It's getting more and more difficult to protect your credit cards from theft. Thieves and scam artists keep coming up with more clever ruses to obtain the information they need to use your cards fraudulently or obtain credit in your name. Even your identity can be stolen.

Keep Your Credit Cards Safe

Your best protection against credit card fraud is to know where your cards are at all times. Don't carry credit cards with you unless you know you're going to need them. Don't leave them lying around on your desk at work or in your car or anywhere else they could be accessible to others. Keep the PIN for your debit and ATM cards a secret. Don't use personal information such as address, phone number, or birth date as the basis for your PIN; those numbers are too easy for a thief to guess.

Don't disclose your credit card number over the phone unless you're dealing with a reputable company and you're the one who placed the call to them. If someone calls and tells you that you've won a prize but they need your credit card number to verify, hang up. Scammers constantly get more sophisticated. They might use "vishing" scams where a computer dialer poses as your bank and asks you to call in to discuss transactions in your account. When you get a renewal credit card or you cancel a card, cut the card up into small pieces, being sure to cut through the number. Ideally, run old cards through the shredder.

If Your Card Is Lost or Stolen

As soon as you realize your credit card, ATM card, or debit card has been lost or stolen, report the loss immediately to the bank or other issuer in order to limit your liability if the card is used fraudulently. Keep a list of your credit cards and telephone numbers in a safe place so you can access the phone number as quickly as possible.

Under federal law, if you report the loss before any unauthorized charges are made to your card, you can't be held responsible for any charges. If a thief uses your card before you report it missing, the most you will owe for unauthorized charges is $50 per card. If somebody uses your credit card number fraudulently without physically stealing the card itself, you are not liable for the charges.

Even though you called the issuer to report the loss, it's a good idea to follow up with a letter in case you need to prove that you did so. After the loss of your card, review your monthly statements carefully and report in writing any unauthorized charges. Lost credit cards should also be reported to each of the major credit-reporting agencies: Experian, TransUnion, and Equifax. Ask them to place a security alert on your account to intercept possibly fraudulent applications for credit.

Identity Theft

Identity theft occurs when someone uses your personal information such as your name, credit card number, or social security number to commit fraud or theft. Using just your date of birth and social security number, thieves can apply for a credit card in your name, and rack up big charges before you even know the account has been opened. When the balance isn't paid, the delinquency is reflected in *your* credit history. It can take years to prove that the card was obtained illegally and to fix your credit report, and during that time you may be denied credit.

Some thieves will even call your credit card company and report a change of address on your account. Since your bills then get redirected somewhere else, you may not even realize there's an issue with your account until it is too late. Other scams include setting up cellular phone service in your name or opening a bank account in your name.

FACT

For more information on how to avoid from falling victim to identity theft and how to recover if you do become a victim, visit *www.ftc.gov* and *www.privacyrights.org*.

Be careful of how and where you dispose of bank statements, credit card offers, credit card statements, or any document that includes your date of birth or social security number. Consider purchasing a personal shredder and shredding these documents before throwing them in the trash. If you believe you have become a victim of identity theft, file a report with your creditors, the three credit-reporting bureaus, and your local police as soon as possible.

The Credit CARD Act of 2009

Effective February 22, 2010, the Credit Card Accountability, Responsibility, and Disclosure Act limits the credit card issuers' ability to charge credit card holders unfairly. Some highlights of this new law are:

1. Should you be more than sixty days behind on payments, a retroactive increase will be allowed; however, once you have made timely payments for a six-month period, the issuer must restore your rate.
2. If you open a new credit card there may not be any rate increase for the first twelve months.
3. Card issuers must deny any purchase that would put the cardholder over the limit of the card unless the cardholder agrees to pay the over-the-limit fee.
4. Total fees charged on a credit card for the first twelve months cannot exceed 25 percent of the card's limit.
5. Statements must be mailed at least twenty-one days prior to the due date.
6. Credit card issuers may not assess interest charges on balances from previous billing cycles that were already paid. This is known as double-cycle billing.
7. Monthly due dates must always be on the same day of the month. Any weekend or bank holiday due dates must be extended to the next business day.
8. All payments received by 5 P.M. must be recorded as being received on that day. A popular prior maneuver was to end the "banking" day at 2 P.M.
9. Any changes to credit card terms must be accompanied by at least forty-five days' advance notice.

CHAPTER 6

Digging Out of Credit Card Debt

Being over your head in debt can be an overwhelming, hopeless feeling. You may be embarrassed to have others know that you're struggling to pay your bills. You may toss and turn at night thinking about how to get out from under the burden. You're not alone, and with hard work and discipline, you can dig your way out.

Your Credit Report and How It Works

A credit report is a record of your credit payment history as reported to credit bureaus by your bank, credit card companies, department stores, and other businesses you've borrowed from. Potential lenders use the information in your credit report to decide whether they want to take the risk of issuing you credit. If you understand how credit reports work, you can protect your rights and avoid being taken advantage of by unscrupulous credit-repair clinics and so-called credit doctors.

ESSENTIAL

Under the Fair Credit Reporting Act, you have specific rights related to your credit report. You can read about these rights on the Federal Trade Commission's (FTC) website at *www.ftc.gov*.

If you're thinking about buying a house or applying for credit for any other big purchase, you'll need a good credit report. It's always best to know what's on it before your lender does, so you'll have an opportunity to clean up any discrepancies or errors.

What's in a Credit Report?

Your credit report includes the following basic personal information: name, current and previous addresses, telephone number, social security number, date of birth, and current and previous employers. The credit history section includes information about each credit account, including the date opened, credit limit or loan amount, balance, monthly payment, and your payment pattern during the past several years. Bankruptcies, accounts sent to collection agencies, unpaid child support or alimony, tax liens, car repossessions, court records of tax liens and monetary judgments, and the names of businesses or individuals who have obtained a copy of your credit report are also included. In addition, your report contains information obtained from public records, such as your job history, whether you own your home, and whether you've been sued, arrested, or have filed for bankruptcy.

When issues between you and a creditor can't be resolved, the comments and explanations you're allowed to add to your credit report and the creditor's response to your statements become part of your credit report. If an account was turned over to a collection agency, your report will include it as a "collection account" until it's paid in full; then it will be noted as a "paid collection," and will stay on your credit report for seven years from the date of the first missed payment.

Review Your Credit Report

Financial advisors recommend that you obtain a copy of your credit report at least once a year and review it carefully. The Fair Credit Reporting Act allows you to get one free credit report from each credit-reporting company every year. If you've been turned down for credit, housing, or employment because of information in your report, you may be entitled to an additional free copy of your credit report. Some states require that credit bureaus provide free copies or charge a reduced price for residents of that state, so you may find a variety of ways to get more than one free credit report per year from each of the credit-reporting companies.

FACT

Your credit report does *not* include information about your race or national origin, religion, personal lifestyle, political affiliation, medical history, criminal record, or other information unrelated to your credit history and ability to repay debt.

There are three main credit bureaus: Equifax, Experian, and Trans-Union. Because some creditors report to only one of the bureaus, the information in your credit report may differ somewhat from one bureau to the other; experts recommend that you obtain a copy of your report from each of the three major credit bureaus once a year. You can also order a three-in-one report that includes the information from all three credit bureaus, but it may cost more than obtaining the individual reports.

To order your credit reports use the official site created by the three major credit-reporting companies: *www.annualcreditreport.com*. If you use a different site, it's likely that you won't get your credit reports for free. Many imposter sites claim to offer free reports and credit scores, but they will want a fee from you sooner or later.

If you find an error in your credit report, call or write to the credit bureau explaining the error in as much detail as possible using 100 words or less. Provide any documents that help prove your statements. Send everything certified mail, return receipt requested. If you don't get an answer within forty days or so, follow up with them.

How Do Lenders Use the Credit Report?

Lenders use the information in your credit report to evaluate your character, your debt capacity, and your collateral or capital. Their evaluation of your character is based on the stability of your employment and residency history.

To evaluate your debt capacity, lenders look at your living expenses, open credit limits, current debts, and other payments to get a sense of how much debt you can afford based on your spending habits, income, and credit burden. They're more likely to extend you credit that's secured by collateral or a down payment. For example, the car you purchase is the collateral for your car loan. If you default on the loan, the car can be repossessed, so there's less risk to the lender.

Increasingly, lenders have been making their lending decisions by using your credit score, which is a number indicating how likely you are to make payments on time and repay loans. The score is computer-generated and largely based on your use of credit in the past—how long you've used credit, how much you use, and how responsibly you've used it. All in all, they may look at your income, education, job stability, how often you've moved, whether you own your own home, how often you take out cash advances, how close you are to your credit limits, what kinds of things you buy on credit, how many credit cards you have, and past payment history. A computer compares this information to patterns from thousands of other consumers and predicts your level of credit risk.

For a fee, you can now obtain your credit score, or FICO score, named after the Fair Isaac Corporation, the company that developed credit scoring and the largest provider of credit scores to creditors and financial institutions. While there are other credit scores out there, the FICO credit score is most often used by lenders and others. All three major credit bureaus offer this option with your credit report or as a separate option.

To get your FICO score directly from Fair Isaac, visit *www.myfico.com*. Their website also provides details on how the score is composed, and what you can do to improve it. Some of the more common ideas put forth to improve your credit include keeping current with your bills, keeping credit card balances low, avoiding the practice of paying down one credit card by borrowing from another credit card, avoiding the closure of unused credit cards and the opening of new credit cards, and checking your credit report for any inaccuracies.

Paying Down Debt on Your Own

Once you realize and accept the fact that you have too much credit card debt, the question is, what are you willing to do about it? The first step is to put the credit cards away, or better yet, cut them up and cancel them. Then consider the following options to see which ones might work for you.

Use Your Savings or Sell Something of Value

If you have something of value, consider selling it. You may have some stocks, savings bonds, or mutual funds you could cash in. Do you own a collection of some sort that has value? If you're earning less than 3 to 4 percent interest on your savings account while paying 12 to 21 percent on credit cards, you may need to use your savings to pay off debt in order to prevent ruining your credit, but try to leave yourself a savings cushion.

ESSENTIAL

Find out how long it will take to become debt-free and how much you'll pay in interest by making the minimum monthly payments by using the Debt Reduction Planner calculator in the personal-finance section of CNNMoney (*www.cnnmoney.com*).

Use the Equity in Your Home

Using the equity in your home may be another option. If interest rates are lower than your current mortgage rate, and you haven't yet damaged your credit, you may be able to refinance and roll your debts into the new mortgage. If that's not an option, you might be able to get a home equity loan or line of credit to pay off your other debts. Rates on mortgages and home equity loans are much lower than the rates on most credit cards, so besides the obvious slash in the interest rate, you may be eligible to reduce your interest costs even more by deducting the home equity loan interest from your taxes. Don't forget that even if you can deduct 28 percent of mortgage interest if you're in the 28 percent tax bracket, the other 72 percent still comes out of your pocket.

Exercise extreme caution when you consider borrowing against the equity in your home. If you get into trouble financially due to job loss, illness, medical bills, or divorce, you may not be able to make your mortgage payments and the lender may foreclose on your house. Don't jeopardize your most valuable asset if you really can't afford the increased mortgage payments or if you haven't made changes in your spending habits and credit use.

Use the Credit Crunch Method

This method of paying down debt goes by a number of different names, but whatever the name, the strategy is the same. It seriously reduces your interest expense, which could be 90 percent of your monthly payment if you've been paying the minimum, and it allows you to pay off your balances sooner.

ALERT

If you drive an expensive car, consider getting a less expensive one. It's not just that the monthly payment is higher for an expensive car; the repairs and maintenance, special tires, gas, and insurance also cost more. Drive a reliable, inexpensive car for a few years and apply the savings to your credit card balances.

First, to really get a handle on your debt, prepare a schedule of your debts, listing the creditor, the balance due, the interest rate, and the current monthly payment. Rank the debts in descending order by interest rate (highest interest rate first, lowest interest rate last). Each month, pay the minimum balance on all credit cards except the one with the highest interest rate. Pay as much as you possibly can on this card each month until it's paid off. Use all available money for this payment including overtime pay, tax refunds, bonuses, and money generated by reducing expenses.

Then start in on the next debt with the highest interest rate. Pay as much as you possibly can each month, including the amount you were previously applying to debt number one. Continue to pay the minimum balance on the others. Keep moving down the list of debts until they're all paid off. This is the only time you should ever pay the minimum balance on any credit card. The credit crunch method requires month after month of consistency and discipline, but it works.

Finance Companies and Bill-Paying Services

If you don't think you're cut out for the credit crunch method, there are several options for consolidating your debt. Finance companies make your paperwork easier because they pay off all your debt so you make only one payment each month. The problem is that finance companies charge very high interest rates, so you end up paying a steep price for the convenience of writing fewer checks. Some experts believe that unless your debt problems were caused by job loss, disability, or other major life experience, a debt consolidation loan is just postponing the inevitable: bankruptcy.

Stay away from consolidation loans unless the interest rate will be significantly lower than what you're currently paying and you're committed to continuing to pay at least as much as you were before consolidating.

If you use a bill-paying service, all your bills are sent directly to the bill-paying company, which makes payments for you and sends you a monthly transaction report. They also charge you a fee, typically around 10 percent of the total you owe. Bill-paying services don't actually lend you money, so you still have to cough up the cash yourself. At most, they offer the incentive for exercising a little discipline and the ease of writing one check instead of several each month. If you owe $5,000 and the bill-paying service charges 10 percent, that's $500 you'll be paying for the convenience of having them disburse the money you send them each month.

Transferring Credit Card Balances

Another popular method of reducing debt is transferring credit card balances to a card with a lower interest rate so more of your payment is applied to principal and less to interest each month. This approach only helps if you continue to pay at least as much as you were paying before, even though the minimum payment may be less.

Beware the Introductory Rate

Shop around for cards with low interest rates, but beware of come-ons that offer a low introductory rate and then take a big jump a few months later. If you haven't paid off the transferred balance when the rate goes up, you could end up paying more than you bargained for. Most introductory rates are only good for five to nine months, so be very sure you can pay off the balance before then. Also make sure that you qualify for the rate advertised. The 1.9 percent rate in the big bold print may be more like 10 percent for you, depending on your credit history. If anything is unclear after you've read the fine print, call the credit card company and ask questions.

Borrowing from Your 401(k)

Most 401(k) plans include a loan feature that allows you to borrow money from your retirement account and repay it in five years or less at an interest rate determined by your plan administrator, usually a couple of points above the prime rate. Most plans with a loan feature allow you to borrow half of your balance, up to $50,000.

ESSENTIAL

Using your 401(k) to pay off debts is dangerous. Your 401(k) is there to help you in future years. If you start spending that money now, you might end up with nothing in retirement. It's harder to borrow, cut costs, and work more hours in retirement.

Paying Yourself Back

Since you pay the interest back into your own 401(k) account, you may think you can't go wrong with a 401(k) loan, but it's not quite that simple. Taking money out of your account could have a significant impact on your retirement income even though you pay the money back, because you have less money invested to earn interest and dividends or appreciate in value. There could be a double whammy if you reduce your contributions to the plan because you can't afford to make contributions in addition to the loan payments. Even if your loan is repaid in one year, going that long without new contributions will have a long-term impact on how much you accumulate by the time you reach retirement age.

The Danger of Changing Jobs

Perhaps even worse than reducing the potential accumulation of earnings is the danger of being stuck with a loan balance if your employment terminates, whether it's because you've accepted a job elsewhere or you were fired or laid off. If you have an outstanding loan at the time your employment ends, you'll have to pay it back *immediately* to avoid having Uncle Sam slap you with taxes and a 10 percent penalty.

Let's say you borrowed $12,000 and repaid $2,000 before changing jobs. Your loan balance at termination is $10,000. If you can't come up with the money to repay it right away, it will be considered a premature withdrawal. If you're in the 28 percent tax bracket, you'll have to pay $2,800 in income taxes, plus another $1,000 (10 percent) early withdrawal penalty. All of a sudden your low-interest loan doesn't look so good. On top of that, if you have no other way to come up with the money to pay the taxes and you have to take them from your 401(k) plan too, that money will also be subject to taxes and penalties. Either action could decimate the retirement fund that you've worked so hard to build.

Credit-Counseling Service

Nonprofit consumer credit-counseling agencies may consolidate your debts into a single, manageable monthly bill. You pay the agency each month and they distribute the money to your creditors. This type of arrangement is not a consolidation loan, but it has its benefits because creditors will often accept lower payments if you're working with a reputable credit-counseling agency. Services may be free or provided for a very low fee of $10 to $15 a month. Go to the National Foundation for Credit Counseling's site at *www.nfcc.org* to find a qualified credit-counseling agency. You may have to agree not to use credit and not to apply for new credit while you're participating in the debt repayment program.

Negotiating with Credit Card Companies

Credit card companies will often lower your interest rate if you simply ask. Call the company and tell them that you've received credit card offers with lower rates and ask if they can lower your rate so you don't have to switch. If you've been a good customer and have been with the company awhile, you stand a good chance of getting your rate reduced.

High Risk Equals High Rate

Once you start getting black marks on your account, your lender is likely to raise your rate sharply to offset the risk that you might not repay your balance. On the other hand, lenders want you to pay your debts and are sometimes willing to lower your interest rate or waive fees if they believe you're serious about getting caught up. It doesn't hurt to ask. If you get "no" for an answer, call back and ask again. Sometimes getting a different customer service representative can make a difference.

Prioritize Your Bills

Some payments are more important than others. For example, it's important to keep your house, as well as to get to work so that you can earn some money. If your situation is so dire that you can't pay all your bills, prioritize your debts and expenses and pay the most important ones first, in this order:

- Mortgage or rent
- Car loan and auto insurance
- Other insurance (homeowner's, health)
- Utilities
- Loans (banks, student loans, finance companies)
- Credit cards
- Miscellaneous

Talk to the creditors you can't pay fully and let them know you intend to meet your obligations but need some time. They may be willing to give you a month or two and tack the payments on to the end of your loan, reduce your interest rate, or re-age your account so it's not reported as delinquent to the credit bureaus.

Avoiding Credit-Repair Scams

Some companies claim they can "fix" bad credit histories for a large sum. It is legally impossible to alter an accurate credit history. If you find yourself in credit trouble, develop a budget and work with your creditors to pay your debts and re-establish a good credit rating. There's no quick fix.

ESSENTIAL

If you find yourself a victim of a credit-repair scam, contact your local consumer protection agency (click on "Consumer Agencies" at *www .consumerworld.org*), your state's attorney general (click on "The Attorneys General" at *www.naag.org*), or your local Better Business Bureau (information is available at *www.bbb.org*).

With so many people carrying too much debt, credit card-repair scams are rampant. Don't fall for anything that sounds too good to be true. Ads that promise to fix your bad credit, create a new credit identity, or remove bad credit information from your credit report are scams. In addition, some credit counseling services are shady. Stick with Consumer Credit Counseling Services located at *www.nfcc.org*.

Errors in your credit report or outdated information can legally be removed, but you don't need to pay somebody to do it. You can do it yourself by writing a letter to the credit bureau. Negative information can't be removed if it's accurate. Credit-repair clinics may use illegal tricks to get something temporarily removed from your credit report but it will show up again the next month when your lender updates the information provided to the credit-reporting bureau.

CHAPTER 7

Other Credit Issues

Credit card debt gets a lot of attention from financial advisors, and rightly so, but it's not the only debt in town. Understanding other types of debt can help you choose the kind of loan that makes the most sense for you. It can also make you less susceptible to being taken advantage of, and may help you avoid bankruptcy.

Installment, Secured, and Unsecured Loans

All loans are alike in some ways. You borrow an amount of money, called the principal, for a set amount of time, called the term, at a fixed-interest rate or a variable rate. Some loans require the principal to be repaid all at once. Others, called installment loans, require regular payments of a specified amount at predetermined intervals, usually every month.

Secured and Unsecured Installment Loans

Loans can be secured or unsecured, which refers to whether or not they are backed up by collateral. For example, car loans and mortgages are secured loans. Your promise to repay the loan is secured by the car or house you're buying. If you fail to make your payments, the lender can seize the car or house to recoup the money it lent you. Unsecured loans are backed up only by your promise to repay.

FACT

Most people use installment loans when buying a car or boat. Sales contracts are a type of installment loan commonly used when purchasing appliances or furniture. The retailer provides financing or outsources it to a finance company and you make monthly payments, including interest, until the balance is paid.

Revolving Credit

Revolving credit is more flexible than an installment loan. There's a maximum you can borrow, and a minimum you must pay each month, but the rest is up to you. Personal lines of credit are a type of revolving credit account where you qualify for a certain amount and use it at your own discretion by writing special checks provided by the lender. Lines of credit are great if you're not sure when you're going to need the money and want to have funds available quickly. Many people use home equity lines of credit to make improvements to their home or pay down credit card debt.

Department stores often offer revolving credit loans with no interest and no payments due for three to six months on large purchases such as furniture or appliances. If you take advantage of these offers, be sure to pay the entire balance before the interest kicks in. Often these accounts are turned over to a finance company at the end of the interest-free period, and the interest rates are high. Although no payments are required for several months, it's a good idea to make them anyway, or put money aside each month to pay off the balance at the end of the interest-free period.

Credit Insurance

Don't waste your money buying any of the various types of credit insurance from credit card or finance companies. Credit life insurance pays the balance on a loan if you die. Credit property insurance covers damage to the item that's being purchased with the loan proceeds. Credit disability insurance makes your loan payments if you're disabled, and involuntary loss of income insurance makes your loan payments if you're involuntarily unemployed.

Insurance that's tied to one particular debt is an expensive way to insure yourself against losses. If something does happen, only the payments for that particular item are covered. If you feel insurance is necessary, talk to your insurance agent about a broader policy, such as disability insurance that would replace your income if you became disabled or life insurance that would provide a lump sum to your beneficiary instead of to the lender.

Creditors and Debt Collectors

Keep in mind that your creditors want to work with you before you become delinquent on your bills, so call your creditors before you miss a payment. Waiting until your account is already delinquent will hurt your credibility. The creditor may not be as willing to work with you and may turn your account over to a debt collector, which can be an unpleasant experience.

Creditors are also quicker than ever to report late payments to collection agencies because more and more people are filing for bankruptcy and walking away from their debts. If you make arrangements with the creditors ahead of time, they may agree not to report your delinquency to the credit bureau.

If you talk to a creditor over the phone, take good notes, including the name of the person you spoke to, the date and time you talked to her or him, and what arrangements were made. It's a good idea to then follow up with a letter outlining the key elements of your discussion, and to ask that they send you something in writing as well. If you're not successful in getting the creditor to work with you, hang up and try calling again. Sometimes one customer service representative or credit manager will be more helpful or flexible than another.

ESSENTIAL

When negotiating with creditors, don't agree to a plan that you're not sure you can stick to. If you make promises and then can't keep them, the chances of the creditor ever being willing to work with you again are slim. You'll need to do a budget and calculate how much money you can squeeze out of it each month to apply to the account in question before committing to a payment plan.

Debt collectors are third parties hired by a lender to attempt to collect amounts you owe when you're late with your payments; they can be lawyers or companies in the business of collecting unpaid accounts. If your account gets turned over to a debt collector, you can save yourself a lot of grief if you're familiar with your rights under the Fair Debt Collection Practices Act, the federal law that specifies what third-party debt collectors can do.

Collectors are allowed to contact you in person, by mail, telephone, telegram, or fax, but they're not allowed to contact you at inconvenient times, such as before 8 A.M. or after 9 P.M., unless you agree to those times. Debt collectors can't threaten, harass, badger, or abuse you or use false or misleading information. If a debt collector is harassing you or causing other problems, report the incident to your state attorney general's office and the FTC.

QUESTION

Can debt collectors call me at work?
If you or your employer tells the debt collector that your employer doesn't want you to receive collection calls at work, the collector is prohibited under the Fair Debt Collection Practices Act from contacting you at your place of employment.

The Fair Debt Collection Practices Act doesn't apply to employees of the creditor that you owe. They're governed by state laws, which vary from state to state. Consult the consumer information section of your state's website for information about your rights.

Filing for Bankruptcy

Bankruptcy is a federal court process that places you under the protection of the bankruptcy court while you try to repay your debts (Chapter 13 bankruptcy) or removes the debts altogether (Chapter 7 bankruptcy). When you file for bankruptcy, an automatic stay goes into effect; the stay prohibits your creditors from attempting to collect the debt without the approval of the court, even if the bank is in the process of foreclosing on your house. Filing for Chapter 13 in this situation could buy you the time you need to sell the house yourself and pay off the mortgage.

Bankruptcy should not be entered into lightly. It has far-reaching effects on your ability to obtain credit, buy a house, buy life insurance, and sometimes even get a job. There are other factors that might make one type of bankruptcy better for you than another. Consult a good bankruptcy lawyer and provide all the details of your financial situation so she can counsel you concerning the option that best suits your needs.

Chapter 13 Bankruptcy: Reorganization

Chapter 13 bankruptcy involves reorganization of your debts. You'll need to file a proposal with the bankruptcy court detailing your plan for repayment and include a detailed budget, which could be challenged by the court if the judge, the trustee, or a creditor feels you've padded it with nonessentials. Some debts can be erased altogether, others must be partially repaid, and others must be repaid in full. If the court accepts your proposal, it will probably garnish your wages during the repayment period, which usually lasts three to five years. In Chapter 13 bankruptcy, you can prevent the loss of your home by immediately starting to make your regular mortgage payments and any catch-up payments required by your repayment plan.

How Much Will You Have to Pay?

You must pay all of your missed payments on secured debt, such as your house or car, if you want to keep the asset. In general, expect to devote all of your income after expenses to your required payments. The minimum amount you'll have to repay on your unsecured debt is the value of your non-exempt personal property. Each state has its own laws for determining non-exempt property, but in general, you'll be given an "allowance" that consists of several thousand dollars for a car, part of the equity in your home, necessary clothing, necessary household goods and furniture, appliances, and personal effects. You'll have to repay at least an amount equal to the rest. In other words, if you add up the equity in everything you own and deduct the amount of the exempt items, the difference is the least amount you'll owe. You'll have to pay more than this if you have nonexempt expenses such as child support or back taxes.

The courts have discretion regarding how much of your debts you'll have to repay. Some courts don't require you to pay anything on debts that you aren't legally required to repay in full; others will want you to pay as much as possible. You may be responsible for a filing fee unless your income is low enough that you qualify for an exemption. You may also be required to pay several years of interest on the total value of your nonexempt property to compensate creditors for the fact that they have to wait several years to be fully paid.

Before you make the decision to file for bankruptcy, you should know which debts you may be able to walk away from and which you'll still be responsible for. Debts that can't be discharged or forgiven include:

- Child support and alimony
- Debts for personal injury or death caused by drunk driving
- Most student loans
- Traffic tickets and other fines or penalties imposed for breaking the law
- Certain types of taxes owed
- Debts you forget to list in your bankruptcy papers

FACT

In 2005 Congress drastically changed the bankruptcy system. The Bankruptcy Abuse Prevention and Consumer Protection Act of 2005 passed, which made it more difficult for individuals to seek shelter in bankruptcy. Among other changes, it's harder to qualify for Chapter 7, and you have to attend financial counseling sessions.

Eligibility for Chapter 13

Because repayment of some of your debts is the basis for this type of bankruptcy, you have to have regular income in order to be eligible. Regular income can include social security benefits, child care or alimony, and rental income, and, of course, employment or self-employment wages. You also have to have enough disposable income after your basic needs such as housing, utilities, and food to use for debt repayment.

Chapter 7 Bankruptcy: Liquidation

Under Chapter 7, liquidation, you turn most of your personal property over to the court, which appoints a trustee to sell the property and use the proceeds to pay off all or some of your debts. As in Chapter 13 bankruptcy, you're allowed to keep certain exempt property, but to keep secured property such as your house, car, or furniture you're buying on credit, you have to sign a Reaffirmation Agreement stating that you agree to be responsible for those debts. You basically promise to pay on the debt going forward, and you give up the protections of bankruptcy on that property.

Once you've signed the Reaffirmation Agreement, these debts can't be discharged for at least six years. In other words, you can't change your mind in a few years and decide you don't want those assets and don't want to be responsible for paying for them. In order to reaffirm the debt, you have to make any payments necessary to bring your account up-to-date.

Is Chapter 7 Bankruptcy an Option for You?

After the Bankruptcy Abuse Prevention and Consumer Protection Act of 2005, Chapter 7 bankruptcy became difficult to qualify for. The first hurdle is a "means test," which looks at your income relative to others in your area. If you don't qualify under the means test, you can still try to qualify if your income and expenses are in line with the government requirements, but as detailed calculations are needed to decide this, you should retain the services of a bankruptcy lawyer to make sure your calculations are sound. However, the old days of simply convincing a judge that you need Chapter 7 are gone—the new system has specific rules and limits.

Chapter 7 is typically the bankruptcy type of choice for people who have large credit card or other unsecured debt and few assets. If there's a risk that you might lose your home or car under Chapter 7, your lawyer may recommend that you file Chapter 13 instead. If you have more equity in your car or home than the exempt amount allowed by your state, the chance of being forced to relinquish these assets to be sold to pay your creditors is high.

Debts That Can't Be Forgiven or Discharged

Some debts may not be dischargeable in a Chapter 7 bankruptcy if a creditor challenges them. These include:

- Debts you incurred by fraud, such as those obtained with false information on a credit application
- Credit purchases over a certain amount in the sixty days prior to filing
- Loans or cash advances over a certain amount in the months prior to filing
- Debts you owe under a divorce settlement or decree, with certain exceptions

Chapter 7 bankruptcy stays in your credit history for ten years. During that period, you may be denied credit.

Bankruptcy as a Debt Management Tool

Filing for bankruptcy is not going to help you in the long run if you got there by irresponsible spending habits that you haven't changed. On the other hand, if job loss, high medical bills, disability, death, divorce, or other circumstances not entirely in your control have produced a financial burden you have no hope of getting out from under, bankruptcy may be the only way you can get a fresh start. If you file for bankruptcy, the court will place restrictions on how you can spend money and will not allow you to buy what it considers nonessentials.

ALERT

Chapter 13 bankruptcy can actually help you learn financial discipline that may prevent you from ending up in the same situation again, because you'll live under a strict budget for the entire repayment period, which is typically between three and five years.

Preventing Bankruptcies

Many bankruptcies can be avoided by practicing good money management:

- Avoid impulse spending.
- Don't use a credit card unless you have the cash to pay it off.
- Tear up credit card offers you receive in the mail.
- Stick to a realistic budget.
- Don't buy more house or car than you can comfortably afford.
- Protect yourself against loss by having adequate medical, homeowner's, and auto insurance.
- Don't make speculative or high-risk investments.
- Don't incur joint debt with others who have questionable financial habits.

The ten-year period following the filing of bankruptcy may be difficult, as the bankruptcy follows you around whenever you apply for credit or even sometimes when you apply for a job. Before you resort to bankruptcy, there may be things you can do to improve your situation. If your debt isn't totally overwhelming, you may be able to cut back on nonessentials and find the money to apply to debt. You may even want to sell your car or house and buy a less expensive one. If you haven't taken advantage of the latest low mortgage rates, refinancing your mortgage (again) may net you a few hundred dollars a month that you could put toward your debt. As a last resort, you could apply for a hardship withdrawal from your 401(k) plan if your plan allows them.

Consulting a Credit Counselor

Before you take a step as drastic as filing for bankruptcy, consider consulting with a reputable credit counselor. Myvesta (formerly known as Debt Counselors of America) and the National Foundation for Consumer Credit are the best known of these groups. Myvesta (*www.myvesta.org*) assists people over the Internet and by phone, while the NFCC (*www.nfcc.org*) has a national network of 1,450 offices, many of them called Consumer Credit Counseling Services. They provide counseling in person, as well as electronically. You don't have to be in dire straits to use these services. If you need help getting your financial affairs in order or setting financial priorities, give them a call.

These services are free or very low cost, but an important part of the plan is your agreement not to apply for any new credit or incur any additional debt while you're in the program.

Avoiding Financial Scams and Schemes

Nearly every month, several new scams and schemes that try to separate you from your money rear their ugly heads. Some are misleading or take advantage of your vulnerability to charge you outrageous fees. Others are downright dishonest and illegal.

Credit-Repair Scams

You're in debt up to your ears, the debt collectors are hounding you every time you turn around, you can't get any new credit, and along comes a credit-repair clinic that promises to clean up your credit history in days. Doesn't it sound too good to be true? Yet many people, desperate to resolve their credit and debt problems, pay these clinics large fees and walk away with nothing.

Payday Loans and Advance-Fee Loan Scams

In the category of charging outrageous fees, consider payday loans. You need money now but payday is not for another week. You write a check for $375 to the payday loan company. They immediately write you a check for $300 and hold your check for $375 until your next payday. They keep the $75 difference as their fee, a whopping 25 percent interest rate for a two-week loan, which would be equivalent to an over 500 percent annual interest rate!

ESSENTIAL

The FTC's website at *www.ftc.gov* lists current scams and unscrupulous schemes. Before you get involved in anything that sounds too good to be true, check it out with the FTC or one of the consumer groups online that monitor fraud.

In the category of dishonest and illegal, consider advance-fee loan scams. You see an ad from a company that guarantees approval for a loan or other type of credit but requires you to pay a fee before you apply. Most legitimate lenders won't guarantee that you'll get a loan until after they've thoroughly reviewed your application and checked out your credit history. Advance-fee loans are illegal. You'll never see the loan. Similar scams exist for credit cards. You're promised a credit card, guaranteed, even though your credit history is so bad that no lender dares extend you credit. All you have to do is pay a fee up front. Once again, you'll never see the credit card.

Don't Be a Victim

Some scams have been around for years, yet there are new victims every day. "Make money from home" scams, nonexistent charities, investment "opportunities" that promise you a high rate of return or a chance to buy in at a discount—any of these should make you very skeptical.

In addition, no reputable company will require your social security number in order for you to claim a prize you won, and nobody needs your bank account number for any legitimate purpose.

The Consumer Financial Protection Bureau

In July 2010, Congress passed and President Obama signed the Dodd-Frank Wall Street Reform and Consumer Protection Act. The act created the Consumer Financial Protection Bureau (CFPB). The CFPB consolidates most federal consumer financial protection authority in one place. The consumer bureau is focused on one goal: watching out for American consumers in the consumer financial products and services market.

The bureau will operate under the Federal Reserve and its purpose, according to the agency's website, is to:

- Conduct rule-making, supervision, and enforcement for federal consumer financial protection laws
- Restrict unfair, deceptive, or abusive acts or practices
- Create a center to take consumer complaints
- Promote financial education
- Research consumer behavior
- Monitor financial markets for new risks to consumers
- Enforce laws that outlaw discrimination and other unfair treatment in consumer transactions.

The bureau's website (*www.consumerfinance.gov*) specifically states "The CFPB will also be a cop on the beat to patrol the consumer financial services markets." In addition, it will also have authority over all financial institutions in the country including mortgage-, auto-, and credit card-lenders, and also some of the grayer participants in the world of finance, such as payday loan providers, debt collectors, and foreclosure relief services.

Congress specifically charged the CFPB with putting an end to no-income verification mortgages, eliminating prepayment penalties, ending lending employee bonuses for steering consumers into high cost loans, and implementing simpler disclosures for financial transactions.

As is the case with nearly all legislative actions, there are exceptions to who's covered under the CFPB's jurisdiction. Those entities excluded from the bureau's oversight include:

- Merchants, retailers, and other sellers of nonfinancial goods or services
- Real estate brokerages
- Manufactured home retailers and modular home retailers
- Accountant and tax preparers
- Legal practitioners
- Employee benefit and compensation plans
- Persons regulated by the Securities and Exchange Commission, the Commodity Futures Trading Commission, a state securities commission, a state insurance regulator, or the Farm Credit Administration
- Motor vehicle dealers, unless they provide mortgages or extend consumer retail credit without assigning it to third parties
- Tax-exempt organizations

The purpose of the CFPB seems to be aimed at fixing the conditions that led to the financial meltdown in the first place, such as deceptive lending practices, high cost loans, loans with super low teaser rates, overly complicated financial disclosure statements, and giving loans to the nonqualified.

CHAPTER 8

Living with Student Loans

If you're one of the 60 to 67 percent of college graduates with student loans, there's a lot you need to know about repayment and how to keep your interest costs as low as possible. If the thought of paying off the large balances seems overwhelming, or if you're struggling to make the payments, you have options available to you to make it easier.

Stafford Loans

The most common type of student loan is a Stafford loan. These are either subsidized, meaning that the federal government pays the interest while you're in school and during grace and deferment periods, or unsubsidized, which means you're responsible for interest during these periods.

If you didn't pay the interest while you were in school, you'll have a larger loan balance to pay now that you've graduated or dropped out, because the interest was capitalized, or added to the balance of your loan. Your monthly payments will be higher and you'll pay more interest over the life of the loan. You can use the online calculator on the Sallie Mae website at *www .salliemae.com* to estimate the accrued interest on your loan and your new loan balance after deferment.

Grace Periods

The day after you graduate, withdraw, or drop to less than half-time status, your six-month grace period begins (some types of loans have different grace periods). You're allowed one grace period per loan, during which no principal payments are required. Your first loan payment will be due approximately thirty to forty-five days after the end of your grace period.

ALERT

Be sure to notify your lenders of your current address so they can contact you during your grace period to let you know the amount of your monthly payments, the payment due dates, how long it will take you to repay your loans, and the current interest rates.

Deferments and Forbearances

Deferment is one option for relief during a period of financial difficulty. If you qualify for a loan deferment, you won't be required to make principal payments on your loan during that period. If you have an unsubsidized Stafford loan, you'll be responsible for making the interest payments yourself during the deferment period, or the interest will be added to your loan balance. If you have a subsidized Stafford loan, the federal government will make the interest payments for you. You can qualify for a deferment under the following circumstances:

- Unemployment
- Enrollment in school
- Graduate fellowship
- Financial hardship
- Rehabilitation program due to disability

If you don't qualify for a deferment, you may qualify for forbearance, a special arrangement with your lender that allows you to reduce or postpone principal payments temporarily. Interest continues to accrue during this period on both subsidized and unsubsidized Stafford loans, and if you don't pay it during the forbearance, it will be added to the balance of your loan. This costs you more in the long run because you'll be paying interest on the interest.

You can automatically receive a forbearance if you participate in a qualifying program such as a medical or dental internship or residency, or AmeriCorps—or if you're serving on active duty as a member of the U.S. armed forces. You may also qualify for debt-burden forbearance if your student loan payments are high compared to your income. Other forbearances are granted at the discretion of the lender based on your individual circumstances.

FACT

Late student loan payments are reported to the credit-reporting bureaus just like late credit card, mortgage, or car payments. This information may stay on your credit history for up to seven years, unless you rehabilitate your loan.

To request a deferment or forbearance, you have to complete an application available from your lender. Some lenders provide these online. Within thirty days of submitting your application, you'll be notified in writing whether or not your deferment or forbearance was approved.

Repayment Options

If you're trying to minimize your monthly payment, try to balance your immediate need for lower payments with your long-term financial goals, which include paying off debt at the lowest reasonable cost. Review the status of your student loans annually to see if you're taking advantage of all the benefits offered by lenders and if the plan you're in still suits your changing financial situation. Just because the terms of your student loans include a particular repayment plan doesn't mean you're stuck with it; if it isn't working for you, you can apply for a change (you can even do it online). There are several options available:

- Standard repayment: You pay the same amount each month over ten years or less, which results in lower interest costs than most other options, except prepayment.
- Graduated repayment: You repay the loan over the same period but the payments are smaller in the early years and significantly larger in the later years. Because the lower payments include mostly interest and you don't pay the balance as quickly, you'll pay more interest.
- Income-sensitive or income-contingent repayment: If you're eligible for these options, your payments can be based on a fixed percentage of your gross income each month. The percentage is between 4 and 25 percent and your payments are made over fifteen years with the income-sensitive repayment plan and twenty-five years with the income-contingent repayment plan. You have to reapply every year.
- Extended repayment: You can use this plan if you owe more than $30,000 in federal student loans. It gives you lower monthly payments over a twelve- to thirty-year period using either the standard or graduated repayment plan.
- Loan consolidation: This option allows you to combine all of your eligible student loans into one loan with one monthly payment.
- Prepayment: No matter what plan you have, there's always the option of prepaying all or part of your student loans at any time without penalty, which can greatly reduce your interest costs.

Forgiveness of Loans

In limited circumstances, some student loans can be forgiven without requiring repayment. You may be eligible to have part of your Stafford loan canceled if you obtained it on or after October 1, 1998, and you've taught full time for five years in a low-income school. You can obtain an application from your student loan lender.

ESSENTIAL

For more information on the loan forgiveness program for child-care providers, call 1-888-562-7002 or write to the Child Care Provider Loan Forgiveness Program, PO Box 4639, Utica, NY 13504. For information on the nursing forgiveness program, call the Nursing Education Loan Repayment Program toll-free at 1-877-464-4772.

The federal government recently instituted a new program whose purpose is to bring more highly qualified child-care providers into the profession and keep them longer. If you're eligible for this program, you may be able to wipe out part of your undergraduate Stafford loan. To be eligible you must have an associate's or bachelor's degree in early childhood education, must have worked for at least two years as a child-care provider in an eligible facility serving a low-income community, and must have taken out your loan as a new borrower after October 7, 1998. A similar program, the Nursing Education Loan Repayment Program (NELRP), exists for registered nurses who serve in eligible facilities located in areas experiencing nursing shortages.

Federal Perkins Loans

When Stafford loans and other financial sources aren't sufficient to cover costs, Perkins loans are sometimes available. With a Perkins loan, the college decides on the amount of the loan, up to $4,000 per year for undergraduate students, with a lifetime limit of $20,000. Graduate students can borrow a maximum of $6,000 for each year of graduate or professional study, with a lifetime limit of $40,000, including any undergraduate Perkins loans. Although these are the maximum amounts allowed by law, actual awards are usually less because schools try to use their limited funds to assist as many eligible students as possible.

ALERT

Colleges award federal Perkins loans as part of their financial aid programs, based on financial need. The federal government provides most of the funds and the college kicks in the rest. To be considered, you would have checked "yes" in the section of your Free Application for Federal Student Aid (FAFSA) that asks about interest in student loans.

Interest rates are fixed at 5 percent for the life of the loan, which cannot exceed ten years. No interest payments are required while you're a student, as long as you attend at least half-time. There's a nine-month grace period after you graduate, drop below half-time status, or leave school. Repayment begins at the end of the grace period and is made directly to the college.

Terms of the Loan

You may be able to receive a deferment or forbearance on a Perkins loan by applying to your college. During a deferment, you can temporarily postpone payments without accruing interest. If you're not eligible for a deferment, you may qualify for a forbearance, which allows you to reduce or postpone payments for a limited period of time. Interest will accrue during this period and you'll be responsible for paying it.

Part of your Perkins loan may be forgiven or canceled if you work full-time in certain occupations, such as teaching full-time at a low-income school or in certain subject areas where there's a teacher shortage.

PLUS Loans

Parents of dependent students can also take out loans. The Direct PLUS loan is a federal student loan that lets parents borrow money. To qualify the parent must pass a credit check and will be held liable for the loan. Graduate students can apply on their own and approval is based on their own credit score. The annual limit is the student's cost of attendance minus any other financial aid received. The interest rate is fixed (the rate as of February 2012 was 7.9 percent) and repayment must begin sixty days after the loan is disbursed. The Federal Direct Loan program will charge a 4 percent origination fee, which will be added to the loan amount. Stafford loan rates are generally lower than PLUS loan rates and the payment deferral period is much longer, but there are annual limits on the amount you can borrow and the student will be held primarily responsible for repayment.

Keep Track of the Interest Rates

Stafford loan interest rates can be a mystery. Congress periodically adjusts how interest is charged (fixed or variable), and the maximum interest rates. Make sure that you're looking at the most up-to-date information as you research your loan. However, you should double-check the up-to-date information with your lender—it may only apply to loans issued after yours.

Stafford loans obtained through lenders associated with Sallie Mae, the largest education finance company in the United States, may be eligible for decreased interest rates if the first forty-eight payments are made on time. Consider having payments automatically deducted from your checking account each month to ensure you're not late with a payment.

FACT

According to Collegiate Funding Services, average monthly payments among those currently owing student loans were $222 per month for men, on an average remaining balance of $12,900, and $141 per month for women, on an average remaining balance of $10,300.

If you don't have a Sallie Mae loan, consider transferring your loan or refiling it with a Sallie Mae lender to take advantage of Sallie Mae's incentives, such as the interest reduction. Other lenders may offer similar rewards if you set up automatic monthly payments and pay on time for several years. When rates are low, you can take advantage of the opportunity to pay off your loans more quickly by continuing to make the higher payments even though your required payment is lower.

The sooner you start paying off your loans and the larger your monthly payment, the less your loans will cost you in the long run. If you find yourself having difficulty making your loan payments, it's better to be proactive than to make late payments or default on your loans. Call your lender at the first indication that you may have trouble making payments.

Defaulting on Your Student Loan

Student loans are the first real debt many people incur. Late payments or defaults can seriously harm your credit record for many years, but if you pay on time you can build a positive credit history that will help you qualify for a home mortgage, new car loan, or other type of credit. The federal government has made it increasingly difficult to escape your student loan debt, and there is no statute of limitations, so you can be sure it will dog you forever if you don't pay.

What Constitutes a Default?

If you're late with a payment for 270 days, you'll be considered in default of your student loan. Once you're in default, your lender will file a default claim with the guaranty agency, which buys your account from the lender and assigns the loan to a collection agency. The government also notifies all the credit bureaus.

Consequences of Default

If you don't pay your defaulted loan right away, you could have your federal income tax refunds withheld and applied to the loan balance, have your wages garnished, have collection costs of up to 40 percent of the loan levied against you, and face possible legal action. If you have a professional license or certificate of any kind (medical, law, accounting, and so on), it could be revoked. You may no longer be eligible for federal financial aid programs. You also lose your eligibility for federal loans such as FHA and VA loans, which enable many people to buy a house that they wouldn't qualify for otherwise, and you may be denied credit cards or other forms of credit.

The default will show up on your credit report for seven years and could affect your ability to rent a house or apartment, buy a car, qualify for a mortgage, or even find a job. Collection costs that are charged to you could total nearly half your balance, plus there's a 28 percent commission charged by the collection agency and that gets passed on to you. The government may even sue you and take your car, bank accounts, and other valuable property that you own and place a lien on your house, if you own one.

Preventing Default

If you're having trouble making your loan payments, you have several alternatives. You could change your repayment plan, apply for deferment or forbearance, or apply for a loan consolidation, which could reduce your monthly payments by nearly half. If you've tried everything and are still having problems with your loan, contact your borrower advocate, who can act as a liaison between you and your lender and may be able to help find solutions to your problem. Lenders really don't want you to default on your loan, and they'll usually offer you a few alternatives—you just have to ask before it's too late.

Rehabilitating Your Defaulted Loan

Once you've defaulted on your student loans, any unpaid interest is computed and the entire balance of the loan becomes due and payable immediately. Once you reach this point, you have several options to avoid the negative consequences of default:

- You can pay off your entire student loan in one lump sum.
- You can establish monthly payment arrangements with your guaranty or collection agency (rehabilitation).
- You can consolidate your account into one new loan.

When you come to a repayment agreement with your lender, guaranty agency, or collection agency, a new loan is created that wipes out the old, defaulted loan.

The Process of Rehabilitation

Rehabilitation is a federal repayment program offered to student-loan holders who have defaulted on their loans. To rehabilitate your loan, you have to make twelve on-time monthly payments in a row. Then the government agrees to insure your loan once again and your guaranty agency can sell it to a secondary market or lender, removing it from default status. Once your loan has been rehabilitated, you have up to nine more years to repay it. You can only rehabilitate a defaulted student loan once.

ESSENTIAL

Besides removing your loan default from reports to the credit-reporting bureaus, rehabilitating your loan helps you regain your student loan benefits if you still need them and restores your eligibility for student financial aid.

Resolving Student Loan Disputes

Sometimes errors occur in student loan record keeping. If you believe there's an error in your student loan—an incorrect balance, payments not credited, incorrect interest rate, incorrect personal information, or other error—contact the agency that holds your loan. If you can't resolve the issue on your own, contact the Federal Student Aid (FSA) Ombudsman of the Department of Education by calling 1-877-557-2575 or writing to U.S. Department of Education, FSA Ombudsman, 830 First Street NE, Fourth Floor, Washington, DC 20202-5144.

Consolidating Your Student Loans

Decisions about student loan repayments can significantly impact your finances long into the future, so before you jump into a consolidation loan, research your options and make sure you're going to achieve your purpose without any costly surprises.

Benefits of Consolidating

If you have several loans, you may want to consolidate them after you graduate just to simplify your record keeping and bill paying. You may also want to take advantage of lower interest rates, or the longer repayment period you get from consolidating. Consolidating may be a good option for you if you have heavy education debt, want to lock in at a fixed rate, or want to reduce your monthly payments and are willing to pay more over the length of your loan in order to do so.

Under the Federal Direct Consolidation Loan program you can consolidate your loans at a fixed interest rate with only one payment a month. The interest rate on consolidation loans is an average of the interest rates on all your student loans, not to exceed 8.25 percent, so you may benefit from locking in when market interest rates are very low. The federal program also allows you to extend the term of the loan up to thirty years. Obviously a loan period this long would cost you much more in interest, but there are no prepayment penalties, so you can always pay more or pay the loan off early. Before you extend your loan repayment period, use an online calculator to calculate the true cost over time.

Student loan consolidation has other benefits. For example, if you pass away, your student loan is forgiven. Contrast this with using a home equity loan to pay off your student loan—your family would still have to cover the balance of the home equity loan.

You May Not Need to Consolidate

You can consolidate all your loans with one lender at any time without a consolidation loan if you just want to simplify your payments. If a lower interest rate is your goal, remember that after making forty-eight consecutive on-time payments, you may qualify for an interest-rate reduction. This may put you at a lower rate than you could get by consolidating, depending on your current interest rate. To figure out what makes the most sense for you, try Sallie Mae's online loan consolidation calculator in the tools and calculators section at *www.salliemae.com*.

A Tax Break

Up to $2,500 a year in interest on some student loans (Stafford, PLUS, Perkins, consolidation, and private) may be tax deductible, if certain criteria, such as income limits, are met. The proceeds of the loan must have been used for qualified higher education expenses (tuition, fees, room and board, supplies, and other related expenses), and you must have been enrolled at least half-time in a qualified program at an eligible institution.

FACT

A survey conducted by Collegiate Funding Services found that more than half (54 percent) of the student loan holders surveyed had not heard of the Federal Direct Consolidation Loan program, a program enacted by Congress to make repaying federal student loans more affordable.

After 2002, the rule that you could only deduct interest for the first sixty months of your loan has been eliminated. You can now deduct interest no matter how long you've had the loan. Also in 2002, the income limits were increased. For 2012, deductibility phased out if your income was between $55,000 and $70,000 for single taxpayers and $110,000 and $140,000 for couples filing jointly. These limits are increased from time to time to adjust for inflation, so see IRS Publication 970 for up-to-date limits. However, unless Congress votes to preserve the law, the 2002 changes outlined above will no longer be the law after 2012. If you paid more than $600 in interest on your student loans during the year, your lender will send you a Form 1098-E showing the amount paid. To claim the amount on your income taxes, you must file Form 1040 or 1040A, but unlike the mortgage interest deduction, you don't have to itemize in order to get the deduction. If you're married, you have to file jointly.

Income-Based Repayment Plans

Originally effective as of July 1, 2009, this plan (IBR) was designed to cap the monthly payments at a percentage of the borrower's discretionary income based on income and family size. To find out if you qualify, you can access an IBR calculator at *www.studentaid.ed.gov/ibr*. IBR is only available for federal student loans such as Stafford, Grad PLUS, and consolidation loans. IBR is not available for Perkins loans or Direct PLUS loans for parents.

The maximum repayment period is twenty-five years. After twenty-five years, any remaining debt will be discharged. The amount of the debt discharged will be considered taxable income in the year of forgiveness. However, if you are employed full time in public service, the maximum repayment period is reduced to ten years, and the amount forgiven will not be included for tax purposes.

A law was passed in 2010 that cut the monthly maximum payment from 15 percent of discretionary income to 10 percent and accelerated the maximum repayment period from twenty-five years to twenty years. It is only effective for new borrowers of loans on or after July 1, 2014. President Obama subsequently signed an executive order making these new IBR rules available in 2012 for certain borrowers who have at least one federal student loan in 2012 or later and no loans prior to 2008.

Creative Financing for Your Children

If you're starting a family of your own, you may want to consider ways to help your children pay for education. You may have felt (or still feel) a heavy burden from paying off your own student loans and wish to spare your children that misery. If so, it's never too early to look at strategies for making higher education more affordable.

Saving for College

One way to help children pay for college is to accumulate funds that can be used to pay for their education. You can do this in a variety of ways, such as college savings plans, retirement accounts, insurance contracts, and more.

529 Plans

The most recent addition to the college savings arsenal is the Section 529 college savings plan. This is a plan sponsored by each state for the purpose of helping people save for higher education. Higher education can mean college, graduate school, trade school, and a number of foreign institutions.

These plans have become popular for their tax benefits, high contribution limits, and flexibility.

You can put away a lot of money in a 529—hundreds of thousands of dollars per year. However, most folks just put away a few bucks per month. If you use your state's 529 plan, you may be eligible for a state income tax deduction on your contributions. Furthermore, the earnings in the account occur without taxes, like the earnings in an IRA. Finally, if you spend the money on qualified higher education expenses (which are defined quite broadly), you don't have to pay any income tax when you take the money out.

If your child does not go to college, you can always transfer the funds toward another family member without penalty. You can even use the funds yourself—for a graduate degree, for example. Many parents prefer this arrangement to the type of accounts that automatically go to the child at age eighteen. If your child is not mature enough for the money, you get to keep it or do something else with it.

Keep in mind that if nobody uses the funds for higher education, you may have to pay taxes and penalties. The penalties are reduced or eliminated, however, in the event that your child gets a scholarship and doesn't need the money.

Coverdell Education Savings Accounts (ESAs)

You can contribute up to $2,000 per year in this type of account, formerly known as an "Education IRA." This can add up, especially if you have several children (or grandchildren), since you can contribute $2,000 annually to separate ESAs set up for each child (or grandchild). Annual contributions are allowed up until the account beneficiary, or the college-bound child, turns eighteen.

If you are unmarried, your ability to make ESA contributions is phased out between adjusted gross income of $95,000 and $110,000. For joint filers, the phaseout range is between $190,000 and $220,000. ESA earnings build up tax free, and then the money can be withdrawn (also tax-free) to pay the account beneficiary's college expenses. Like contributions to Roth IRAs, ESA contributions are nondeductible, but the tax-free withdrawal privilege makes up for that. If the beneficiary doesn't attend college or doesn't incur enough expenses to exhaust his or her account, the balance can be rolled over tax free into another family member's ESA.

You can also take tax-free ESA payouts to cover the account beneficiary's elementary and secondary school (K-12) costs. Eligible expenses include tuition and fees to attend private and religious schools, room, board, uniforms, and transportation. Other eligible expenses include books and supplies, academic tutoring, computers, peripheral equipment and software, and even Internet access charges. You have until April 15 of the following year to make your ESA contribution for the tax year in question. For example, you can make your 2012 ESA contribution as late as April 15, 2013.

Advanced Strategies

If you think that you or your child will have to borrow to pay for education, set the stage early. Keep an eye on how assets are titled as soon as possible. Assets in your name or the child's name can affect how your child qualifies for loans, scholarships, and gift aid. If your parents want to help their grandchild, plan ahead on how their assets can accomplish this. For example, 529 accounts can often receive favorable student aid treatment, so have grandma and grandpa consider 529 contributions.

If you're self-employed and your kids are old enough to do some work, put them to work. You can pay them for tasks such as filing, stuffing envelopes, and cleaning. You'll get a tax deduction, and they'll have earned income that they might put into an IRA or college savings plan. For example, the child could fund a Roth IRA, and take the contributions back out (without taxes or penalties) at college time. However, any income or assets in the child's name will hurt his or her chances of receiving needs-based financial aid.

CHAPTER 9

Show Me the Money: Work and Career

Salary is not always the most important indicator of job potential. Knowing how to evaluate a prospective employer, determine your worth in the job market, negotiate the best salary and benefits, and request a raise will help you optimize job potential. In today's volatile market, it's equally important to know how to protect yourself financially if you lose your job.

Choosing a Job with Potential

Salary is a very important factor in choosing a job, but it's not always the most important one. Evaluate the total compensation package: salary, insurance, paid leave, stock options, retirement plan, and other benefits. Once you've placed a dollar value on the employer-provided benefits, evaluate other aspects of the job. Remember that there are some things you can't put a price tag on, such as training and experience. The best jobs will prepare you for the next step in your career by teaching you valuable skills and providing on-the-job training.

Evaluating a Potential Employer

When evaluating a potential employer, find out as much as you can about the industry. What's the history of growth in the industry and what's the anticipated future need for goods and services produced or provided by that industry? Is the industry trendy? Is it subject to government regulation? If so, what's the possible impact on the company?

ALERT

There may be times when you need a job—any job—and you don't have the luxury of being selective, but you don't have to stay in one that's a dead end. Continue your search even after you find employment if the job doesn't provide you with what you need.

Also find out as much as you can about the company or organization. Detailed information, including current financial information, is easily available at your local library or online if the company trades publicly. Is the company financially stable? What are its size, reputation, and growth potential? In addition, if you know anybody who has worked for the organization, find out what you can about the company culture and atmosphere and the quality of management.

Evaluating the Job

What do you know about the job itself? Is there a training program or opportunity to obtain additional education? What are the day-to-day tasks and duties? Who will you report to and what is that person's leadership style? What are your potential coworkers like? Does the job require travel, weekend work, or working long hours? What is the salary and benefits package? If the salary seems low, are there benefits that compensate for it?

Your Worth to an Employer

When you get a job offer, how will you know if the salary is reasonable? Before you enter the job market, whether it's your first job out of college or a new step on your career path, you need to know what the going salary is in your geographical area for someone with your education, training, and skills.

The *Occupational Outlook Handbook,* produced by the Bureau of Labor Statistics (BLS), is an invaluable source of information on salaries in hundreds of different occupations. It also provides descriptions of what workers do on the job, working conditions, training and education needed, and expected job prospects in a wide range of occupations. In addition, the BLS provides information on wages, earnings, and benefits for many occupations by region, state, and metropolitan area. Visit BLS online at *www.bls .gov*, and see Appendix B for more web resources for your salary research.

Negotiating Your Salary and Benefits Package

Much has been written about negotiating salary and benefits, but most of it boils down to knowing what you're worth in the marketplace, identifying which benefits are important to you, and putting a price tag on the benefits offered by your prospective employer so you can evaluate the real value of an offer. When meeting with prospective employers, find out what benefits and perks the company gives employees in the position you're applying for, what an average pay increase is, and what benefits the company might add to sweeten the pot if they're not able or willing to offer the salary you'd like.

Experts caution job seekers to delay discussing salary until well into the interview process and to avoid telling interviewers your current salary. You shouldn't be pegged at a salary range that's lower than the going rate just because you're underpaid in your current job, and discussing salary too early in the process can stick you with a lower than acceptable offer or, conversely, take you out of the running if your current salary is too high.

To find out how much you'd need to earn in a new city to equate to your current salary, use the cost of living calculator at *www.homefair .com*. Enter the city and state you're moving from and to, your current salary, and whether you'd prefer to own or rent.

Evaluating Your Employee Benefits

Employer-provided benefits are a significant part of any compensation package and can have a profound effect on your finances. Employers often provide a wide range of benefits, including the following:

- Retirement plans, such as the 401(k)
- Section 125 cafeteria plans
- Group health, life, dental, and disability insurance plans
- Tuition reimbursement
- Flexible-spending accounts
- Stock option plans
- Bonus plans
- Vacation, holiday, and sick-leave benefits

All of these benefits, as well as others not mentioned, have a monetary value that you should consider when evaluating your salary or comparing job offers. Some benefits, such as 401(k) and cafeteria plans (which have nothing to do with food), also have tax benefits that can save you additional money by reducing your taxes.

Insurance Coverage

Most people with health insurance are covered under a group plan offered by their employer or their spouse's employer. Although employers are charging employees more as prices continue to increase dramatically each year, employer-provided health insurance is still a bargain. If you aren't offered coverage through your employer you can purchase an individual policy, but these can be expensive—especially as you get older, or if you have a family. Whether you're married or single, you need health insurance to protect yourself against financial disaster in the event of a serious illness or accident.

If you're fortunate enough to have employer-provided coverage, calculate its monetary value by first finding out what the company pays for your medical, dental, life, and long- and short-term disability on a monthly or yearly basis. Some ways to ascertain this information might be to consult your employment contract, your pay stub, or ask your employer's human resources department. If you contribute to the cost, subtract your contribution from the total. If your contribution is pretax (as in a cafeteria, or section 125 plan), factor in your tax savings by adding your social security tax rate of 7.65 percent (up to $84,900 in earnings, after which it's only 1.45 percent), your federal tax rate, and your state tax rate. Multiply the total percentage times the amount you pay toward your insurance coverage to calculate your tax savings.

For example, if you're in the 28 percent federal tax bracket and a 7 percent state tax bracket, add these two percentages plus the 7.65 percent social security tax. Your total tax rate is 42.65 percent. If you contribute $100 per month toward your insurance, your real cost is $57.35 ($100 × 42.65 percent = $42.65 in savings; $100 – $42.65 = $57.35).

ALERT

Being young is no guarantee of health. If you don't have full insurance coverage, purchase a high-deductible policy to protect yourself against major medical expenses. The higher the deductible, the less expensive the policy, so consider one with a $1,000 to $5,000 deductible until you find a job with insurance.

Flexible-Spending Accounts (FSAs)

FSAs, or reimbursement accounts, are an employer-provided benefit that allows you to set aside pretax contributions to pay for eligible medical expenses that aren't covered by your health insurance, including premiums (unless they're paid with pretax money), deductibles, copays, and any other health cost considered an allowable medical expense by the IRS. For a complete list of allowable medical deductions, see Publication 502, *Medical and Dental Expenses*, in the Forms and Publications section of the IRS website (*www.irs.gov*), or request a printed copy of this publication from the IRS by calling 1-800-829-3676.

You benefit from an FSA because your contributions are deducted before taxes are calculated, thus reducing your taxes. Using the same tax brackets as the health insurance example, if your total tax percentage (federal, state, and social security) is 42.65 percent, every dollar you put into an FSA will cost you only fifty-seven cents. If you have significant medical expenses you can save a lot of money, so don't overlook this great benefit. Don't contribute more than you think you'll use, because under IRS regulations, you forfeit any unused funds at the end of the year. If you get stuck at the end of the year with an unused balance, visit your local drugstore and stock up on bandages, aspirin, cough syrup, and any other goods you think you'll use in the coming year.

401(k) and Other Retirement Plans

If your employer provides a 401(k) plan, you'd do well to participate—remember, your contributions are usually tax deferred (except for social security taxes). If your employer matches a percentage of your contribution, add this to your compensation total when calculating the value of your benefits. Most employers match between fifty cents and $1 for every dollar you contribute, for up to 3 to 6 percent of your salary. If you earn $40,000 a year and contribute $200 a month and your employer match is 75 percent for up to 6 percent of your salary, your employer will kick in another $150 a month up to a maximum of $2,400 a year. Under this example, your employer is actually paying you an additional $1,800 a year ($150 × 12 = $1,800).

Employee-Ownership Plans

The world of employee stock-ownership plans, stock option plans, employee stock-purchase plans, and incentive option plans is confusing at best, and it's difficult if not impossible to evaluate the potential worth of stock and stock options offered by your employer. Stock options are a popular method of attracting employees in high-tech companies and are becoming more common in other industries as part of total compensation plans.

Stock Options

Stock option plans are a way for companies to attract, share ownership with, and reward employees. A stock option gives an employee the right to buy company stock at a specified price during a specified period after the option has vested. Companies use the vesting period to motivate employees to stick around. Let's say you receive an option of 500 shares at $10 per share and the stock price goes up to $20. You can exercise the option and buy the 500 shares at $10 each, sell them for $20 each, and pocket the $5,000 difference. If the stock price never rises above the option price, you don't lose money but you don't make any, either.

ESSENTIAL

If you're offered stock options, be sure you understand which type they are and how they work. You can find detailed information about the various types of plans at the National Center for Employee Ownership website at *www.nceo.org*.

Employee Stock Purchase Plans

Employee stock purchase plans (ESPPs) offer employees the chance to buy stock, usually through payroll deductions during an "offering period" at a discounted price. The employee can then sell it right away and take the profit created by the discount, or hold on to it in expectation that its value will increase.

Employee Stock Ownership Plans

Employee stock ownership plans (ESOPs) are a type of benefit plan that is regulated by the federal government in which a trust is set up to acquire some or all of the stock of the company and sell the stock to employees. Because ESOPs receive tax advantages, they're not allowed to discriminate in favor of key or highly compensated employees, so most employees get to participate. ESOPs are typically used as a type of retirement plan, or as an exit strategy for the boss in small companies. Be cautious about investing the bulk of your retirement funds in company stock no matter how well established the company is.

Incentive Stock Options

Incentive stock options (ISOs) allow employees to purchase shares of stock at some time in the future at a specified price. The employee pays tax on the gain upon sale or disposition of the stock, not upon receipt or exercise of the option. Nonqualified stock options don't have the restrictions of other options and don't receive any special tax consideration. When employees exercise nonqualified options, they pay ordinary income tax on the difference between the grant price and exercise price.

Asking for a Raise

If you already have a job but feel underpaid, you may be thinking about asking your boss for a raise. If this is the case, you need to be prepared to convince the powers that be that you not only deserve one, but that you're worth it. Don't make the common mistake of basing your request on your need for more money or your inability to meet your financial obligations. Businesses do not base salary increases on employees' personal needs; they base increases on employees' worth to the company, the quality of their work, company pay scales, and budgetary concerns.

QUESTION

What's the number one rule for requesting a raise?
Don't give ultimatums. They'll put your boss on the defensive, and may force you to quit your job or eat crow. Your goal is to convince your boss that you're worth more money because you do an exceptional job or you've accepted additional responsibility that warrants an increase or promotion.

Evaluate Yourself

First, perform an evaluation of your skills, productivity, job tasks, and contribution to the company. Look at your job duties and performance from the company's perspective and base your approach on the company's needs. If you have a written job description, dig it out, along with copies of your last two or three written performance reviews. Jot down the major tasks you perform that may not be part of your formal job description. The goal is to show or remind your boss of your tangible contributions to the company, so make a list of your accomplishments, and if possible, the dollar value of each to the company. For example, you might say: "I saved the company $20,000 this year by researching and negotiating contracts with new vendors."

Determine the Going Rate for Your Job

Next, you need to determine the going rate, both inside and outside the company, for what you do. Ask your company's human resources department if there are company-wide salary ranges for your position and several related positions above yours. Review these, along with the salary information and compensation surveys you obtained from the BLS website. National information can give you an idea of what jobs similar to yours typically pay, but salaries vary from one region to another. Be sure to consult some local information as well by reading help-wanted ads, talking to friends and associates, or making a call to your local human resources organization, such as the Society for Human Resource Management (SHRM; *www.shrm.org*).

Know Your Company's Policies and Financial Status

To increase your chances of getting the raise you want, you need to know several things about your company. What is the company's financial condition? Is it struggling to stay afloat? Is there a budget crisis? What is the policy on salary increases? Are all employees reviewed at the same time each year? Does your department have a budget for salaries that it needs to stay within? If so, you're in direct competition with the other employees in your department for limited funds, and you should work on making yourself stand out above the crowd.

Pick Your Time Carefully

Timing is everything. If you've only been at your job for a few months, asking for a raise probably won't go over very well. However, if you find after a few months that the company hired you at a salary well below that of others in your position and with your experience, it may pay to discuss this with your supervisor. If you've been formally or informally disciplined or chastised recently, wait at least a few months before asking for more money.

Don't ask to meet with your boss during the busiest time of the month or busiest days of the week, which for most people are Monday and Friday. It's to your advantage to arrange an appointment at a time that's convenient with your manager.

Consider Benefits in Lieu of Salary

Not all companies are in a position to raise salaries. However, your employer may be able to offer you additional benefits instead, such as extra paid leave, tuition assistance, stock options, overtime, or a promotion, if one is warranted. When comparing salaries, it's important to consider the financial value of these and other benefits and perks. If your company pays for all or part of your health insurance, this is as good as money in your pocket. The same is true of a 401(k) match.

ESSENTIAL

The average employer spends 42 percent of salary costs on employee fringe benefits such as insurance, vacation and other paid leave, retirement contributions, and tuition assistance, including mandatory benefits such as state and federal unemployment insurance and workers' compensation insurance. The average employee making $40,000 per year receives $16,800 in benefits.

Losing Your Job Without Losing Your Shirt

The average worker changes jobs at least half a dozen times. In this era of corporate takeovers, downsizing, mergers, layoffs, and most recently, stunning corporate corruption, nobody is immune from sudden job loss.

Prepare for the Possibility of Job Loss

You don't need to be paranoid, but being prepared for the possibility of job loss will make it easier to deal with if it does happen. To be prepared, you need to know your net worth, set up a budget, save, and keep your debt low.

FACT

According to the U.S. Department of Labor's Bureau of Labor Statistics, during 2011 there were over 6,000 mass layoff events in the United States resulting in over 1 million new unemployment claims. Mass layoffs involve at least fifty people at a time.

You should also have a feel for the stability of your job. How are your employer's competitors doing? Are they experiencing layoffs? Layoffs in your industry can be a good indication of the instability of your job, even if your employer has not yet made any cuts. If job layoffs have already occurred where you work, you should have your resume updated and be looking around for possible job opportunities that fit your skills. Compile a list of references, with job titles, telephone numbers, and addresses, and line up letters of recommendation. It's also a good idea to get contact information from coworkers, vendors, and customers so you can use it for networking purposes.

Next, acquaint yourself with your employer's severance policy. Do laid-off employees receive severance pay? If so, is it based on years of service or other criteria? Will you be paid your accrued vacation balance upon termination? What will happen to your benefits if you lose your job? Will you be able to continue your health insurance benefits under the Consolidation Omnibus Budget Reconciliation Act (COBRA)? How much will it cost? It's foolhardy to go without at least catastrophic health insurance, so know what your other alternatives are if you can't afford to elect COBRA coverage (note that COBRA is often much more expensive than the monthly deduction from your paycheck—you have to pay the entire bill without the help of your employer). An illness or accident while you're uninsured could leave you no alternative but bankruptcy.

If the Worst Happens

If you get the pink slip, apply for unemployment on the first day of your layoff so you'll receive the maximum benefits for which you're eligible. Some people are reluctant to file for unemployment because they feel it's a type of welfare, but it isn't. Your employer contributes to your state's unemployment insurance fund as well as a federal unemployment fund. You earned those benefits by working. If you need them, use them.

Unemployment benefits are typically about half of your regular earnings, up to your state's cap, paid for a maximum of twenty-six weeks. Your state's cap is based on the average wages in your state. For instance, the state maximum benefit in Massachusetts, effective October 2, 2011, is $653 per week, while South Dakota's is $323 a week. You'll be required to prove that you're actively seeking work while receiving unemployment benefits, and you must be ready, willing, available, and able to work. Unemployment benefits are subject to federal income tax, so you'll need to claim them at the end of the year. Be prepared for the additional taxes you may owe as a result.

During a period of unemployment, resist the urge to use your credit cards unless absolutely necessary for critically important expenses. If you can't make ends meet, contact your creditors, tell them you've lost your job but are actively seeking employment, and request an arrangement that allows you to make reduced payments for a limited time.

So You Want to Be Your Own Boss?

At some point in your career, you may decide that you'd like to start your own business instead of working for someone else. Let's assume you've already thoroughly researched the viability of your idea for a business, prepared a business plan, and are confident that you have the skills, discipline, and work ethic necessary to be successful on your own. Here is what else you need to consider:

- Can you live without a steady income for an undetermined period of time? Before you give up your day job, you should have a healthy savings account to fall back on while you build a customer base, especially if the business is seasonal or cyclical.

- Will there be start-up costs? Do you have a solid, detailed estimate of what they'll be? Have you prepared a budget detailing projected monthly costs and estimated sales? Talk to your banker and find out what financing options are available, if any, and what's required in order to qualify for them.

- Have you thought about the legal form your business will take? Read up on the subject or talk to an accountant about the pros and cons of being a sole proprietorship versus a partnership or corporation.

- Have you familiarized yourself with the laws regulating your business and made a plan to comply with local ordinances and laws regarding business licensing, safety, workers' compensation, and sales tax?

- Have you talked to your insurance agent? If you're running a business out of your home, you may need a rider to your homeowner's insurance policy. If you have employees, you'll need workers' compensation and liability insurance. If you have inventory, you'll want property insurance.

- What about the tax issues? You'll be required to file quarterly federal and state estimated taxes for yourself or, if you have employees, you'll need to register to withhold and submit income and other taxes to the state and federal government and file quarterly and annual payroll tax returns. Who will do your payroll and prepare and file these reports? Do you need to hire an accountant or payroll service or will you do this yourself?

ESSENTIAL

You will likely have to set up a double-entry bookkeeping system. Talk to an accountant if you don't know how. The easiest way to do your accounting is to buy an inexpensive but robust program such as Quick-Books or Peachtree, which can more than adequately handle the accounting for most small or midsize businesses.

The True Cost of Happiness

Your job is where you spend most of your waking hours. Therefore, it's a significant part of your life. Even if you just view it as a way to pay the bills, it affects you in many ways. If it makes you unhappy, evaluate the alternatives. Maybe you can afford to take a lower-paying job that you'll enjoy.

If you're stressed and unhappy at work, you may be setting yourself up for bigger problems. You may have higher medical expenses down the road (for you as well as your family), which could offset the benefits of your larger paycheck. Keep the big picture in mind and consider the rest of your life as you evaluate your employment situation and choices.

CHAPTER 10

Moving On: Finding New Living Space

Whether you're seeking a new place to live in the same town or moving to a new city for a job opportunity or change of scenery, there are financial issues to consider before you take the plunge. The more you know about the costs associated with your move, the better you can plan for the financial impact.

Your Housing Options

Looking for your first apartment or upgrading to a better one? Take a few minutes to think about what's important to you in your living space, such as access to public transportation or being able to own pets. Identify the things you won't compromise on. This will help you quickly rule out places that don't meet your minimum standards. If you can't find a suitable apartment in your price range, consider sharing a house or apartment with a roommate, or renting a studio or efficiency apartment.

You'll need to have two months' rent saved up before you rent an apartment: one month's worth for the security deposit, plus the first month's rent. Some landlords require that you also pay the last month's rent up front, for a total of three months' worth of rent.

How Much Rent You Can Afford

As a general rule of thumb, allow no more than 30 percent of your gross income for housing. If you're making $35,000 a year, you shouldn't pay more than $875 a month for rent. You'd be more comfortable at 25 percent, or $729 a month. If some or all of the utilities are included, you could pay higher rent.

Finding an Apartment

If you're looking in your own town, you probably know about some of the apartment complexes in your area. It's more difficult if you're moving to a new city, especially if you don't have the luxury of being able to go there to find housing before you move. A number of methods can make it easier.

Word of Mouth and Classified Ads

If you know people in the neighborhood you're considering, ask them for recommendations. You'll learn important information that might not be readily apparent when you walk through the building, such as noise levels, and the safety of the neighborhood. The local newspapers in most towns and cities advertise apartments for rent. You might even grab independent newspapers that you find in coffee shops and pizza joints for a wider variety of inexpensive places. On the Internet, try *www.craigslist.org* or special sections of local papers' websites that have listings not found in the hard-copy editions.

Using a Real Estate Agent

The benefit of using real estate agents is that they're familiar with where the apartment complexes are and with the neighborhoods they're in. The easiest way to find realtors with rentals is by searching the Internet. Go to a good search engine and type in "real estate agents" or "realtors" and the name of the city and state. While you're searching, keep an eye out for agents who offer relocation packages with information about the city you're going to be living in. This could be helpful once you move.

Apartment-Finder Services

Apartment finders or locators are companies that specialize in knowing all the apartment complexes in a given area. They work with apartment property managers to keep up-to-date on apartment availability, and save you the time and hassle of making phone calls to each individual complex to get information. Try to avoid using an apartment-finder service that costs money. Some of them charge an entire month's rent.

ESSENTIAL

Two of the larger online apartment-finder services are Apartments.com (*www.apartments.com*) and ApartmentGuide.com (*www.apartment guide.com*). Both have millions of listings nationwide, many with photos and floor plans, plus helpful articles on moving and settling in.

The better services will have a real estate agent contact you when you fill out an online form indicating your housing requirements. Some will even have your utilities hooked up for you without charge once you find an apartment you want.

Signing the Lease

Remember four little words: read the small print. You need to protect yourself by knowing all the rules and regulations of living in your new space and of leaving it. If there are provisions in the lease that you object to, see if you can work out a compromise with the landlord. Cross out the unwanted language for any changes the two of you agree to, initial and date the change, and have the landlord do the same. Don't rely on oral agreements. They're difficult, if not impossible, to prove.

If there's something you don't understand, ask the landlord or property manager to explain it. Don't make any assumptions. A few things you might want to ask up front are:

- Is there an on-site manager?
- What kind of routine maintenance is performed and what am I personally responsible for?
- How much notice do I need to give when leaving?
- How is trash handled?
- What utilities and other services are included in the rent?
- Are there provisions in the lease that allow the rent to be raised during the lease term?

Don't be embarrassed if you have a lot of questions. Landlords expect questions, and once you sign the lease, it's too late. Make sure that the answers you get from your landlord correspond with the lease document.

FACT

Most landlords check your credit report and rental history, and charge you a fee of $10 to $35. Most will also verify your income to ensure that it's at least three times your monthly rent, so if rent is $800 a month, your monthly income would have to be at least $2,400.

Breaking Your Lease

Getting out of your lease before the end of the lease term, which is usually twelve months, can be difficult and expensive. You can be held responsible for paying the rent for the remainder of the lease. Find out if there are circumstances that would release you from your obligation. What if you got a job transfer? Had a baby? Some landlords will allow you to break the lease for a fee. Others may allow you to sublet to another tenant. Some landlords will allow you to sign a month-to-month lease. If you sign a month-to-month lease, be aware that the landlord can terminate the lease or raise the rent on short notice. Usually you're still obligated to give written notice of your intention to move out ten to sixty days in advance.

Deposits and Other Charges

When you rent a house or apartment, you're usually required to pay a security deposit equal to one month's rent, which the landlord will hold until you move out. At that time, any expenses for cleaning or repairs beyond normal wear and tear and any unpaid rent will be deducted from your deposit and the balance will be returned to you. Most states have laws about how landlords have to treat security deposits. Usually they have to place them in an escrow account or an account separate from their normal operating account. The landlord may be required to pay you interest on the deposit, and is required to return it to you within a specified time after you vacate the apartment.

Getting Your Security Deposit Back

Get a detailed receipt for any security or other deposits you pay. The receipt should show the date and amount paid, the name of the person you paid it to, the name of the landlord (if different), the address and apartment number the deposit is for, and a statement that it's a security deposit. Save the canceled check for the security deposit when your bank returns it in your monthly statement. This and your receipt are the best proof that you actually paid the deposit.

During the first week or so that you live in rented housing, go through every room and make a detailed list of everything that's broken, dirty, or damaged in any way, including chips in cabinets or tubs, holes in walls, broken windows, missing or broken knobs, tears in or stains on carpets, chips or rips in linoleum, burns, and so on. If possible, take pictures of the damage. Send a copy of the list to your landlord and keep a copy with your pictures to use, if needed, when you leave.

ESSENTIAL

Don't give your landlord an excuse to make a deduction from your security deposit when you move. If the apartment isn't clean or you leave things behind for the landlord to get rid of, he will charge you for the cost of cleaning or removal and deduct it from your deposit.

Clean the apartment thoroughly before you move out and repair any damage you caused. Remove all of your belongings and any trash. Ask your landlord to walk through the apartment with you and give you a signed statement about the condition you left it in. You may even want to take pictures of the condition of the apartment before you leave, in case you have to go to small claims court to get your security deposit back. Be sure to leave your landlord your forwarding address so he can mail your deposit.

Pet Deposits

If you find an apartment that allows pets, you may be required to pay a pet deposit in addition to your security deposit, to protect the property owner against any damages your pet may cause. Pet deposits can range from $100 to a full month's rent, and are often nonrefundable or only partially refundable.

ALERT

Rentlaw.com (*www.rentlaw.com*) has links to each state's laws governing rental housing, information about tenants' rights and landlords' obligations, and articles with advice and information about many aspects of moving. Check out the laws in your state before you sign a lease.

Some states prohibit landlords from charging extra deposits for kids or pets or charging for credit checks. This doesn't mean your landlord won't try to charge you.

Utility Deposits and Hookup Charges

You may be required to pay a refundable deposit and nonrefundable hookup charges to one or more utility companies, including electric, gas, water, sewer, and cable TV. Many electric companies require a deposit of several hundred dollars. If you can prove you had electric service recently in your name in another location and you had a good payment record, the utility company may waive this requirement. To prevent paying for utilities used by the previous tenant, if possible take utility readings as soon as you move in. (Ask your landlord how you can do this.) When you move out, be sure to request your deposit back from the utility company.

Renting with Roommates

If you plan to rent an apartment with one or more roommates, your landlord may require separate deposits from each one of you. You have several choices. All of you can sign the lease, which will make you all jointly and severally liable for rent and damages. This means each one of you is fully responsible for all of the rent and all of the damages, if any. If one of you fails to pay the rent, the others will have to come up with her share or face eviction.

Another option is for one of you to sign the lease and "sublet" rooms to one or more roommates. You collect the rent from the others and pay it to the landlord. If one roommate fails to pay the rent, you evict him, deduct the rent from his security deposit, and find a replacement. Before you enter into this type of arrangement, make sure your complex allows subletting.

In any case, it's a good idea to design a written contract spelling out each person's responsibilities, including the amount of rent each will pay, who will share responsibility for damages, how payment for utilities will be divided, how long the rental agreement will last, and who will be liable for rent if one person leaves.

Renters' Insurance

Most renters have the mistaken belief that they don't need renters' insurance and that the property owner is responsible for any damages to the property. The owner's coverage doesn't protect you against damage that you or your guests cause to the property. If you overrun your bathtub and water leaks into the apartment below, you're liable for the costs, unless you have renters' insurance.

The building owner's coverage also doesn't protect you against personal injury lawsuits if someone is injured in your apartment. And it doesn't provide for replacement of your belongings if they're stolen or damaged by fire or water. Renters' insurance does all of this, and is well worth the cost—which is surprisingly low.

How Much Coverage Do You Need?

Even if you don't have much furniture or large household appliances, you'd be amazed at how much your belongings would cost to replace. For starters, you probably have several thousand dollars' worth of clothing. Take a detailed room-by-room inventory of your belongings, write down a brief description of each item, and estimate what it would cost to replace it. Include clothes in your inventory.

ESSENTIAL

To obtain an estimate of what you would pay for renters' insurance, go to *www.insurancequote.com*, choose "Renters," and complete the online form to the best of your ability. You'll receive the best quote from licensed insurance agents in your area.

Replacement Cost or Actual Cash Value?

When buying insurance, it's a good idea to buy coverage for replacement cost rather than actual cash value. Replacement cost coverage is just what it sounds like: if something you own is stolen or damaged by fire or water, the insurance company will pay you what it will cost to replace it with an item of similar quality. Actual cost value coverage assumes that your belongings lose value with time and usage, and pays you only the depreciated value of the items.

Deductibles

The deductible is the amount you agree to pay out of your pocket before the insurance company covers the rest of your loss. The higher the deductible is the less expensive the insurance. When choosing a deductible, you're deciding how much risk you're willing to take and balancing risk and cost. Most property deductibles are between $250 and $500 per year.

Cost of Living Differences

If you're planning a move to a new city, it's important to know the difference in the cost of living. What sounds good in your hometown may not pay the bills in a new location, depending on the cost of living in that city.

Many sites on the Internet provide "cost of living" calculators. You enter the city you're moving from and the city you're moving to, and your current salary, and the calculator will tell you how much you'd have to earn in the new city to equal your buying power where you are now. We all know that cities such as New York are outrageously expensive compared to many other parts of the country, but you may be surprised at the cost of living in some smaller or more remote cities.

Automotive Costs Related to Moving

Excise tax on automobiles is one of the biggest surprises people face when they register their car in a new city. This tax is based on the value of the vehicle and can amount to many hundreds of dollars on newer or more expensive models. When you're planning your move, call the city clerk's office and ask about the cost of registering your vehicle and whether excise taxes are charged. They'll be able to tell you how much you can expect to pay on your particular make, model, and year. Many cities collect excise taxes annually when you reregister your car. The only comfort is in knowing that the tax will decrease each year as the car depreciates. If you itemize deductions on your income tax return, you can deduct excise taxes.

Auto insurance costs can vary dramatically from one city to the next. Obviously you'd expect rates to be higher in large cities, but the size of the city is not the only thing that determines rates. If you're thinking of moving to a new city, call an insurance agent there (you can find agents on the Internet) and get a quote on coverage for the make and model of your vehicle so you don't have any unpleasant surprises when you arrive in your new location.

Tax Issues Related to Moving

You may be able to deduct some of the expenses of moving from your taxable income, even if you don't itemize expenses. There are two rules you must satisfy. The distance test requires the new job to be located at least fifty miles from your old residence. The time test requires you to work full-time in the new location (not necessarily at the same job the whole time) for at least thirty-nine weeks in the twelve months following your move.

FACT

If your former home was twenty miles from your job location, your new job location must be at least seventy miles (50 + 20) from your old home in order to meet the distance test for deducting moving expenses from your income.

If you're a new college graduate taking your first full-time job, the work location must be at least fifty miles from your former legal residence, which is the address you use when you file your income taxes, not your school address, so it's probably your parents' home. If you return home after college, you won't qualify for this deduction. If you're married, either you or your spouse can qualify, but you can't add your work times together to pass the thirty-nine week test.

Applicable Expenses

If you meet both of the tests, you can deduct the costs associated with physically moving your belongings from your former legal residence to your new home. This includes the amount paid to a moving company or the cost of a truck rental if you do it yourself. If you use your own car, you can deduct actual expenses for gas and oil or mileage at a rate published by the IRS (fifty-five and one half cents per mile in 2012). Keep a mileage log and save it with your tax papers for the year. You can also deduct airfare, train, bus, and lodging expenses (but not meals) while en route for you and any dependents that you take with you. Keep receipts for everything.

Employer-Sponsored Move

Employers use one of two methods of covering your moving costs. In the first method, your employer gives you a moving allowance for you to use as you see fit, and adds the amount to your taxable income when they issue your W-2 at the end of the year. You can offset some or all of this income by claiming your allowable expenses. In the second method, you pay the expenses yourself and submit a claim to your employer for reimbursement. Only expenses your employer reimburses you for that aren't IRS-allowable will be included on your W-2.

Not all moving-related expenses are allowable. For instance, temporary housing at the new location, house-hunting trips, meals en route to your new home, and long-term storage of your household belongings are not allowable deductions. For details on the moving expense deduction, see IRS Publication 521, *Moving Expenses*.

CHAPTER 11

Buying a Home

Buying a home is the most expensive purchase you'll ever make. It's also an emotional and stressful experience for most people. There's a lot of information you have to absorb to make wise house-buying and financing decisions, from deciding if owning is really for you to understanding the nuances of home mortgages.

Getting Ready for Home Ownership

Before you start house hunting, establish a record of paying your bills on time. Avoid taking out any new loans or applying for any new credit cards in the months before you start looking for a house. Pay off as much debt as possible to help you qualify for the loan and to give you more expendable income after you move in.

Check your credit report. It's the first thing a lender will do when you apply for prequalification or a mortgage. Make sure there's nothing in the report that's inaccurate or will raise a potential lender's eyebrow, and be prepared to explain any late or missed payments.

Review your entire financial situation. If you haven't already prepared a net worth statement, now's the time to do it. Ditto for a budget. Make sure you can really handle the mortgage payments on top of the other debt you owe, and that you have a realistic feel for what other expenses you'll incur from home ownership.

Avoid Becoming House Poor

You may think buying your dream house is worth any sacrifice, but years of doing without the enjoyment of vacations, new cars, eating out, decorating, or a myriad of other simple pleasures can make your dream house feel like a jail. It can also put a strain on your relationship with your spouse or partner. A good rule of thumb is to buy a house that costs less than two and a half times your income. If your income is $50,000 a year, try to keep your home price under $125,000.

Prepare the Down Payment

A down payment is the amount of money you pay up front when you buy property, and it reduces the amount of money you need to borrow. The larger the down payment, the smaller your loan and monthly payments will be, but it's difficult to save enough for a sizeable down payment and closing costs that require cash (real estate transfer taxes, escrows for property taxes and insurance, title insurance, attorney fees, loan origination fees, and so on). Luckily, you have a few options.

One is to go on a crash budget for a few months by cutting your spending to the bare minimum and saving as much cash as possible. Another method is to sock away all the extra money that comes your way: income tax refunds, over-time, bonuses, cash gifts, or—if you're lucky—lottery winnings. You may have a relative who's willing to lend you money, but it's not legal to borrow money for your down payment unless you identify the loan as a debt and can still qualify. Otherwise your lender will require a statement that the money is a gift.

ESSENTIAL

If you're selling a house, use any equity you have in it to apply to the down payment on the new house. Borrowing from your 401(k) may be another option, since you may get additional time to repay the loan, but weigh the decision carefully.

How Mortgages Work

A mortgage is a legal contract that describes the terms of the loan obtained to buy a piece of property. It stipulates that if you don't meet the repayment terms of the loan, the lender can take your property and sell it to get his money back. This process is known as foreclosure.

Principal and Interest

Mortgage payments are divided between principal (the amount you bor-rowed), and interest (the cost of borrowing the money). Each month a little bit more gets applied to the principal balance (very little!). On a traditional thirty-year mortgage, the payments for the first twenty years or so will be more interest than principal. For example, on a thirty-year $100,000 mort-gage at 7 percent interest, your payments the first year would total $7,983, of which $6,967 would be for interest and only $1,015 for principal. At the end of the year you would still owe a balance of $98,985. Over the life of the thirty-year mortgage, you'd repay the $100,000 you borrowed plus $139,509 in interest, for a total of $239,509.

Private Mortgage Insurance

If it weren't for private mortgage insurance (PMI), which protects the lender in case you're unable to make the payments on your loan, you might not be able to buy a house for many years. Most lenders require a 20 percent down payment, so on a $100,000 loan, you'd be required to come up with approximately $25,000 for the down payment and closing costs. PMI, which ranges between $40 and $100 per month, helps you buy a house with as little as 5 to 10 percent down and is folded into your loan payments.

Under federal law, your lender is required to automatically terminate PMI when your equity reaches 22 percent of the original appraised value of your home. To calculate what percent equity you have in your home, divide your loan balance by the appraised value and deduct this number from 100.

If you bought your home after 1999, your lender must terminate your PMI when you reach 20 percent equity, if you request it. Some businesses offer a service to help you get your PMI dropped, but don't waste your money. Just call your lender and ask if you're paying PMI and if so, when it can be canceled. Then be sure to call again when that time arrives. If you have an FHA or VA loan, PMI isn't required because the federal government has already agreed to protect the lender if you default on your loan.

Types of Mortgages

You may think that all mortgages are alike, but they actually come in many shapes and sizes. There are several different terms, fixed-interest rate and variable-interest rate, balloon mortgages, government-backed mortgages, and more. To choose the best one for your personal situation, you should be familiar with at least these basic types.

Mortgage Terms

Most mortgages are for fifteen, twenty, or thirty years with an interest rate that's fixed over the life of the loan. Payments on fifteen- and twenty-year loans are somewhat higher than those on traditional thirty-year loans, so it requires higher income to qualify for the shorter terms. The benefit is that you build equity faster, pay off your mortgage years sooner, and save many tens of thousands of dollars.

To illustrate the difference between a thirty-year and a fifteen-year mortgage, take the example of a mortgage for $150,000 at 6 percent. The payment on a fifteen-year loan would be $1,266 per month, and the total interest paid over the life of the loan would be $77,841. The payment on a thirty-year mortgage for the same amount at the same interest rate would be $899 per month (a decrease of $367) and the total interest paid over the life of the loan would be $173,757 (an increase of $95,916). Moreover, interest rates on shorter-term mortgages are generally lower than those on longer-term mortgages, so the difference between the two loans in the example would actually be even greater.

QUESTION

Should I choose a shorter or longer mortgage term?
If you can swing the payments comfortably, the shorter terms are definitely worthwhile. If you're a disciplined saver, you may be able to do just as well with a thirty-year loan if you invest the monthly savings in stocks or mutual funds.

Adjustable-Rate Mortgages

The interest rates on adjustable-rate mortgages (ARMs) vary. They often start out as much as 1.5 to 2 percentage points lower than the prevailing market rates and increase or decrease at predetermined intervals. The amount of increase or decrease depends on whether they're tied to Treasury bills, CD rates, or some other financial index. The rate is fixed for a certain period (between six months and five years) and then adjusted periodically, perhaps every year or two. The amount the rate can increase at each interval is usually 2 percentage points, and there's often a lifetime cap of 6 percentage points.

In a time of rising interest rates, it can be disturbing to know that your rate can increase every year. Before taking out an ARM, be sure that you can afford the highest payment possible under the terms of the loan. ARMs might be a good option if you know you'll only be in the house for a few years, but if you use one because you can't qualify for a conventional mortgage, you're risking the possible loss of your house.

Balloon Mortgages

Balloon mortgages have lower interest rates than traditional mortgages, but the loan term is only for five to seven years. At the end of that time, the entire balance is due, and you have to either pay it off or refinance at the rates that are in effect then. If you plan to sell your house, pay it off, or refinance it within the time frame of the loan, this might be an option for you.

Interest-Only Mortgages

If you want a lower payment, you might look toward interest-only mortgage options. With a traditional mortgage, your monthly payment consists of interest and principal. It is designed so that you'll pay off the entire loan at the end of the loan term. By eliminating the principal portion of your payment, you spend less each month. Of course, you never pay down any of your loan with an interest-only mortgage. You'll owe just as much after ten years as you did on the day you bought your house. In other words, you don't build any equity with each monthly mortgage payment—you just service the loan.

This type of loan option allows a borrower to pay only the interest on the mortgage in monthly payments for a fixed number of years, usually five to seven. After that point, the buyer has the option to refinance, pay off the higher balance or face what could be a significantly higher monthly payment. These loans are a good idea for people who want to use such loans strategically, for example, for people expecting a windfall that can wipe out their debt at the end of the term or at least will be earning enough to make the new payments painless.

Negative-Amortization Loans

Some loans allow you to pay even less than the monthly interest. These allow you to enjoy a lower monthly payment, but they are extremely risky. A loan with negative amortization actually sets payments at a level that fails to cover the principal and interest due—or creates an option where a borrower can pay less than the principal and interest due whenever they feel like it—which makes the total loan balance rise instead of fall.

Negative-amortization loans have a significantly lower monthly payment at the start (maybe the first year or two) as compared to more conventional loans. Unfortunately, the day will come when you have to settle up—usually with dramatically higher monthly payments. What a shock it is to look at a mortgage statement and find out that six months, a year, or two years in, you owe more than you originally borrowed!

There are two scenarios where negative amortization can make sense. The first scenario involves experienced real estate investors who understand their particular markets and properties so well that they know they'll be able to unload their investment on a specific timetable. The second involves individuals with a similarly superior knowledge of the market and solid finances who know they won't have any trouble selling or refinancing into a more stable loan product later.

Government-Backed Mortgages

Government loans such as FHA and VA loans make home ownership possible for people who might not otherwise qualify for a mortgage. The federal government insures the loan, which is issued by a regular lender. FHA loans allow a smaller down payment than regular mortgages (3 percent rather than 10 or 20 percent), allow a higher debt percentage, and allow you to borrow the down payment and closing costs from a family member, which you can't do legally with a regular mortgage. VA loans are for veterans and don't require any down payment. They have even less stringent requirements on the income-to-debt ratio than FHA loans.

ALERT

The more you borrow relative to the price of the home, the higher the interest rate, so when you make a small down payment, don't expect to get the best rates. Lenders charge higher rates because there's more risk that you'll default if you have little equity in your home.

Even though they're insured by the government, FHA and VA loans are not always your best bet. If you have good credit, you should take a look at conventional loans from a bank or mortgage broker for comparison.

Choosing the Best Mortgage for You

As you can see, there are many mortgage options, so it's important to understand how each of the basic types would impact your payments. Don't underestimate the impact of interest rates on your monthly payments. A $100,000 loan at 7 percent interest for thirty years would cost $665 per month. The same loan at 8 percent interest would cost $734 per month, a difference of $24,840 over the life of a thirty-year mortgage.

For most people, a standard thirty-year mortgage is a good choice. You'll know what to expect each month, and you're not taking any wild risks. If you really want to save on interest costs, you can go for the fifteen-year mortgage.

FACT

The website of HSH Associates (*www.hsh.com*), the largest publisher of mortgage rates and other financial information in the United States, can help you quickly track down the best mortgage rates offered by lenders located near you. Rates for borrowers with perfect credit are separate from rates for those with "bruised" credit.

The interest-only option and any loan with negative amortization are much more complicated. If you have an investment plan that's more attractive than building equity in your home, the interest-only route can make sense. Negative-amortization loans (sometimes found in "option ARM" programs) are extremely dangerous. You may be able to make the monthly payments today, but be prepared for a disastrous shock down the road.

Federal Truth in Lending Act and the APR

The federal Truth in Lending Act requires lenders to disclose the annual percentage rate (APR) and the total finance charges to borrowers in writing. The APR is the average annual finance charge. It's more meaningful than the interest rate alone because it includes costs such as loan origination fees, private mortgage insurance premium, and points.

The APR levels the playing field by allowing you to quickly and painlessly compare loans that have different rates and fees. It's a much more accurate indicator of the cost of the loan. Be aware, however, that it can't be used as an accurate comparison of borrowing costs on adjustable-rate mortgages.

Paying Points

Points are a percentage of the loan amount that you pay up front to "buy down" the interest rate on a mortgage. One point is 1 percent of the loan and usually lowers the interest rate by ¼ percent. One point on a $100,000 loan would be $1,000, two points would be $2,000, and so on. A 7 percent loan with one point is not necessarily better (or worse) than an 8 percent loan with no points. Remember, you have to look at the APR to compare rates and fees. Paying points in order to get a lower interest rate may be worthwhile if you're planning to stay in the house for five years or more. The lower interest rate saves you a lot of money over the long term, but if you sell in less than five to ten years you won't have time to recoup your costs.

The Home-Buying Process

Once you've decided you want to be a homeowner, you must determine how much house you can afford. There are two parts to this. The first is to follow a budget for at least three to six months so you know your spending habits and how much money you have to work with. The second is to estimate how much money the bank is likely to lend you so you don't waste time and emotional energy looking at houses or neighborhoods you can't afford.

Calculate Your PITI

To estimate how much you can expect to borrow, use the two basic guidelines that banks and mortgage companies follow. The first guideline is that principal, interest, taxes, and insurance (PITI) shouldn't exceed 28 percent of your gross income (your pay before taxes). Let's say that your gross income is $50,000 a year. Your principal, interest, property taxes, and insurance shouldn't exceed $14,000 per year, or $1,166 per month.

Property taxes can vary drastically between states and even between towns in the same state, so call the town or city tax assessor and ask what the typical taxes would be on a house that's in your approximate price range. The sales listing for a home you're looking at may also yield some historic information—but things could change. You may be able to afford to buy the house but unable to afford the taxes.

Let's assume that the property taxes on a $100,000 house are $1,800 per year, or $150 per month, that homeowner's insurance is $400 per year, or $33 per month, and that PMI is $50 per month. You would qualify for $933 per month in principal and interest payments ($1,166 – $150 – $33 – $50 = $933). So how much house can you buy for $933 per month? Try plugging several different interest rates into one of the mortgage calculators found at websites such as CNNMoney (*http://money.cnn.com*) or Quicken.com (*www.quicken.com*).

Consider Your Long-Term Debt

The second guideline is that PITI plus all your other long-term debt shouldn't exceed 36 percent of your gross income. Your long-term debt (car loans, credit cards you won't have paid off within the next ten months, furniture or equipment loans, student loans, child support and alimony, and so on) shouldn't exceed 8 percent of your income (36 percent – 28 percent for PITI = 8 percent for other debt). Again, using the example of $50,000 in gross income, your monthly payments toward long-term debt other than your PITI shouldn't exceed $333 per month ($50,000 × 8 percent = $4,000 ÷ 12 months = $333 per month). If your debt payments are more than this, you'll need to come up with a larger down payment so you don't have to borrow as much.

ESSENTIAL

If you make a small down payment, your lender may only use the lower percentages for PITI and long-term debt to protect itself against the possibility that you might default on your loan. However, there's a growing trend for lenders to automatically use the 28 percent guideline for PITI.

Check the Mortgage Calculator

Play around with an online mortgage calculator that will help you determine how much you can afford to pay for a house. Moving.com (*www.moving.com*) has an excellent calculator for this under "Tools & Resources." There are also several helpful calculators related to the home-buying process at Mortgage101.com (*www.mortgage101.com*) under "Calculators."

Getting Preapproved or Prequalified

It's a good idea to apply for your mortgage early in the process instead of waiting until you find a house you like. Prequalification means the lender has looked at your credit report, income, and level of debt and determined that you appear to qualify for a loan.

ALERT

Mortgage brokers bring lenders and borrowers together but do not lend money or service loans. Their fee is added to the cost of your loan. If you don't have great credit, you may get a better rate through a broker than through a bank, but watch out for the fees.

Preapproval, which means that the lender has approved you for a specific loan amount, gives you the most credibility with the seller, who may be deciding between two or more offers and doesn't want to accept an offer from someone who may not qualify for the financing. You'll need to present a heap of paperwork to the mortgage company during the application process, including the following forms:

- W-2 forms for the prior two years
- Federal tax returns for the prior two years
- Documentation for any other income you're claiming, such as overtime, bonuses, child support, or alimony
- A list of all your debts, such as credit cards, student loans, car loans, child support, or alimony, and the name of the creditor, balance owed, and minimum monthly payment
- Copies of bank statements
- Proof of assets, such as stock or mutual fund statements and car and real estate titles
- Proof of rent or mortgage payments (canceled checks)

Making and Negotiating the Purchase

Once you've found the house you want to buy, the next step is to make a bid. The bid will include the amount you are willing to pay for the house, the amount you will need to finance, and the time frame needed for the purchase. It would be wise to prequalify for the mortgage amount you feel you will need for the purchase so that the seller knows you will most likely get the financing you require.

Should the seller agree to the terms of the bid, the formal contract process will begin. It is common practice at this point for the prospective buyer to arrange for a home inspection of the premises from a qualified home engineer. This way you can determine if the "guts of the place" are sound (the heating, electrical and plumbing systems, the foundation, roofs, walls, ceilings, etc.). It would be wise to accompany the home engineer on the inspection so that you can ask whether certain problems are due to normal wear and tear or are serious problems that the seller must address in the contract of sale.

The real estate contract should contain a few standard clauses, such as a list of whether certain items (window treatments, lighting fixtures, wall to wall carpeting, air conditioning units) are to remain on the premises after closing. In addition, the contract should contain confirmation that the heating, electrical, and plumbing systems, as well as all appliances, will be in working order for closing. All contracts should be conditioned upon two things: your ability to secure a specific amount of financing within a predetermined time period and the seller's ability to deliver a marketable title.

There is also the matter of the down payment that must be paid to the seller's attorney. Such an amount will be held in an escrow account until the closing and the title is delivered to the home buyer. Should you fail to secure the financing through no fault of your own or the seller fails to deliver a marketable title, then the down payment should be returned to you. The amount of the down payment can be negotiated. Historically, 10 percent of the purchase price was common, but with today's real estate prices, you might be able to negotiate this number down.

Once all parties have executed the terms of the contract, you must obtain a mortgage commitment from a financial institution (your bank) and have an abstract company search the land records to ensure that the seller is able to deliver a marketable title.

Closing the Deal

After your bank gives you a mortgage commitment and you have worked out all of the title issues present on your title report, you will be ready to schedule the title closing. Just prior to the scheduled closing date, though, it is important to walk through the house to ensure that all of the seller's commitments have been fulfilled. You must bring a paid homeowner's insurance policy as well as photo identification to the closing.

The seller will prefer payment in the form of a cashier's check or a certified check. These forms of payment are guaranteed by the bank or credit union on which the check is drawn. If there is a pre-existing mortgage on the premises, you must make sure that one of those checks is made out to the seller's lender so that the mortgage is satisfied at closing. Once you receive an executed deed, you'll get the keys to your new home!

Understanding Closing Costs

Closing costs are all of the costs associated with the transfer of the property, the processing of your mortgage, and the fees charged by those who make it all happen. Closing costs include:

- Attorney's fees (both your attorney and the lender's attorney)
- Title Insurance policies for you and the lender
- Property taxes and homeowner's insurance placed in the lender's escrow account (so that they're available to pay when due)
- Real estate commissions
- Lender fees such as appraisal, processing fees, points, origination fees, land surveys, and interest from the settlement date until your first payment is due
- Deed and mortgage recording fees and mortgage tax

Closing costs vary by location but are typically 3 to 6 percent of your loan, so if you're buying a $100,000 house, you can expect closing costs to be between $3,000 and $6,000. Like the down payment, closing costs must be paid at the time of purchase. Federal law requires lenders to provide you with a good faith estimate of your closing costs before you go to settlement.

Home Ownership Tax Savings

When you own a home, you can deduct the mortgage interest and a few related costs from your taxable income by itemizing your deductions on Schedule A of Form 1040. By the end of January each year, your lender will send you a Form 1098 showing the amount of mortgage interest you paid during that year. Points you paid at closing are deductible the first year you own your home if they're considered a prepayment of interest and meet a number of other requirements. For a complete list of the requirements and limitations on deductibility of home mortgage interest, see IRS Publication 936, *Home Mortgage Interest Deduction*. If your points don't meet these requirements, you can deduct them over the life of the loan. Most of the other costs paid at closing are not tax deductible.

FACT

According to a study by the Center for Housing Policy, many low- and moderate-income families are spending half their income on housing instead of the recommended 28 percent because wages haven't kept up with the increase in housing prices.

Real Estate Property Tax Deduction

You can also deduct real estate property taxes from your taxable income. If property taxes are included in your mortgage payment and paid by your lender, claim the amount the lender actually paid out during the year, not the amounts included for taxes in your monthly mortgage payments. Your lender places these funds in an escrow account for safekeeping and uses the funds to pay your real estate and insurance. Frequently real estate taxes are adjusted at the closing so that the purchaser may have actually paid more or less than the real estate taxes paid to the government in the year of closing. Your attorney's closing statement should disclose the amount of this adjustment and whether it should be added to, or deducted from the amount paid to the government during the year in order to determine your proper real estate tax deduction.

If your local real estate taxes include charges for services such as trash removal or water and sewer, this portion of your taxes is not deductible.

Look carefully at your copy of the real estate tax bill to determine how much you can deduct. The bill should identify services separately from taxes, which are based on the value of your property.

Calculating Your Tax Savings

To calculate how much you'll save by deducting mortgage interest and property taxes, you need to know your marginal tax rate for federal and state income taxes. You can get these rates from the tax rate schedules in your tax return packets or from the IRS website (*www.irs.gov*). In 2012, a married couple filing jointly with an income of $110,000 had an average tax rate of 17.8 percent. We'll assume a state tax rate of 6 percent, for a total of 24 percent. Multiply this rate times the amount you can claim on your income tax return for mortgage interest and property taxes to get the amount you save in income taxes. If you were married with a 26 percent combined tax rate and $10,000 in deductions, you'd save $2,600 in taxes ($10,000 × 0.26 = $2,600), a monthly savings of $217. If your mortgage interest is $1,000 a month, your actual after-tax cost is $783 ($1,000 − $217 = $783).

Moreover, you may save more than this example if owning a home allows you to itemize for the first time. When you itemize, you can also deduct state income taxes, charitable gifts, investment expenses that exceed 2 percent of your adjusted gross income (AGI), and medical and dental expenses that exceed 7.5 percent of your AGI. You can file a new W-4 to claim more exemptions and have less tax taken out each week or leave your withholding as it is and get an income tax refund at the end of the year.

Be Prepared for Other Expenses

Mortgage payments aren't the only expense to consider when evaluating whether you can afford to buy a house and how much you can afford to spend. There are also property taxes, homeowner's insurance, repairs and maintenance, utilities, sewer and water bills, major appliances, landscaping and yard maintenance costs, and more. Utilities can be very expensive if you live in a cold region of the country such as the Northeast, where bone-chilling winters drive up heating costs, or in the South, where hot, humid summers run up air-conditioning bills.

If you've been renting and are considering buying a house, try to think of all the things you'll need to buy that you didn't need when you had a landlord. You may need a lawnmower, weed whacker, chipper/shredder, leaf blower, rototiller, or other lawn and garden equipment; a washer and dryer, a new stove or refrigerator, or other household appliances; a snow blower or snow plow. Then there are the items that aren't absolutely necessary but that you'll want to have as soon as possible, such as window coverings (blinds, shades, or curtains), and new or additional furniture. If you're buying a fixer-upper, you'll need money for materials even if you intend to do most of the work yourself.

ESSENTIAL

Buy a less expensive house than you can afford. Then you'll have money for other things and won't be as likely to get in over your head with credit card and consumer debt. You'll even be able to make extra principal payments on your mortgage or larger retirement account contributions.

Most people use all the cash they can scrape together for the down payment and closing costs, and then end up having to use credit to buy the things they need or want for the new house. If you plan ahead and know how much house you can really afford, you can avoid being house poor—unable to afford anything but the house payment.

Owning a Condo

Some people decide to own a condo or townhome as opposed to a single-family home. You can share some costs with others, and you don't have to do as much of the work yourself. In exchange for these benefits, you have to pay homeowners association dues (HOA dues) or some similar fee. HOA dues pay for your property's insurance (but not for insurance on anything inside your unit), yard work, some utilities, and more.

When shopping for a condo, make sure you consider the HOA dues in your budget. You might talk about mortgage costs with a lender, but don't forget that you'll owe an extra $100 to $500 per month for HOA dues. Higher

HOA dues often mean that you get more from the HOA, but not always. Work with your real estate agent to understand how the HOA works and if it's going to be worth it.

Owning a Co-Op

When you purchase a co-operative apartment, you do not technically own real estate. Instead you own shares in a corporation that owns the real estate. You become a tenant in a designated apartment in the building by signing a proprietary lease with the corporation. The co-op board of directors makes sure that the offering plan and the by-laws of the co-op are enforced. Each tenant is charged a maintenance fee that pays for the ongoing maintenance of the building along with real estate taxes, insurance, and the mortgage on the building. Although you do not technically own the real estate, for tax purposes you are entitled to deduct any interest associated with a co-op loan taken to purchase the premises as if it were a real estate mortgage. Additionally, any part of the monthly maintenance attributable to the payment of real estate taxes on the building or mortgage interest on the co-op's mortgage will flow to you so you can deduct those amounts as itemized deductions on your tax return. Usually, the managing agent of the co-op will issue a statement informing the shareholders as to the portion of the maintenance charge properly allocable to mortgage interest and real estate taxes. Before you purchase a co-op, it is important to analyze the current financial statements of the co-op carefully in order to determine whether the current maintenance charge is sufficient to support the co-op's ongoing carrying costs.

CHAPTER 12

Living with a Mortgage

If you own a home, you may have questions about refinancing your mortgage to pay for home improvements, consolidate debt, or reduce payments. You may wonder when to refinance, what kind of loan to choose, how to prepay your mortgage, or how to go about selling your house. You may even be facing foreclosure and need urgent help.

Planning Home Improvements

Whether you've just bought a fixer-upper and need to do some renovations, you're trying to make room for a growing family, or you just want to increase the value of your home by remodeling, you have several options for financing the improvements. Before you approach a lender, make a detailed plan of the work you want done and get bids from several contractors.

Whenever you use your home as collateral, as in a mortgage or home equity loan, you risk losing it if you can't make the payments. That's why it's so important to get detailed, accurate cost estimates from reputable, experienced contractors. If the contractor's work is incomplete or shoddy and you have to hire someone else to finish or fix it, you still have to repay the loan.

Shop for financing at established financial institutions and compare rates and fees from several different lenders. Contractors sometimes offer to arrange financing with a particular lender. The contractor usually receives a commission from the lender for the referral and you can end up paying for it in higher interest rates or fees you wouldn't incur at your local bank or credit union.

FACT

According to estimates from the U.S. Department of Commerce, in the year 2007 Americans spent $226.4 billion on repairs and improvements to their homes. Many big-ticket improvements don't pay for themselves when it comes time to sell, so choose them wisely.

The Best Way to Find a Contractor

Ask friends, neighbors, and coworkers who have remodeled or made home improvements. Who did they use? Once you've identified several possible candidates, check them out with the local Better Business Bureau or consumer protection agency to see if they've had complaints filed against them and, more importantly, whether they resolved any problems satisfactorily.

Get at least three detailed written estimates that spell out exactly what will be done, the type and quality of materials that will be used, and the cost, based on your written description of your project. Compare the bids carefully. Don't automatically choose the lowest bid without discussing each bid with the appropriate contractor so you can determine why they differ. If a bid is significantly lower than the others, you may want to toss it out. The contractor may be bidding inferior materials or planning to take labor-saving shortcuts that compromise the quality of the work.

Once you've chosen a contractor, ask for the name of his insurance agent and call to verify that he carries workers' compensation insurance and coverage for property damage and personal liability in case of accidents. You don't want to be held financially responsible if a worker is hurt on your property. It's also a good idea to call your state and local government and find out if contractors have to be licensed or bonded. If they do, check to make sure the contractor has complied.

ESSENTIAL

Before hiring a contractor to build or renovate your home, educate yourself about contractor fraud so you know what to look out for. Visit *www.contractorfraud.net* for information on popular contractor scams and advice on finding and using reputable contractors.

The Payment Schedule

Never pay a contractor the entire cost of the project up front. He'll probably request a down payment, the amount of which may be limited by state law. Try to keep the first payment to no more than 10 to 20 percent. Additional payments should be tied to completion of measurable milestones, so you're paying for the work that's actually been accomplished. Include these milestones in your contract to ensure that your contractor understands and agrees to them. You should be holding at least 15 percent of the contractor's money until the job is finished to your satisfaction and you have written proof that all subcontractors and suppliers have been paid.

Mechanic's Liens

One of the biggest concerns about hiring a contractor who uses subcontractors is the possibility of what's known as a mechanic's lien. If the contractor doesn't pay his subcontractors or suppliers, they can demand payment from you directly even though you already paid the contractor for the subcontracted services or supplies. If you don't pay, they can place a lien on your home and force you to sell it to pay them if you can't come up with the money any other way. Never settle for a contractor's promise that he'll pay everybody.

You can protect yourself by asking your contractor to provide lien waivers or lien releases from all his subcontractors and suppliers before beginning work. A lien waiver is a simple form that the subcontractor signs stating that he won't ask you for money you've already paid the contractor. If the subcontractor won't sign a lien waiver before performing the job, you could meet with the contractor and subcontractor together and write a check to each one separately. Then get the subcontractor to sign a lien release, which is similar to a lien waiver but states that the subcontractor has been paid.

Building a Home

It may be that you're not interested in improving your home, but in building it yourself. This is a huge undertaking and will require a commitment of time and money.

FACT

Debt consolidation is the number-one reason people use home equity loans. According to the Consumer Bankers Association, 44 percent use the loans to pay off credit card and other consumer debt and 25 percent use the money to make home improvements. Other uses include buying a car, education costs, or a major purchase.

If you've decided to buy a custom-built house, interview several builders. Ask for references from the ones you like and call the recent home buyers who used the builder. If the project is still in progress, ask if you can see it. Try to look at a finished house as well. Call your local Better Business Bureau, consumer protection agency, and state attorney general's office to see if there have been complaints about the builder, and if so, the nature of the complaints and whether the builder rectified the problems. Before you sign a contract, verify that the builder has property, liability, workers' compensation, and builder's risk insurance.

There are special loans for building your own home. You may need to take out two separate loans: a construction loan and a regular mortgage. An interim construction loan provides money to the builder and subcontractors while your house is being built. During the building process, you pay only interest on the loan. When the house is completed, the construction loan is converted to a regular mortgage. You'll probably need a commitment letter from the permanent mortgage company in order to get the interim loan because the commitment letter pledges to pay off the construction loan when the home is finished. Some lenders now offer the two types of loans together with only one closing, so you save closing costs.

Home-Equity Loans and Lines of Credit

The two most common methods of financing home improvements are cashing out the equity in your home by refinancing and taking out a second mortgage or home-equity line of credit. Home-equity loans, a type of second mortgage, have a fixed term, usually between five and fifteen years, at a fixed-interest rate. You borrow one lump sum of money and make regular monthly payments over the life of the loan.

Home-equity lines of credit are a type of revolving credit, like a credit card. You're allowed to borrow a certain amount over the life of the loan, and you don't have to borrow it all in a lump sum. Some lenders give you special checks; others provide a type of credit card that you use to access the money. As you pay off the principal, you can borrow more. For example, let's say you have a line of credit of $15,000. You borrow $6,000, leaving $9,000 of available credit. You pay off $3,000, making your available credit $12,000 ($15,000 − $6,000 + $3,000 = $12,000). The interest rate is variable so your payments change depending on the current rate and your outstanding balance. At the end of the loan term, any unpaid balance is due. If you sell your house, the balance is due at the time of sale.

Which Type of Loan Is Best for You?

Home-equity loans are best suited for times when you need a lump sum amount. Lines of credit are best if you need the money at intervals, so you borrow only the amount you need, when you need it. Lines of credit can be dangerous if you have trouble controlling credit card debt because they work in much the same way as credit cards. But there's one very important difference: With a home-equity line of credit your home is at stake. If you get in over your head, you could lose your home.

Home-equity loans are attractive because their rates are higher than interest rates on first mortgages but much lower than credit card interest rates, and interest on home-equity loans may also be tax deductible. Closing costs for home-equity loans are similar to those for first mortgages. Expect to pay 2 to 5 percent of the loan amount.

You can't use the APR to compare home-equity lines of credit and home-equity loans. The APR for a line of credit doesn't include points and fees, so it will be misleadingly low if you try to compare it to the APR for a home-equity loan.

Should You Get Your Loan Online?

Even if you're not comfortable with the idea of handling the entire mortgage process online, don't hesitate to use the Internet to research rates and fees being offered by various lenders. Lenders who offer the most competitive rates tend to be online. You may not want to complete the lengthy loan application form online, but you can call the lender and give the information over the telephone. You may be able to track the progress of your loan online. At the very least, you can use the Internet to educate yourself quickly and painlessly about various mortgage products and current rates.

QUESTION

Where can I find the best mortgage interest rates and costs?
Research or apply for mortgage loans online at E-Loan (*www.eloan .com*), LendingTree (*www.lendingtree.com*), Bankrate.com (*www .bankrate.com*), or REALTOR.com (*www.realtor.com*).

Escrow Accounts

An escrow account is a special account your lender sets up if your mortgage payments will include amounts for property taxes and homeowner's insurance and the lender or mortgage servicing company will be disbursing the money when these bills become due. If you have trouble saving for large expenses, escrow accounts can make it easier because each month you pay one-twelfth of the annual amounts needed. However, you're paying the money before it's really due and in most cases not earning any interest on it.

Lenders can easily make mistakes in escrow accounts, so it's important to keep an eye on them and make sure all the money is accounted for and that you're not paying more than is necessary. By law, there has to be at least one month per year when the balance in your account is no more than one-sixth of your annual expenses paid from escrow. Once a year your lender will perform an escrow analysis to determine how much money should be deposited into the account for the coming year in order to cover the expenses that will be paid. If you have more than $50 in excess of what's needed, you should receive a refund. If you have a shortage, one-twelfth of the amount needed may be added to your monthly payments for the next year.

Refinancing Your Mortgage

When you refinance your mortgage, you take out a new loan at a lower rate or for a different term and use the proceeds to pay off the original mortgage. Most lenders require you to have at least 10 to 20 percent equity in your home before you can refinance.

When Does It Pay to Refinance?

How do you know if the difference in interest rates is enough to make refinancing worthwhile when you include the costs of closing on the new loan? The old rule of thumb was that interest rates should be at least 2 percentage points below your current rate, but the low-cost refinancing that many lenders now offer makes that guideline obsolete. Refinancing may make sense if you have a second mortgage or home-equity loan with a higher rate. You can save money by rolling both your first and second mortgages into one new loan with an overall lower rate. Refinancing also makes sense if you want to take advantage of lower interest rates to shorten the term of your loan, from thirty years to fifteen years, for example, for around the same monthly payment.

Sometimes refinancing doesn't make sense. If you've had your mortgage for more than ten years, for example, you could end up paying a lot more in interest by refinancing at a lower interest rate. That's because in the early years of a mortgage most of your payment goes toward interest and very little is applied to your principal balance. By the time you've been making payments for ten or more years, you've started to make some dents in the principal, and if you refinance with a new thirty-year loan, most of your payments will once again be interest. Consider not just the monthly payment, but also the total interest costs over the life of the loan added to the total interest costs you've already paid. Online calculators can help you quickly determine the total interest under different scenarios.

ALERT

Be aware that you may not qualify for the low interest rates you see advertised. When you apply for refinancing, the lender will do a credit check, and if your credit isn't what it should be, you'll pay a higher rate.

The Time Frame Issue

The first question to ask yourself when you're thinking about refinancing is how long you expect to live in the house. If you plan to move within the next three years or so, you may not have enough time to recoup your closing costs. Assuming you'll be sticking around, the next thing you need to do is get a detailed, written estimate of your closing costs from the lender.

To figure out how long it will take you to pay off the cost of refinancing and really start saving money, deduct the new, lower monthly payment from your current payment to find your monthly savings. Multiply your monthly savings by your combined effective state and federal tax rate to get your tax cost and subtract this from your monthly savings. The reason for this adjustment to your savings is that your new loan with the lower payment reduces the tax benefit you had under the old loan. Now divide the total of all the fees and closing costs on the new mortgage by your net monthly savings after the tax adjustment. This is how many months it will take you to pay off the cost of refinancing.

For example, let's say that your closing costs are going to be $3,000. Your current monthly payment is $875 and your new payment is $750, a monthly savings of $125. If your combined effective state and federal tax rate is 20 percent, decreasing your interest payments by $125 per month will increase your taxes $25 per month ($125 × 0.20), so your net savings are $100 ($125 – $25). Your closing costs of $3,000 divided by your monthly savings of $100 equals thirty months, the time it would take to repay your closing costs and start saving money. Before you refinance, check with your lender and make sure there's not a prepayment penalty on your current mortgage. If there is, it may cost you more to refinance than it's worth.

Look at the Big Picture

When it comes to mortgages and home equity loans, the bottom line is to look at the big picture. If you're on a tight budget and can barely qualify for a thirty-year mortgage, you may not have any other options, but if possible, look beyond the monthly payments to your overall financial plan. What will benefit you the most in the long term? Even if you'd love to have a fifteen-year loan to build equity quickly but can't quite swing it, you may be able to make extra principal payments on your thirty-year loan. You'd still come out ahead without the monthly commitment to higher payments.

ESSENTIAL

Remember that your home is a place to live, not an ATM. Cash-out refinancing can be a useful tool or a dangerous trap. Don't use the technique to increase the amount you can spend each month or for a trip to the beach.

Cash-Out Refinancing

Some people refinance for more than the value of their current mortgage if they have a lot of equity in their home. This is called cash-out refinancing. Let's say you paid $125,000 for your house and your mortgage is $100,000. Your house has appreciated in value and is now worth $175,000. You might refinance for $140,000, pay off the balance on your $100,000 mortgage and pocket the difference of $40,000 or more. You'd still have 20 percent equity in your home ($140,000 ÷ $175,000 = 80 percent). Don't forget that your monthly payments would be significantly higher, so make sure you can afford them. If you're planning to borrow anyway to make improvements to your home, this may be the way to go instead of taking out a second loan to pay for the renovations. In the event that you cash out for purposes other than home improvements the tax deductibility of the mortgage interest related to the refinancing may be limited. See IRS Publication 936 for the details.

Tax Deductibility of Mortgage Interest

Many people do not realize that mortgage interest isn't necessarily tax deductible in full, even on one's primary residence. The government recognizes two different types of mortgage interest: acquisition indebtedness and home-equity indebtedness.

With acquisition indebtedness, you may not deduct interest for more than $1 million of debt related to the acquisition of your primary home plus one vacation home. Acquisition indebtedness means a mortgage incurred in order to acquire, construct, or substantially improve a qualified home. If you are married and filing separately, the limit is reduced to $500,000 per spouse. With home-equity indebtedness, you may not deduct interest related to more than $100,000 of this kind of debt. Home-equity indebtedness is defined as a mortgage incurred for purposes other than to acquire, construct, or substantially improve your home. This limitation also applies to acquisition indebtedness to the extent it exceeds the $1 million limit described above. If you are married and filing separately, the limitation is reduced to $50,000 per spouse.

You should also note that for purposes of calculating your alternative minimum tax (AMT), all home-equity indebtedness deducted for ordinary tax purposes must be added back. The alternative minimum tax is a way to ensure that taxpayers pay at least a minimum amount of tax. The AMT has a completely different set of calculations than the regular tax. For the regular tax, you add up your total income, subtract various deductions and personal exemptions, then calculate the tax. You can claim various credits against the regular tax to reduce your tax even further. The AMT, however, does not allow the standard deduction, personal exemptions, or certain itemized deductions. Also, some income that is not subject to the regular tax is added for AMT purposes. Your tax under AMT rules may be higher than your tax under regular tax rules. For example, let's say you borrowed $800,000 to buy your primary residence and another $600,000 to buy a second home. Your acquisition indebtedness amount is only the interest related to 1 million/1.4 million of total interest paid, or five-sevenths of total interest paid.

In another scenario, let's say you paid off your mortgage on your home years ago but are somewhat strapped for cash so you borrow $400,000. You use $300,000 to improve your residence and $100,000 to pay your student loans. Three-quarters of the interest paid is to be characterized as acquisition indebtedness since it was used to improve the home. The rest of the interest would qualify as home-equity indebtedness since it did not exceed $100,000. However, that interest would be added back in determining your AMT.

In addition, if you borrowed $450,000 in example two and bought a fancy sports car with the extra $50,000, then only 100,000/150,000, or two-thirds of the home-equity indebtedness would have been deductible for ordinary tax purposes. IRS Publication 936 contains all of the details related to mortgage interest deductibility.

Prepaying Your Mortgage

You can shave thousands or tens of thousands of dollars off the long-term costs of your mortgage by prepaying. There are several ways to do it. You can add a little extra to your regular monthly payment, make one extra payment a year, or pay half your regular payment every two weeks, which equates to paying an extra full payment each year.

If you had a thirty-year mortgage for $100,000 at 7 percent interest and you paid an extra $25 every month, you'd cut more than three years off the length of the mortgage and save over $18,000 in interest. Please note that when mortgage rates are significantly lower than other consumer borrowing rates, it makes more sense to pay off your high-interest credit card debts first.

When you make extra payments, be sure to tell your lender to apply them to the principal. Don't pay a company that offers to set up a prepayment plan for you for a fee. Before making prepayments, check with your lender and read the fine print of your loan documents to make sure your lender won't penalize you for prepaying part of your mortgage in the first three to five years of the loan. These prepayment penalties are rare in the primary mortgage market (lenders who directly negotiate mortgages with borrowers), but common in the subprime market (investors who buy and sell pools of mortgages from lenders, which makes mortgages more accessible to those with less than perfect credit). Even if your loan does have a prepayment penalty, you'll probably be allowed to prepay up to 20 percent of your mortgage in any twelve-month period without incurring a penalty.

Facing Foreclosure

The number of home foreclosures is at an all-time high, and the rising popularity of interest-only loans and ARMs allows borrowers to buy bigger, more expensive houses. If you fail to make your mortgage payments for ninety days, your lender will probably start foreclosure proceedings to take over your house and sell it to get back the money they lent you. If the house sells for less than you owe on it, they could sue you for the difference. Obviously foreclosure is a major black mark on your credit record and will affect your ability to obtain credit in the future.

ALERT

You may find lower refinancing interest rates than your current lender advertises, but don't rule your lender out without talking to your loan officer. Sometimes banks and credit unions will waive certain fees or offer a slight rate discount for current customers.

Act Quickly to Prevent Foreclosure

There are things you can do to help prevent foreclosure. If you anticipate having trouble making payments, contact your lender immediately and explain your situation. Your lender may be willing to come up with a new payment plan that takes your current situation into consideration. You may be able to refinance the loan, extend the term, or spread the missed payments out over several months. If you have an FHA mortgage, you may have other alternatives as well. Your lender doesn't want to foreclose, but the lender can't work with you unless you're willing. For instance, Bank of America, Wells Fargo, and Citibank have all recently announced loan forgiveness programs to reduce mortgage balances as much as 30 percent. Although debt forgiveness will usually result in taxable income to the debtor, federal income tax law will specifically exclude the debt forgiveness if:

1. The house is your principal residence
2. The mortgage was used to purchase build or substantially improve the residence
3. The loan did not exceed $2 million

The Short Sale Alternative

A short sale is when a sale is arranged for less than the outstanding mortgage. Obviously, the seller's lender must agree to the terms of this transaction. Generally a seller will qualify for a short sale only if she can show some sort of financial hardship and a house that is "underwater" financially, i.e., the debt to which the home is subject exceeds its fair market value. Financial hardship can be due to death, disability, divorce, unemployment, bankruptcy, etc. Since a third-party lender is involved in the transaction process the real estate contract period is usually substantially longer than normal. The lender might favor a short sale over a loan foreclosure since they would not have to go through the eviction and auction process, which can be quite costly and time-consuming.

ESSENTIAL

A new program makes it somewhat easier to qualify for a short sale, called the Home Affordable Foreclosure Alternatives (HAFA) program. You can find details at *www.makinghomeaffordable.gov*.

Tax Ramifications

Usually if a debt is forgiven, that amount will be included in the debtor's taxable income unless the debtor is insolvent both before and after the debt forgiveness. However, a law in existence from 2007 to 2012 gives debtors relief from this provision for up to $2 million of debt forgiven if the home qualifies as a qualified principal residence indebtedness. This would include any debt incurred in acquiring, constructing, or substantially improving a principal residence, and any debt secured by the principal residence resulting from the refinancing of debt incurred to acquire, construct, or substantially improve a principal residence, but only to the extent the amount of the debt does not exceed the amount of the refinanced debt.

CHAPTER 13

Getting Deals on Wheels

Buying a car is a big deal that can cost you big money. Whether you pay cash up front or lease or finance your new car, there are pitfalls to steer clear of and information to gather to avoid paying too much. And maybe you should consider buying a used one, anyway. The Internet has revolutionized how people buy cars and made it possible for you to educate yourself before you head to the dealer.

New or Used?

As gratifying as it is to buy new, you can save a lot of money by buying a car that's one to three years old. That's because cars depreciate dramatically in the first two years—as much as 30 to 40 percent. The car that you paid $20,000 for just two short years ago may be worth only $12,000 now. If you plan to keep it for eight or ten years, it's a moot point, but if you like to trade cars every few years, it could cost you a lot of money.

If the cost is important to you, consider a vehicle that's one to three years old. Ask your dealer to notify you of models you're interested in that are coming off leases. People who lease are more likely to take good care of the car to avoid extra charges, and mileage on leased cars tends to be lower as well because they have mileage restrictions. Former rental cars are not a good buy because they're ridden hard and usually have high mileage for their age. When you buy a used car from a dealer, be sure to haggle over the price.

In general, today's cars are built better than the used cars of yesterday. Dealers and manufacturers now offer warranties on used cars that are in good condition, so you don't have to buy new to get quality. The dealer's profit margin on a used car is considerably greater.

FACT

According to *www.edmunds.com*, most new autos lose 20 to 30 percent of their value once they've been sold. Buying a used car can get you most of the value of a new car at a discounted price. To buy used, you should look for autos that are roughly two years old for optimal value.

Do a Background Check

There's always a chance with a used car that you're buying somebody else's problems. Carfax.com (*www.carfax.com*) will check its database of over 2 billion records and produce a report that reveals hidden problems that may affect the safety or resale value of the car. You may find that the car was turned in under the lemon law, salvaged after being totaled in an accident or flood, used as a taxi, or that the odometer was rolled back. To use this service, all you need is the vehicle identification number (VIN) of the car, usually found on a metal plate inside the windshield. The cost is $24.99 for a single report or $29.99 for unlimited reports for thirty days.

Trade In or Sell It Yourself?

You almost always come out ahead by selling your old car yourself. If you want to trade the car in, discuss the possibility only after you've already negotiated the best possible price for your new car. Tell the dealer that you'd rather just focus on buying a new car; that way, if you decide later to get a quote for a trade, you know there's no shuffling going on between the price of the new car and the trade-in amount.

Paying for a New Car

When you're ready to buy a new car, you have three basic methods of paying for it: cash, loan, or lease. Most people don't walk into a dealership and plunk down $20,000 to $30,000 in cash for a new car, but if you're one of the few who are able to do this, or if you're financing part of the car but making a very large down payment, there's only one important factor you need to consider:

Paying cash will save you several thousand dollars in interest charges. But before you use your cash to avoid paying 5 to 7 percent interest on a car loan, you should have all your credit card or revolving credit loans paid off. It doesn't make sense to use cash if you have credit cards with higher interest rates than those of new car loans.

Financing Through a Bank or Other Lender

Most people finance the car through the dealer or their own bank and make monthly payments. The car is collateral for the loan, meaning that if you miss a payment, the lender can repossess it. The typical car loan used to be three years, but five-year loans have become very common. This makes a new car more affordable because you can spread the payments out over a longer period, but it also costs more in interest charges. This can make you "upside down" on your loan if you decide to trade the car in for a new one in a few years. Being upside down means you owe more on the loan than it's worth. If you try to sell the car while you're upside down, you'll have to pay cash in addition to the balance on your loan. You can prevent this by using the shortest loan period possible, preferably three or four years.

Car manufacturers often promote special offers such as very low-rate financing or even 0 percent interest loans, but dealers who offer these low rates won't always negotiate on the price of the car. You may find it's cheaper to negotiate a lower price and get your financing elsewhere even if the interest rates are higher. In fact, you're better off arranging your financing yourself through a local bank or credit union, especially if you don't have great credit. Financing through the dealer opens you up to the risk of their "shifting" costs around.

Don't make your decision based on the monthly payment alone. The price of the car, the length of the loan, and the APR influence the payment. You could have what seems like an affordable monthly payment but end up paying far too much for the car by the time you pay it off.

What about Leasing?

A lease is like borrowing a car rather than buying it. You make monthly payments for the period of the lease, usually three to five years. At the end of the lease term, you have the choice of returning the car to the dealer, buying it, or in some cases, renting it from month to month. Even though you don't own the leased car, you're responsible for insurance, regular maintenance, and repairs not covered by the warranty. You will need to keep detailed records of service and repairs and the dealer will probably ask that all services be performed where you bought the car or another dealership of the same manufacturer. If you lease only for the length of the warranty, you'll never have to pay for major repairs.

ESSENTIAL

Search the Internet for "lease versus buy calculators." Some of the best calculators are available at *www.bloomberg.com* (go to "Investment Tools," then "Calculators") and *www.bankrate.com*. Also, Lease-Guide.com (*www.leaseguide.com*) offers an online Lease Kit that rates cars for leasing purposes and helps you analyze any lease you're thinking of entering into.

When you lease, you're paying only for a portion of the car's value, the part you "use up," known as depreciation. In a closed-end lease (a lease with a specific term), the price you'd pay to buy the car at the end of the lease is determined ahead of time. In an open-end lease, the car is priced at the end of the lease based on market value and the condition of the car.

The Benefits of Leasing

Leases require relatively little cash up front, usually $500 plus one month's payment as a security deposit and the first month's payment on the lease. Instead of the sales tax being paid up front as it is in a loan for a new car, a portion of it is paid each month. If sales tax in your state is 5 percent, the sales tax on a $20,000 car is $1,000. If you lease, that's $1,000 you don't have to borrow or cough up all at once. Leasing may be a good option for you if you like to have a new car every few years and don't want to incur the costs of buying and selling, or you don't have the money to come up with a down payment on a new car.

On the Other Hand

Leases may not be a good option for you if you put more than 12,000 to 15,000 miles per year on your vehicles. All leases include a mileage allowance, usually between 12,000 and 15,000 miles per year. If you exceed the allowance, you'll have to pay a fee at the end of the lease (often between ten and twenty cents per mile), which can add up to a significant amount of money. If your lease allows 12,000 miles per year and you average 14,000 per year for four years, the 8,000 extra miles at twenty cents per mile would cost you $1,600 in addition to your lease payments.

Understanding Leases

Read all the fine print and ask questions to be sure you understand what you're getting into. Leases have three basic components:

- Capitalized cost
- Residual value
- Interest rate or money factor

The capitalized cost is the price of the car. It's important to negotiate the lowest possible capitalized cost in order to reduce the size of your payments. Tell the salesperson that you want to negotiate the price of the car just as you would if you were buying it outright.

You have no direct control over the residual value, but you can influence it by choosing certain makes over others. Cars that depreciate quickly will cost you more to lease than those that hold their value. Remember, you're paying for the depreciation on the vehicle, so if you choose a car that depreciates quickly, it comes out of your pocket.

The third component of a lease is the interest rate, which dealers aren't obligated to reveal to you. If the dealer won't tell you the interest rate, you can calculate it yourself.

To calculate the lease's interest rate, or money factor, go through the following steps:

1. Subtract the residual value from the capitalized cost to calculate your depreciation.
2. Divide the depreciation in step one by the number of months in the lease to calculate your monthly depreciation charge.
3. Subtract the monthly depreciation in step two from the monthly payment quoted by your dealer. This is the monthly interest charge.
4. Add the residual value and the capitalized cost to get the total capitalized cost and residual.
5. Divide the monthly interest in step three by the total capitalized cost and residual in step four to get the money factor.
6. Multiply the money factor in step five by 24 to get the interest rate implicit in the lease (24 has nothing to do with the length of your lease—it's a mathematical constant).

Compare this interest rate to the going rates for new car loans in your area to make sure it's in the ballpark.

The Bottom Line on Leasing

The most important thing to remember about leasing is that you should never judge a lease solely by its monthly cost. If you let the dealer know that you understand how leases work and the components that go into the lease price, you'll be able to walk out with a better deal.

Don't enter into a lease lightly. They are very difficult and expensive to get out of if you terminate them early. Also be aware that you will have to pay for any damages or abnormal wear and tear on the car when you turn it in.

Negotiating the Price

There are two main keys to negotiating a price on a new car. The first is to keep the purchase, your trade-in, and the financing as three totally separate transactions. The second is to start with the invoice price (the dealer's cost) instead of trying to chip away at the manufacturer's suggested retail price (MSRP). Starting at the invoice price, subtract any manufacturer's rebates that you found on Edmunds.com to get the dealer's real cost (include rebates the dealer receives from the manufacturer but doesn't pass on to you). Make an offer of 5 percent above that and don't allow yourself to be pressured into paying more.

ALERT

The dealer profit on options is higher than the profit on the base car, so there's more room to negotiate on options. You should go to the dealership armed with information on dealer cost not only for the car, but also for any options you're thinking of adding.

Manufacturer's Rebates

Manufacturers often offer rebates, sometimes to buyers and sometimes to dealers. If you don't know about a rebate to the dealer, you could end up paying more for the car than you should, even if you're paying only 5 percent over the invoice price. You may also be able to get good deals at the end of the model year, when dealers are trying to get the current year's models off the lot to make room for next year's models.

The Dealer's Real Cost

The MSRP is just that: a suggestion. Dealers don't expect you to pay it but will gladly take your money if you don't try to negotiate. Dealers receive rebates, allowances, discounts, and incentive awards that reduce the cost of the cars they sell. If the salesperson shows you the actual invoice price and tells you he's not making any money on the deal, he's not being entirely up front with you.

Don't Pay for More Than What You Want

If you can't find a car with the options you want, try calling around to other dealerships, or consider ordering a car. You'll have to wait longer, but why pay for features you don't need or want just because the car is sitting on the lot? On the other hand, if the dealer is willing to negotiate a good deal because it wants to move cars off the lot, it may be worthwhile to buy a car with extra features. The only way you'll know whether or not it's a good deal is to know the dealer's cost on the car and each option. Once you've determined what car you want to buy, call around to several dealers and ask for their best price. Compare their estimates to information found on websites such as Edmunds. com (*www.edmunds.com*) or Autobytel.com (*www.Autobytel.com*). The more information you're armed with and the more you appear to know about how new-car pricing and selling works, the better off you'll be.

FACT

Car-buying services such as those offered by Costco (*www.costco.com*) and Autoweb.com (*www.autoweb.com*) negotiate special member-only prices with dealerships all over the country. For example, if you're a Costco member you can research the cars on its website, do side-by-side comparisons of different models, set up an appointment at a participating dealership, and automatically get the no-haggle price.

The True Cost of Ownership

You may be tempted by the looks of certain cars or trucks, or the affordable price of a particular model, but there's more to consider than appearances and cost when buying a new car. What's the repair record of this make and model? Are there problems with certain components of the car, such as the brakes or the transmission? What does it cost for routine repairs and maintenance? What kind of mileage does it get? What does it cost to insure? How is its safety record?

You can buy a new car for $10,000, but if it's not well made or doesn't have a good repair record, you are likely to end up pumping money into repairs. If, on the other hand, you buy a more expensive car with a good repair record, you may save money over the life of the car. *Consumer Reports* does extensive research on the repair records of many makes and models, so do your homework before you buy.

ESSENTIAL

Even the color of your car can affect your insurance rates. For instance, red sports cars cost more to insure because insurance companies assume drivers of red sports cars will drive at excessive speeds and therefore get in more accidents.

Extended Warranties

When you buy a new car you'll be offered an auto service contract to help protect you against the expense of major repairs. If the dealer tells you that your lender requires you to purchase an auto service contract to qualify for financing, call the lender directly to verify this. Prices on service plans vary greatly and you'll almost always pay much more if you buy it through the dealer. Read the contract carefully and make sure you're not duplicating coverage that's already offered by the manufacturer. Most new cars come with at least a one-year, 12,000-mile warranty, and some come with a three-year or 36,000-mile warranty. Any service plan you buy should kick in after the manufacturer's warranty runs out, or "wrap around" the manufacturer's warranty. Otherwise you're paying for duplicate coverage.

You'll need to know what repairs are covered (some plans explicitly disallow certain items or repairs), how long the contract lasts, whether repairs must be made by a certain company, and whether parts and labor are included. Most dealer plans are mechanical breakdown plans, not wear-and-tear plans. They cover only things that actually break, so something like piston rings that need to be replaced wouldn't be covered. You want a plan that includes both breakdowns and wear and tear.

Where to Look

You should check out the company providing the service contract, because if they go belly up, you're out of luck unless they've put aside funds to insure your contract. One of the largest warranty service providers is Warranty Direct (*www.warrantydirect.com*), which *Forbes* magazine named as one of the Top 200 Small Public Companies. Their plans are nearly half the price you'd pay through the dealer and you're buying directly from the source with no middleman markup. With their service plans, you can take the car to any Automotive Service Excellence (ASE)–licensed repair facility you choose, whether it's an auto dealership, repair shop, or private mechanic. The warranty company will pay the repair shop directly.

Buying Credit Life Insurance

Credit life insurance pays off the balance of your loan if you die. When you finance a car through a dealership, you'll almost certainly be asked if you want to buy credit life insurance. Sometimes it's even added in without you being told, so be sure to look at every line on the financing sheet. Most consumers are better off not buying this coverage.

ALERT

Consumers are overcharged more than $400 million a year for credit life insurance, according to the Consumer Federation of America, which warns that credit life insurance is grossly overpriced and is therefore "a ripoff."

You'll probably also be encouraged to buy credit disability insurance, which would make your car payment for you if you became disabled and couldn't work. The credit disability through your lender only covers your car payment. If you can't get life or disability insurance any other way (through your employer or an individual disability policy), you might consider credit life or credit disability if you're concerned about your family's ability to make the car payment if you die or become disabled.

QUESTION

Where can I find more tips and information about car buying?
Check out websites such as *www.carbuyingtips.com, www.carinfo .com,* and *www.edmunds.com* for comprehensive advice on all aspects of buying, selling, and leasing cars. Read up on car dealer scams, too.

CHAPTER 14

Marriage and Family

You're tying the knot, and there are decisions to make about merging your finances. Later, you may find yourself planning for a baby, deciding if you can afford to be a stay-at-home parent, and trying to raise financially savvy kids. And although you probably don't want to consider the possibility, you may need to know how to protect yourself if your marriage ends in divorce.

Tying the Financial Knot

Once you've decided to tie the knot, discussions about money shouldn't be far behind. When you get married, you take on all his or her financial baggage as well. You need to know just how heavy that baggage is.

Talking about Money

You may want to start out by first discussing how your parents handled money and how you feel about its role in your life. For some people, money symbolizes love or security; for others, it symbolizes power or control. It can be spent freely or hoarded and saved. Explore your feelings about money together.

After you've had a few initial discussions about money in general, initiate a discussion about your respective financial situations. Figure out whether either of you have any of the following:

- Large debts
- Student loans
- Credit card debt
- Child support or alimony obligations
- A bad credit record
- Past bankruptcy
- Investments
- An inheritance
- A trust fund

Get copies of your credit reports and go over them together. If your spouse-to-be won't talk about money, consider counseling. How can you work toward common goals if one of you can't or won't talk about money?

It's important to realize that each of you will probably have goals that the other doesn't share. Acknowledge that they're important too, and try to find a way to work toward these individual goals as well as those you have in common.

Spender Versus a Saver

Spenders often marry savers, so this is a common issue. If you're a saver and you open the credit card statement to find that your spouse has bought several hundred dollars' worth of hunting gear when you were planning to use that money for some much needed auto repairs, an argument is almost inevitable. If your spouse constantly nags at you and blames the constant drip of your ATM habits for the huge leak in the budget by month's end, another argument is on its way. When there's a saver and a spender in a relationship, you have to come to a compromise you can both live with.

FACT

There are a number of good books about money and relationships, including *Money Harmony: Resolving Money Conflicts in Your Life and Your Relationships* by Olivia Mellan and *Couples and Money: A Couples' Guide Updated for the New Millennium* by Victoria Collins, PhD, and Suzanne B. Brown.

Who Will Do What?

How will you handle your banking? Will you keep separate bank accounts and split the bills between you? Will you share a joint account that all of your income goes into and all of your bills are paid from? It's very difficult to keep track of the transactions that two people make to a single bank account. Many couples find that a joint account for household expenses and individual accounts for each spouse's personal spending works very well ("His," "Hers," and "Theirs"). It allows each of you to have discretionary money for expenditures that you don't have to explain or justify to each other.

ALERT

If one person in a relationship controls the other's spending, it gives the controlling person a parental type of power that's not healthy in a marriage, and can cause resentment to build in the spouse who has no financial power in the relationship.

Often there's one person in a marriage who is more interested, motivated, or adept at paying the bills, balancing the checkbooks, tracking expenses and investments, and maintaining a budget. Talk about it. You may both quickly agree on the obvious choice for these tasks or you may decide to share the responsibility. Regardless of who does what, sit down at least once a month and review your finances together.

Maintaining Credit in Your Own Name

Virtually all financial experts agree that after marriage you should maintain credit in your own name. Keep a credit card in your name only, and use it occasionally, but always pay off the balance each month. If you find yourself on your own through death or divorce, you'll have immediate credit available. It can be difficult to obtain credit for even the most basic needs, let alone a large purchase like a car or house, if you don't have a credit history that doesn't include your spouse.

Do You Need a Prenuptial Agreement?

Prenuptial agreements may have a negative connotation, but nearly everybody could benefit from one. These agreements designate how your assets and liabilities will be handled in the event of a divorce, but can also be used to protect the interests of children from a previous marriage or spell out other important issues. If you plan to have children of your own, your agreement may contain arrangements for child support, education, or even religious upbringing.

Anybody who owns a business or professional practice, has received valuable gifts or inheritances, has a trust fund, owns a home, has a retirement plan, has substantial savings or investments, or wants to protect the inheritance of children from a previous marriage should draw up a prenuptial agreement. Most states will give a spouse a right of election of about one-third of a deceased spouse's estate unless such right is waived in the nuptial agreement.

If one of you expects to inherit money or other assets, you may want to keep your inheritance separate, but most states will consider it marital property to be divided at divorce, unless you have a nuptial agreement. These agreements can be written after marriage, but are much easier to work out ahead of time.

For a prenuptial agreement to be legally binding, each of you must have your own independent lawyer and each must fully disclose all of your assets and liabilities. Prenuptial agreements shouldn't be viewed as planning for a marriage to fail. They're just good common sense.

Planning an Affordable Wedding

According to *Brides Magazine*, the average wedding in the United States costs around $26,500. How can you keep your wedding costs under control? First of all, do a budget. Make a list of everything you can think of that you'll need for the ceremony, rehearsal dinner, and reception and your estimate of what each item will cost. Refine your budget as you get price quotes, and identify the things that are most important to you. Small compromises can often add up to big savings.

ESSENTIAL

Tipping is often an overlooked wedding expense that could bust your budget. Don't forget to plan for tipping caterers, limo drivers, parking attendants, and musicians 10 to 20 percent if you're happy with their services.

The Wedding Budget

The biggest factor influencing your costs is the number of guests that attend. If your average cost per person for food, drink, linens, cutlery, china, and other things you have to rent by the person is $50, knocking twenty people off your guest list will save you $1,000 plus tips.

Consider a buffet or hearty hors d'oeuvres instead of a sit-down dinner. Bar costs can be higher than food costs, and the markup on alcohol provided by your caterer is significant. It's cheaper to do it yourself but you'll have to assume the liquor liability. Talk to your insurance agent to see if your homeowner's policy will cover it. One option for limiting bar costs is to provide tickets for guests that they can turn in for drinks. If they want more alcohol after using their tickets, they pay cash. Or you can choose to have a cash bar where everyone pays for his own drinks.

The busiest wedding season is May through October and the most popular day for weddings is Saturday. Reception sites are usually less expensive if you book a wedding in the off-season (November through April) or on any day other than Saturday. Entertainers and photographers may also charge less during the off-season.

Rings and Things

Although the rings are important, don't spend more money on them than you can reasonably afford. You can buy a beautiful ring for a fraction of the cost that experts recommend you spend and upgrade your rings as a sentimental gesture as time goes on and you refine your preferences.

What about the Marriage Tax Penalty?

Your wedding present from Uncle Sam may be higher taxes, known as the marriage tax penalty. This is a scenario when you pay more in taxes because you are "married filing jointly." If both of you make $100,000 per year, you might pay more as a married couple than you would as singles, even though you're talking about $200,000 of income either way.

In general, couples are penalized if they both earn a similar amount of money. Couples may benefit if their income levels are very different—for example, one partner might not work, or one partner might have an extremely high salary. Besides higher taxes, if you both checked "married" on your new W-4 at work, your payroll departments will calculate withholding based on the standard deduction for married individuals. You'll have taxes withheld as though you were entitled to twice the standard deduction and your taxes will be underwithheld significantly. To prevent this from happening, after you get married you should file new W-4s with your respective employers with one of you checking the married status and the other checking the single status. This will help correct your withholding so you're not hit with a huge tax bill in April. You can also use the IRS's withholding calculator at *www.irs.gov* to figure out exactly how you should set up your withholding.

Beneficiaries, Name Changes, and Wills

After the wedding, there are several financial issues you should take care of right away. Go through the documentation for your retirement plans, life insurance policies, bank accounts, and investment accounts. If you want your spouse to be the beneficiary, file change-of-beneficiary forms. Most private pension plans require that your spouse be named as primary beneficiary unless a waiver is executed by the spouse. Also look for accounts you want to add your spouse's name to as joint owner, or where you need to change the name of the person to notify in an emergency. If one of you owns property, decide whether you want to change the deed to include both your names. It should be noted that property acquired before the marriage would not be considered marital property in the event of a divorce. However by changing the form of ownership to include both names you have converted separate property to marital property.

ALERT

If you have a complicated financial situation or a large net worth, consult an estate-planning attorney about ways to protect your estate from higher taxes if one of you dies.

If you change your name when you get married, apply for a new social security card, vehicle title, and driver's license in your new name. Notify banks, insurance companies, brokerages, and others about your name change. Be aware that if you add your name to your spouse's existing credit card, you'll be equally responsible for the debt that he or she brought into the marriage.

Have a will drawn up, or if you already have one, have it updated or rewritten. If one of you has children from a previous relationship, it's especially important to spell out guardianship and custody issues.

Planning for a Baby

Your home is not the biggest investment you'll ever make—your kids are. You probably won't use cost as a determining factor in whether you decide to raise a family, but you can still benefit financially from some advance planning.

Insurance Issues

The most immediate issue when you're thinking of adding a new member to your family is how much of the associated cost will be covered by your health insurance. Estimate how much you can expect to pay out of your own pocket, based on the coverage provided by your health insurance policy. If you're covered under an HMO, you'll probably have a copay for each doctor visit (usually $10 to $25) and a copay for the hospital admission for the delivery (usually a minimum of $250 to $500). Be sure your doctor and the hospital are in your HMO network or you could be faced with some very large medical bills.

If you have an indemnity plan instead of an HMO, you probably have a deductible (usually $200 to $1,000) that you have to pay out of your pocket before the insurance kicks in. After the deductible, a typical plan will pay 80 percent of all other allowed charges, and you'll pay 20 percent, up to a maximum out-of-pocket expense (usually $1,000 to $3,000). After you've satisfied the out-of-pocket maximum, the insurance will pay 100 percent of usual and customary charges. Sometimes charges are only partially paid by insurance because they exceed the usual and customary cost for that service or procedure in your area, but if you ask, doctors will sometimes write off the excess.

FACT

The U.S. Department of Agriculture estimates that in 2010, one child cost a husband and wife couple $163,440 (if your annual income was under $57,600) and over $377,000 (if your annual income was higher than $99,000) from birth to the age of eighteen, not including any provision for private school or college costs.

Find out how much it will cost to add your new family member to your group medical insurance policy as a dependent. If you and your spouse have separate insurance policies, figure out if it makes sense for one of you to transfer to the other's policy. Dependent coverage may be cheaper if you're all on one policy, especially if one spouse has a cafeteria (section 125) plan and pays premiums with pretax dollars. If you or your spouse has an option of contributing to a flexible-spending account (FSA) at work, you could come out ahead by doing so.

Income and Expense Issues

Think about how you'll manage on one income during maternity leave and possibly reduced income during the pregnancy. Are you covered by short-term disability insurance? If so, you'll receive between 60 percent and 70 percent of your regular income for approximately six weeks following delivery, or sooner if you're deemed medically unable to work during your pregnancy.

Arrange child care well in advance. It takes time to interview potential providers and check them out with other parents who have used them. Child care is a huge expense, so figure the costs into your budget ahead of time and come up with ways to make cuts elsewhere if necessary. Child-care expenses are eligible for a tax credit as long as you provide the caretaker's employer ID or social security number to the IRS.

Start a baby fund to cover unexpected costs, and contribute to it monthly and shop for bargains on baby equipment and supplies, but don't skimp on items that affect safety, such as high-quality car seats.

Can You Afford to Stay Home?

Before you jump to the conclusion that you can't afford to live on one salary so you or your spouse can stay home and raise your kids, consider the cost of working:

- Day care, after-school care, day camps, babysitters
- Work clothes and shoes, dry cleaning, uniforms, special gear
- Additional wear and tear and more frequent maintenance on your car, plus gas and auto insurance
- Transportation costs such as bus fares, parking, and toll fees
- Coffee and vending machine snacks or sodas at work, office gift pools, lunches out
- Professional fees such as licenses or certificates, continuing education courses, dues or subscriptions

Estimate all of these costs, add them up, and deduct the total from your net pay (after taxes). This is how much the second income is contributing to your household budget.

For an example: Assume you earn $15 an hour and work thirty hours a week, for a gross weekly pay of $450. Taxes deducted are between $123 and $182, depending on your tax bracket, leaving you a net pay of $327 to $268. Child care is likely to be between $125 and $187 per week, and its costs are growing at double the rate of inflation. Subtract the average of these two child-care figures, $156, from your net after taxes, leaving you with $112 to $171 per week. Now subtract an estimate of all your other work-related expenses as previously listed. That's what you're really getting out of that second income, before you even look at the marriage tax penalty.

ALERT

The Average Family's Guide to Financial Freedom by Bill and Mary Toohey isn't about staying home with your kids. It shows how an average family, with kids, in debt, and on a modest income, can take control of their finances and sock away a small fortune.

You may find you're working for minimum wage or worse after your costs of working are deducted from your net pay. If you can't make ends meet without the extra money, however little it is, try going back to your budget and see where you can make cuts. *You Can Afford to Stay Home with Your Kids* by Malia McCawley Wyckoff and Mary Snyder is a step-by-step guide to the most effective cost-cutting strategies that make it possible to live on one income. The book walks you through the financial-planning process necessary to make staying at home possible.

Raising Financially Savvy Kids

You need to take an organized approach to teaching your children sound financial principles and personal-finance skills if you don't want them to grow up to live from paycheck to paycheck, be financially dependent on you, get deeply into debt, or develop destructive attitudes about money.

You can start with teaching your kids about the basics of spending, banking, and saving when they are around the age of five. Let them make their own bank deposits and withdrawals, make purchases, and decide what to spend their money on (within reason).

Kids should receive an allowance by the time they're in school. The purpose of the allowance is to teach them about managing money. Help them decide how much of each week's allowance they'll put in the bank. They'll quickly learn that if they spend it now, they won't have it when something they really want comes along. As your kids get older, adapt your teaching to their age and ability to understand. Teach older kids how to invest by using the Internet to research stocks or mutual funds and set up a mock stock portfolio so they can track their stocks' performance. Teach your teenagers how to balance a checkbook and how to track their earnings and expenditures.

ESSENTIAL

Smart-Money Moves for Kids by Judith Briles helps parents teach their kids about the value and proper use of money. *Allowances, Dollars and Sense* by Paul Lermitte presents a proven system for teaching kids about money. It's easy to read and includes exercises, worksheets, and checklists.

Teach Good Consumer Habits

One of the most important things you can teach your kids is how advertising can influence their buying decisions, and how they can resist giving in to the advertiser's message that buying its product makes kids look cool or makes them feel good. Help them realize that brand-name jeans, for example, are identical to other jeans, except for the label, but cost a lot more.

The Financial Impact of Divorce

You've probably heard that 50 percent of all marriages end in divorce. If yours is one of them, it helps to be aware of some of the financial issues. For example, if you and your spouse agree to a division of your debt, be sure to make this a formal arrangement by contacting each creditor and asking them to legally transfer the debt to you or your spouse and release the other from liability. If you're going to be responsible for a debt, your spouse shouldn't be listed as an authorized user (for example, on a credit card) and he or she shouldn't be held responsible if you fail to pay it off—and vice versa. Some couples obtain individual consolidation loans and pay off their portion of the joint debts so the accounts can be closed. This is ideal for a clean split, but if it's not possible, and your spouse incurs large amounts of debt, inform the lender in writing that you're no longer responsible for any new charges.

Good references on divorce include *Divorce & Money: How to Make the Best Financial Decisions During Divorce* by Violet Woodhouse and Dale Fetherling, and *Using Divorce Mediation* by Katherine E. Stoner, a complete manual on how to mediate your divorce and avoid prolonged court battles and huge legal expenses that you'll spend years paying off.

Be sure to consider how divorce will impact your health insurance. If you have coverage under your spouse's policy and he or she works for a company with more than twenty employees, you're eligible to continue under the same plan for up to thirty-six months by electing COBRA coverage. You'll have to pay the amount the coverage costs the employer plus an administrative fee of 2 percent. If you don't notify your spouse's employer of the divorce within sixty days, you lose your right to this benefit.

FACT

Certified divorce planners are professionals who give financial advice that lawyers aren't qualified to give, such as the short- and long-term financial impact of a proposed divorce settlement, tax consequences, dividing retirement plans, and stock option or insurance issues. They serve as your advocate in achieving a financially equitable divorce settlement.

Child Support

If your marriage is headed for divorce and you're the custodial parent, file for child support as soon as you and your spouse separate. Your spouse has no legal obligation to pay child support unless there's a court order from a divorce, marriage dissolution, establishment of paternity, or legal separation. An attorney or your local child support agency can help you get a court order. Child support judgments are issued as of the date of filing and are not retroactive.

Unfortunately, having a court order is not always enough. The Association for Children for Enforcement of Support (ACES) estimates that there's $41 billion in unpaid child support for over 30 million children in the United States. If your ex-spouse is delinquent in child support, the Child Support Enforcement Agency (CSEA) in your state is required to help you collect payment by serving your ex-spouse with papers requiring him or her to meet with the district attorney and arrange a payment schedule. If your ex-spouse refuses, he or she could serve jail time. The CSEA will provide you with a free attorney if necessary.

Other measures include taking the parent's tax refund, garnishing wages, taking unemployment insurance proceeds, seizing assets, suspending a professional or business license, and in some states, revoking a driver's license. The government can even take your lottery winnings if you owe back child support. If your spouse lives out of state, there are methods of locating him or her and having the courts in the two states work together to enforce the child support judgment.

Tax Consequences of Divorce

Generally, alimony is tax deductible to the spouse who pays and is included in the taxable income of the recipient spouse. However, just because you and your ex-spouse decide a payment qualifies as alimony does not make it so. You must comply with the tax law that describes a payment as alimony only if:

1. The payment is made in cash (paying bills for the ex-spouse will not qualify)
2. Received pursuant to a divorce decree or separation instrument (including court order)
3. Between members of different households
4. The obligation must cease at the death of the recipient spouse

Other payments to the spouse will be deemed a property settlement and neither deductible to the paying spouse nor included in the recipient spouse's income. Child support payments are treated the same way as the property settlement payments. The spouse entitled to the dependency deduction for the children ($3,800 per child in 2012) depends on which parent is the primary custodial parent regardless of who furnishes the financial support. However, the primary custodial parent may execute a waiver form to allow the other parent to take the deduction.

CHAPTER 15

Unwed but Not Unwise

Millions of couples live together without the benefits of marriage, many unaware of the legal and financial consequences of their arrangement. If you're living with your partner, you should consider the issues involved with mingling your assets and sharing your expenses and take steps to protect yourself in case your relationship ends.

Moving In Together

Before you move in together, inform your partner of any skeletons in your financial closet, such as bad credit, a past bankruptcy, a lien on your house, unpaid child support, or a tax lien. Since you'll be mingling finances to some extent, it's only fair to be up front about these things. It's likely your partner will find out about any financial issues once you're living together anyway. You can always change the way you do things after you've lived together for a while, but don't wait until then to discuss how you're going to handle the money issues that affect you both, from spending habits to investments and financial goals.

ESSENTIAL

The Myvesta Foundation offers a brochure called *Living Together: A Financial Contract for Unmarried Couples*. It's available from their website at *www.myvesta.org/articles*.

Nonmarital Agreements

People take for granted the legal rights afforded to married couples. If one of the couple dies, the other inherits their joint property and may receive social security or retirement benefits. If the couple divorces, their assets are divided between them. Unfortunately, these same rights don't apply to unmarried couples, so financial planning may actually be more critical for them than for those who have tied the knot.

Why Do I Need a Nonmarital Agreement?

It may not sound romantic, but it's wise to have a written agreement that spells out how property, other assets, and shared expenses will be handled if your relationship ends. The best legal protection for unmarried couples living together is a nonmarital agreement, also referred to as a cohabitation, relationship, or "living together" agreement. It's a written contract that gives each of you legal control over your property and finances if the relationship ends, and it can save you attorney's fees and court costs if there's any disagreement about who gets what.

There are obvious financial benefits to living together, such as sharing rent and utilities, but there are also dangers involved. If you're in your twenties and haven't accumulated many assets yet, a nonmarital agreement may seem totally unnecessary. But if you're in a committed relationship that you expect to be long term, a nonmarital agreement is important.

FACT

Regardless of how many years you and your partner live together unmarried, when you split up, you're legally entitled to only property that is in your own name or was specifically designated yours by written contract.

If your relationship ends, you may get stuck with the bills for things you and your partner bought together. If the apartment or house you share was leased in your name based on your joint income, you may find you can't afford the rent after you and your partner split. You may have lent your partner money or cosigned on a loan, only to be left holding the bag. If you buy a house together, you could be the one out on the street but still responsible for paying the mortgage.

What's Covered in a Nonmarital Agreement?

Nonmarital agreements can cover a wide range of issues but are especially critical if you're buying a house together, purchasing other large assets with joint funds, coming into the relationship with previously owned property or assets, or if one of you has a lot of debt. The agreement can accomplish the following:

- Address how property you own and what you accumulate together will be handled if you no longer live together
- Cover how gifts or inheritances will be dealt with
- Include provisions for support after separation or death, or an agreement to waive the right to palimony. Palimony is generally defined as an allowance for support made between unmarried individuals who

have cohabitated and are now living separately based on an express or implied promise by one of the parties to the other.

- Spell out who's responsible for the mortgage and who gets to take the tax deduction for interest
- Stipulate that property be kept separate
- Indicate who gets to keep a rental apartment if you split up
- Discuss how credit cards and other debt will be handled

It's a good idea to include a clause stating that mediation will be used for resolving any disputes and that if you still can't come to an agreement after mediation you'll go to formal and binding arbitration.

What Happens Without a Nonmarital Agreement?

If you can't settle issues at the end of your relationship regarding who owns what, you may end up in court. In most states the court will first ask if there's a written contract, and if there isn't, the court will try to determine if there was an oral agreement (difficult to prove). If not, the court will examine your actions to try to determine if there was an implied contract. If there's proof that you've shared expenses and assets equally, for instance, or that you shared a bank account, the court could rule that there's an implied contract and enforce it as such. One of you may end up paying a settlement or support payments to the other, even in the absence of a written or oral agreement.

ALERT

You should be aware that if one of you is still legally married to someone else, you might not be protected legally regardless of what you do. Some states won't enforce agreements or promises you make to your live-in partner if one of you is still legally married.

This is a general overview of nonmarital agreements and is not offered as legal advice. Sometimes laws in a particular state will override anything you write in an agreement, so you may think you're protected when in fact you may not be.

Common-Law Marriages

Common-law marriages between heterosexuals are recognized to some extent by fifteen states and the District of Columbia. Several of those states only recognize common-law marriages that began before a certain year. In a common-law marriage, you're considered married even though you've never gone through the formalities. There are four requirements:

1. You have to live together.
2. You have to present yourself as a married couple, for instance by using the same last name or referring to your partner as your husband or wife.
3. You must intend to be married.
4. You must live together for a significant number of years.

The number of years it takes before you're considered married by common law is not clearly defined in any of the fifteen states that recognize common-law marriages (New Hampshire only recognizes common-law marriage in relation to inheritance rights should either party pass away). There's also no simple way to determine if you're married by common-law, and it usually only comes up if you have to go to court for a legal matter related to your relationship. Common-law marriage is not something you should rely on to give you any kind of legal protection.

FACT

There's a common misperception that if you live together for seven years you're married by common law. No states specify a minimum number of years. Instead, they specify criteria they would qualify you as being "married." For example, if you live together and tell everybody you're married, you might qualify.

If you become married by common law and later decide you want to end your relationship, you have to go through a regular legal divorce. To avoid becoming common-law married when it's not your intention, if you live in a state that recognizes common-law marriages, you and your live-in partner may want to sign a statement saying it's not your intention to be married.

Mingling Your Assets

If it's important to discuss the mingling of your assets and finances when you're planning to get married, it's even more important if you're moving in together without the legal benefits of marriage. Even if you don't think it's necessary when you first move in together, if you find that you're accumulating joint property, consider clarifying who owns what in a legal document.

Making Joint Purchases

Some couples use a joint purchase agreement when they buy large items together. Joint purchase agreements spell out what will happen to an item purchased with joint funds if the relationship ends for any reason, without addressing the broader issues usually included in a nonmarital agreement.

ALERT

Never purchase a major asset jointly that doesn't have your name on the title or deed. The person whose name is on those papers is the person who legally owns the property, and you could end up losing whatever money you've put in to it.

If you don't have a written agreement about how assets purchased together will be dealt with if your relationship ends, you should document your contribution for these assets. When you buy an asset together, get a receipt as evidence that you contributed toward ownership of the asset. Better yet, pay your portion by check and make a notation on the check itself, such as "50 percent of the jointly owned bedroom furniture."

Buying a House Together

If the two of you decide to buy a house together, in addition to making sure that both of your names are on the deed, you should make sure the deed also indicates your preferred method of jointly holding property. Specify either "joint ownership with rights of survivorship" or "tenants in common."

Joint Ownership with Rights of Survivorship

The simplest method of transferring property is joint ownership with rights of survivorship, which means that if one of you dies, the other automatically inherits the property. For estate tax purposes, it will be presumed that if there is a joint tenancy between unmarried individuals, the deceased tenant owned the entire property. It is up to the surviving tenant to prove that they made a contribution toward the purchase of the property in order to avoid its total inclusion in the deceased tenant's estate. You don't have the option of leaving your share at your death to someone other than your partner since joint ownership provisions in the deed will override any bequest in your will. In a joint tenancy with rights of survivorship between unmarried parties either party could legally force a sale through the use of a partition proceeding.

Tenants in Common

Being tenants in common means that each of you owns half of the house. If you die, your share will go to the person or persons indicated in your will (if you have one), or else to your next of kin. This method of ownership allows for owners with unequal equity. For example, you may own 75 percent of the house and your partner may own 25 percent. Each of you can sell or give away your share or leave it to one or more individuals of your choice, such as kids from a previous relationship. Having a will is critical if you own property as tenants in common.

Who Gets the House If You Break Up?

Your nonmarital agreement should spell out what will happen if both of you want to keep the house when you break up. How will you decide who goes and who stays? Does the person who gets the house buy out the person who's leaving? How is the buyout price calculated? Is it half the equity in the house, or is an amount deducted equal to the realtor fees that would have been paid if the house had been sold? If one of you contributed more to the purchase of the house than the other, your nonmarital agreement should spell out how this will be compensated if you break up.

Sharing Expenses

While the actual method you decide on for sharing expenses may be unimportant, to avoid disagreements later, you should discuss up front how you want to handle this issue. Will you divide housing costs and day-to-day expenses equally or contribute to a household fund in proportion to your income? The latter may be the fairest method if one of you earns significantly more than the other. For example, let's say one of you makes $40,000 per year and the other makes $20,000. The one that makes twice as much will contribute $2 for every $1 the other contributes to the joint household fund.

FACT

The number of unmarried couples cohabitating in the United States increased 72 percent from 1990 to 2000, to over 5.5 million couples, according to the U.S. Census Bureau. It's estimated that less than half of cohabitating unmarried couples will get married.

What will your banking arrangements be? Will you share a checking account, deposit both your checks into it, and pay all your household bills from it, or will you maintain separate accounts and settle up with each other as bills come in? If you choose to maintain separate accounts, it's a good idea to document your intention to share expenses by paying your portion of bills directly rather than paying your partner your share in cash or by check. This documents the implied contract (mentioned previously) and could protect you if your relationship ends in court. If you decide to have a joint bank account, be aware that either of you could legally take all the money out of the account. Many people have ended a live-in relationship by walking away with the cash and leaving their partner high and dry.

Taxes for Unmarried Couples

Unlike married couples, unmarried couples can't file joint returns. This can help you or hurt you depending on how your income falls in with the "marriage tax penalty."

Home Mortgage Interest Deduction

When you own a house together, the issue of who will get to claim the mortgage interest and property tax deductions for federal income tax return purposes has to be addressed. You could split the deductions in half, but you might not benefit as much from this method if one of you makes significantly more than the other, because the deductions will create more tax savings for the person with the higher tax rate. It might make more sense to let that person claim the entire deduction and compensate the other person in some monetary way.

ESSENTIAL

For a comprehensive guide to the legal and financial implications of living together, see *Living Together: A Legal Guide for Unmarried Couples* by attorneys Ralph Warner, Toni Ihara, and Frederick Hertz, available from Nolo.com (*www.nolo.com*). Click on Search and type in the keywords "Living Together Guide."

Head of Household and Earned-Income Tax Credit

If a dependent child lives with you and your unmarried partner at least six months a year, and you provide more than 50 percent of the cost of maintaining the household, you can claim head of household status on your income tax return. This allows you to take the child and dependent care credits to reduce your taxes. See IRS Publication 17 for detailed information on the "head of household" status and a checklist to see if you're qualified to claim it.

If your income is below the limit, you can also take the earned-income tax credit, which offsets your income tax liability and can sometimes supplement your income by allowing you to get back more than you actually paid. If you have a dependent child living with you, you may want to consult a tax accountant before filing your income tax returns.

Other Issues

Other issues that unmarried couples face include wills, trusts, and advance directives. Dying intestate means dying without a written will. Each state has laws that designate the method of distributing your property if you die intestate, and there's a good chance your property won't go to the individuals you'd want to receive it. That's why a will is important even if you're single. If you have kids, it's absolutely critical, because your will is the instrument for indicating who you'd want to take guardianship.

If you're married, in most states your spouse and children automatically inherit your property if you die intestate. If you're unmarried without children, and die intestate, your property will be left to your next of kin as determined by the state. Your partner will not receive anything. Without a written nonmarital contract, the only way to leave property to your partner if you die is through a will or beneficiary designation (on your retirement account or life insurance policy).

An advance directive is a legal document identifying the treatments and lifesaving measures you want if you become ill and there's no reasonable hope of recovery. There are two basic types of advance directives: a living will and a durable power of attorney for health care. In a living will, you state the kind of health care you want under certain circumstances and the kind you don't want. For example, if you're terminally ill, you may not want to be resuscitated if you stop breathing. In a durable power of attorney for health care, also called a health care proxy, you designate somebody close to you to make decisions about your health care if you're unable to make them for yourself.

CHAPTER 16

Minimizing Income Taxes

Filling out the forms properly is not even half the battle when it comes to taxes. You also want to avoid penalties and keep as much of your money as possible by taking advantage of every tax-saving strategy available to you. That requires a basic understanding of how taxes work and an awareness of significant tax-reduction opportunities.

Federal Income Taxes—the Basics

By having income taxes withheld from your paycheck each pay period, you're really prepaying an estimate of the taxes you'll owe for the year. You settle up your bill with Uncle Sam when you prepare your tax return after the end of the year.

The W-4 Form

The amount you have withheld is calculated based on your filing status (married or single) and the number of withholding allowances you claim on the W-4 form you file with your employer. You should file a new W-4 with your employer if you:

- Got a big refund last year
- Owed over $100 last year when you filed your tax return
- Got married or divorced
- Had a child
- Can no longer claim a dependent that you claimed last year

Most people have too much tax withheld and let the IRS borrow their money interest-free all year. You could be earning interest on that money or saving between 12 and 20 percent in interest charges by using the extra money to pay down credit card debt.

ALERT

The only time it makes sense to have more withheld than you're going to owe is if you find it impossible to save money on a regular basis. You could accomplish the same thing by having a fixed amount automatically deducted from your check each month and deposited in a savings account.

Exemptions

An exemption is a fixed amount you deduct from your taxable income for yourself, your spouse if you're married, and each eligible dependent you claim on your income tax return. In 2012, each exemption was worth $3,800, so if you're married but have no kids, you can claim $7,600 if you file jointly. There are different tests employed for the dependency deduction depending on whether you are claiming a qualifying child or qualifying relative. See Section 3, Part One, of IRS Publication 17 for details.

Marginal and Effective Tax Rates

Your income is taxed based on taxable income brackets, ranging from 10 percent to 35 percent. The higher your income, the more tax brackets you'll cross, with the income that falls within each bracket being taxed at the rate for that bracket.

▼   2012 TAX BRACKET LIMITS

Filing Status	10 percent	15 percent	25 percent	28 percent	33 percent*
Single	$8,700	$35,350	$85,650	$178,650	$388,350
Married filing jointly/ Qualifying Widow(er)	$17,400	$70,700	$142,700	$217,450	$388,350
Married filing separately	$8,700	$35,350	$71,350	$108,725	$194,175
Head of household	$12,400	$47,350	$122,300	$198,050	$388,350

*Income in excess of these amounts is taxed at 35 percent

For example, if you're single and your AGI is $40,000, your tax would be calculated as follows:

The first $8,700 at 10 percent = $870.00.

The next $26,650 (the difference between $35,350 and $8,700) at 15 percent = $3,997.50.

The next $4,650 (the difference between your AGI of $40,000 and $35,350) at 25 percent = $1,162.50.

That means your total tax burden would be $870 + $3,997.50 + $1,162.50 = $6,030.00.

Your effective tax rate (or average tax rate) is the tax rate you actually pay on your total income, considering that part of your income isn't taxed at all due to exemptions and the standard deduction or itemized deductions, and that part of your income may fall in different tax brackets. To calculate your effective federal tax rate, divide your total federal income taxes for the year (from your latest tax return) by your total income. If your marginal rate is 25 percent, your effective tax rate may be between 15 and 17 percent.

FACT

If all this talk about marginal tax rates seems confusing, just remember that if your marginal rate is 25 percent, then 25 percent of any additional earnings will go to the IRS, and additional tax-free or tax-deferred deductions will produce savings of 25 percent. This is important information for tax planning.

Your marginal tax rate is the rate you pay on your highest dollars of income. Look up your total income (including capital gains, interest income, and so on) in the tax bracket table. Your marginal rate is the percentage shown in the column that your total income falls into. For example, if your income is $40,000, your marginal tax rate in 2012 is 25 percent. Your marginal tax rate tells you two important things: how much you'll gain by reducing your taxable income, and the true after-tax cost of a tax-deductible expense.

For example, if you want to increase your tax-deferred contributions to your employer's 401(k) plan by $100, you could quickly calculate your real out-of-pocket expense by using your marginal tax rate of 25 percent and your state tax rate, which we'll assume is 6 percent for purposes of the example. Since 401(k) contributions aren't subject to federal or (in most states) state taxes, the $100 could go into your account with only $69 coming out of your pocket (savings of 25 percent + 6 percent = 31 percent; $100 – 31 percent = $69). You'd save $31 in federal and state income tax by reducing your income $100.

You can also quickly calculate the real value of additional income, such as overtime, bonuses, or a second job, which will be taxed at your marginal tax rate. If your marginal federal tax rate is 25 percent, $1,000 in extra income will net you around $593.50 (7.65 percent for social security taxes

[5.65 percent for 2011 and 2012], 25 percent for federal income taxes, and 6 percent for state income taxes for purposes of our example, for a total tax rate of 38.65 percent; $1,000 × 38.65 percent = $386.50 in taxes; $1,000 − $386.50 = $613.50 net pay).

Standard and Itemized Deductions

When it comes to deductions, you have two choices. You can take the standard deduction, which is a fixed dollar amount that you deduct from your taxable income, or you can itemize deductions. For 2012 the standard deduction is $5,950 if you're filing single, $11,900 for married filing jointly, $5,950 for married filing separately, and $8,700 for head of household.

ESSENTIAL

So many deductions have disappeared over the years that if you have no mortgage interest or very low mortgage interest, you probably won't be able to itemize unless you are in a state or city with high income taxes or have extremely large medical expenses or charitable contributions.

If your actual allowable deductions total more than the standard deduction, you'll save money by itemizing. To see if you qualify, use a copy of Schedule A from Form 1040 to list the amounts of each of the deductions that apply to you, such as home mortgage interest, real estate taxes, state income taxes, and personal-property taxes. If the total is more than the standard deduction, itemize.

Preparing Your Tax Return

The average person is more than capable of completing Form 1040EZ and Form 1040A (the short form). Form 1040 (the long form) is definitely more challenging but is much less so thanks to the availability of robust tax preparation software programs and online services. The biggest requirement is time.

Types of Federal Tax Return Forms

There are three versions of the U.S. Individual Income Tax Return Form 1040:

- Form 1040EZ: The simplest form, for those under age sixty-five with no dependents, no itemized deductions, no more than $1,500 of taxable interest income, no advance earned-income tax credit (EITC), and taxable income from line six of less than $100,000. There are a few other little caveats, so be sure to read the instructions with the form to make sure you qualify to use the form.
- Form 1040A: Only slightly more difficult to complete than the 1040EZ. You can use this form if you don't itemize deductions, your taxable income is less than $100,000, you claim only certain tax credits (see the form instructions for a list), and you had income from only the following sources: wages, salaries, and tips; interest and ordinary dividends; capital gains; taxable scholarship and fellowship grants; pensions, annuities, and IRAs; unemployment compensation; taxable social security; Alaska permanent fund dividends.
- Form 1040 (the long form): Nearly three-quarters of all taxpayers use this form. There are a number of special circumstances that require you to use the long form, so be sure to read the instructions.

Using Tax Software on Your PC

Doing your own taxes is easy using tax software such as TurboTax by Intuit or TaxCut by H&R Block. You can buy the software from Staples or other office supply stores or download the program online for around $30 for the basic version. This type of software handles both simple and complex returns with ease, although it does take a bit of time. The programs walk you through an interview process by asking you questions, do all the calculations, and produce your finished tax return and any necessary schedules, plus worksheets to keep in your file as backup. You can either print the return and mail it or file it electronically. Both federal and state versions are available.

Using Web-Based Software

If you don't want to buy new tax software every year, you can use web-based software. It's no longer significantly cheaper than buying your own, so the main advantage now to web-based software is that you don't have to be on your own PC to work on your return. You can do so from any computer that has access to the Internet. You don't have to complete your return in one sitting; you can come back to it as often as you want until you're ready to hit the "Send" button.

ALERT

There are a few instances where you can't file the entire return electronically. If your return includes one of several schedules that require another person's signature—for instance, noncustodial parents claiming exemptions for their kids—you'll have to file a paper copy of the form along with transmittal Form 8453 within three business days after the IRS acknowledges it has received your electronically filed return.

Using Paper and Pen

For technophobes or those with the simplest of tax returns, there's nothing more satisfying than preparing tax returns with pen and paper. However, if you file electronically, you can get your money in nine to sixteen days if you have your refund automatically deposited to your bank account. If you file a paper return, expect it to take at least twice that time, depending on when you file.

Hiring a Tax Accountant or Service

Approximately half of Americans use a tax-preparation service of some type. Three-quarters of a million of them pay a tax preparer to complete the very simple Form 1040EZ. Many others use a preparer for the 1040 form. While it pays to use expert help if you have a complex tax situation, you can save yourself $100 to $200 or more by preparing your own return if you use the short form. Having a very complex return done professionally could cost $1,000 or more. The more organized your records are and the more information you can give the preparer about your personal situation, the less it will cost.

There are times when it's almost certainly a good idea to seek professional tax assistance—for instance, if you exercised incentive stock options, had complex investments, have a home-based business, own rental property, or had a major life transition such as marriage, divorce, a baby, or started your own business. The qualifications of tax preparers vary immensely, and you'll pay more if you choose someone who is over-qualified to handle the complexity level of your return. Certified public accountants, tax attorneys, and enrolled agents (certified by the Treasury Department) are the only professionals who can represent you in an audit if that ever becomes necessary, but you can also use other trained preparers suited to your needs.

ESSENTIAL

You can search for tax professionals near you by visiting the National Association of Tax Professionals website at *www.taxprofessionals.com* and using the search feature. The site provides members' names, addresses, telephone numbers, and e-mail addresses.

Finding a Reputable and Skilled Preparer

Start by asking friends, family, coworkers, and other professionals for recommendations. If you can't come up with a recommendation this way, try contacting the local chapter of a professional association such as the American Institute of Certified Public Accountants (AICPA). Once you've identified someone you'd like to use, talk to her on the phone and ask about her qualifications, background, and fees. Find out whether she works full- or part-time doing tax consulting, how many years of experience she has, and whether she participates in continuing professional education. The latter is important because tax preparers need to keep up with yearly changes in tax laws. When you've made a decision, make an appointment well in advance of the filing deadline.

Making Tax-Wise Financial Decisions

Think about how much of your income goes toward taxes. If you're in the higher tax brackets, you may be handing nearly half of every dollar you earn to Uncle Sam, but there are things you can do to keep more of your hard-earned money.

Reducing Your Taxes

One of the easiest ways to reduce your taxes is to take advantage of tax-free or tax-deferred employer-provided fringe benefits, such as:

- Benefits provided under cafeteria plans and flexible-spending accounts that allow you to take benefits in lieu of cash (tax-free)
- Medical and accident insurance paid by your employer (tax-free)
- Educational assistance programs (tax-free)
- Retirement plans such as 401(k) and 403(b) that allow you to make contributions (tax deferred)
- Incentive stock options (tax deferred)
- Employee stock purchase plans (tax deferred)
- Group term health insurance up to $50,000 (tax-free)
- Transportation subsidies such as mass transit incentives (tax-free)
- Employer-provided meals and lodging under certain circumstances (tax-free)

ALERT

Owning a home is another one of the best tax shelters available. Not only do you get to deduct your mortgage interest from your taxable income, you also get to keep up to $250,000 ($500,000 for married couples) of profit when you sell, without paying any taxes on the gain.

Another way to reduce taxes is to be sure you take all the credits and other tax reductions you're entitled to, such as the child credit (in addition to claiming the child as a dependent), education credits, head of household status, or earned-income tax credit if you qualify.

Taking Advantage of Tax-Saving Strategies

Bunching and accelerating deductions are two time-honored approaches to cutting taxes. Both require an awareness of what your tax situation is before the end of the year. If you're close to being able to itemize, bunching your deductions may put you over the threshold. Bunching is a strategy that involves timing your payments of deductible expenses by pushing as many deductions as possible into one year. When you bunch, you fatten up your deductions for one year and slim them down the next year, or vice versa. If you're close to having enough medical expenses to meet the 7.5 percent of income requirement, and there's a medical procedure you're planning, having it before the end of the year could put you over the limit and reduce your taxes. Please note that the medical expense phaseout is raised from 7.5 percent to 10 percent of AGI beginning in 2013 as one of the subsidies for the new Affordable Care Act.

FACT

Most people have too much tax withheld from their paychecks and get a refund at the end of the year. In 2011, the average federal tax refund was $2,913. That's roughly $250 per month that could have paid down debt or been deposited into a retirement account.

Accelerating deductions is similar to bunching, but you increase your deductions in the current year by paying tax-deductible bills that aren't actually due until the following year. For example, pay your property taxes before the end of the year instead of waiting until they're due in the following year, to push the deductions into the year you'll be able to take advantage of them.

Keeping Good Tax Records

You should keep detailed and organized records as though you expect to be audited. Then if you ever have to prove your income or deductions you won't be scrambling to find receipts and other documents, and facing possible disallowances from the IRS.

Records to Keep

Hang on to any documents that identify your sources of income (W-2s, 1099s), help determine the value of assets (brokerage and mutual fund statements), and prove your deductions (receipts or invoices *and* canceled checks, property tax statements, mortgage interest statements, and proof of any business expenses if you file Schedule C). Checks alone may not prove the deductibility of an expense. The best proof is an itemized invoice accompanied by a canceled check proving that you paid it.

Keep your tax records in a separate file for each year. After six years you can throw the backup documents away if storage space is an issue, but keep your income tax returns, retirement account statements, home purchase or sale documents, and stock or other investment documents indefinitely.

Home Ownership Records

Even though profits (up to $250,000 for singles and up to $500,000 for married couples) on the sale of your primary residence are no longer taxable, you should keep all records related to the sale and purchase of your home(s), including settlement papers and documentation for improvements or additions to your home. To calculate whether you can claim exemption from taxes if you make a gain on the sale of your house, you have to be able to accurately document its cost basis. If you bought or built your home, the original basis is the price you paid, plus any closing costs. Improvements you make to your home increase your basis as long as they pass the IRS requirements of adding to the value of the house, extending its useful life, or adapting it to a new use. You must differentiate between improvements and repairs. Repairs can't be added to the basis of your home. If you hire contractors to do improvements, the entire cost can be used to increase your basis; if you do the work yourself, you can only add the cost of supplies.

Surviving an Audit

There are a few simple steps you can take to reduce your chances of being audited, but if you're one of the 0.5 percent who get chosen randomly for the experience, don't panic. Being prepared is more than half the battle.

ALERT

Some characteristics of a tax return, such as filing Schedule C for self-employed individuals or experiencing dramatic swings in income, will increase your chances of being audited. But as long as you reported everything accurately and have documentation to prove it, you have nothing to worry about.

The most basic thing you can do to reduce your chances of being audited is to make sure there are no math errors on your return. Too many math errors will red flag your return for review. Make sure social security numbers for you and your dependents are accurate. If you won't be able to file your return by the April 15 deadline, file for an extension before the deadline. Attach an explanation for anything that's not obvious. For example, if you report an amount that differs from the amounts on your W-2 or 1099s, explain the reason. Be sure to sign your return.

How Are Returns Chosen for Audit?

The IRS uses something called the discriminant function system (DIF), which assigns a score to key elements on your return. If the total score for your entire return is greater than the IRS guidelines, the computer will kick your return out for review by an IRS agent. If the agent feels your return should be audited after reviewing it, you'll be contacted. A very small percentage of returns are chosen completely by random. File close to the filing deadline rather than early. There's some evidence that people who file early may have a greater chance of being randomly selected for audit.

What to Do If You're Audited

During an audit you'll be asked to substantiate certain items by producing receipts or other proof. You may be able to do this by mail. If the IRS requests a face-to-face audit, you have the right to have a representative (your accountant or tax preparer) attend with you or in your place. If you attend, keep your emotions under control, don't volunteer any information, and don't act defensive. Treat the agent respectfully. Have all of the requested documents with you and organized in a logical manner. It may be best to let your representative answer all questions or meet with the IRS agent without you. If your representative can't answer a question, he will ask you later and get back to the agent.

When You Can't Pay Your Taxes

It's a disturbing moment when you finish your tax return and realize you owe additional tax and don't have the money to pay it. Don't compound the problem by filing your tax return late. File by the due date or file for an extension even if you can't pay the tax due. Penalties for late filing can add up to 25 percent to your tax bill.

You have a number of options for coming up with the cash later. Try to take out a bank loan for the amount you owe. The interest rate is usually lower than the rate charged by the IRS. If that doesn't work, consider using your credit card or applying for a new card with a low introductory rate and paying the balance off before the rate goes up.

Your first step should be to request an extension of time to pay from the IRS. It is the most economical way to delay your payments—less expensive than an installment loan with the IRS. You can usually find out immediately (online) whether or not you qualify for this program.

Another option is to request an installment agreement with the IRS by completing Form 9465, Installment Agreement Request, and attaching it to your return. You can also make your request online at *www.irs.gov*. State the amount you can pay monthly toward your tax debt. If your request is approved, you'll have to pay interest at up to 0.5 percent per month, and you may have to pay additional penalties.

Your last resort is the Offer in Compromise program. You can make an offer to the IRS and see if they'll accept it. Your odds of success here are very slim—the IRS will grant your request only if your financial situation suggests that the IRS can never collect from you. You'll also have to pay a fee and submit a portion of your proposed settlement amount up front.

Be Prepared in the Future

To ensure that this doesn't happen to you again, review your withholding every year and make sure you're having enough taken out to cover your income. If you receive income that taxes weren't withheld from, make quarterly estimated tax payments or increase the amount of your withholding at work to compensate.

You can avoid incurring tax penalties for underpaying taxes by estimating your tax liability before the end of the year to allow time to catch up if you've underwithheld. If your tax status has changed during the year, do a projection of your taxes using your new status as soon as possible after the change takes place. To avoid penalties, you must pay at least 90 percent of your tax for the current year before December 31, or at least as much as your total tax liability for the prior year.

FACT

Tax Freedom Day illustrates how much of the average American's budget goes toward paying for government services. It's the day by which you will have worked enough to pay your tax obligations for the year, starting from January 1. According to the Tax Foundation, in 2011 Tax Freedom Day was April 12 for the average American. Of course, depending on where you live and what your state's average income is, your tax freedom day may be much earlier or later than this national average.

If it looks as if you may not have had enough tax withheld, change your withholding by filing a new W-4 with your employer to have additional tax taken out each pay period through the end of the year. After the start of the new year, complete another W-4 to adjust your withholding back to a more normal amount. The withholding calculator on the IRS website will help you determine what your withholding should be and is more accurate than the worksheets used on the W-4 form.

Credits and Deductions

When managing your taxes, it's important to understand the difference between a credit and a deduction. Credits are dollar-for-dollar reductions of your income tax liability. In other words, a credit reduces the amount of tax you owe by the amount of the credit (a $500 credit reduces your tax bill by $500). Credits are usually much better for you than deductions.

Deductions reduce the amount of income that you get taxed on. A $500 deduction does not reduce your tax bill by $500. Instead, it reduces your taxable income by $500. You pay less in taxes, but you don't give a dollar-for-dollar reduction. If you pay taxes at 25 percent, a $500 deduction might save you $125 in taxes (25 percent of $500).

Education Benefits

In your twenties and thirties, you should particularly keep your eye out for education benefits. You may be finishing college or pursuing an advanced degree. The best way to make sure that you take advantage of these benefits properly is to talk with an accountant or tax preparer.

American Opportunity Tax Credit

If you are in your first four years of postsecondary education, look into the American Opportunity Tax Credit. This program offers a tax credit of up to $2,500 in 2012. It is one of the most powerful education benefits, as you get a dollar-for-dollar credit on the first $1,500 of qualified expenses. You'll have to qualify with certain income, enrollment, and other characteristics. The credit is refundable up to $1,000 in excess of your income tax liability so those college students paying their own tuition should file an income tax return even if they had no income for the year.

Lifetime Learning Credit

The Lifetime Learning Credit allows you to earn a credit even if you are in graduate school, and for some continuing education expenses related to your job. The maximum credit is $2,000, but you only get credited 20 percent against your education expenses (so you have to spend $10,000 to get the entire credit). Be mindful that both of these credits are subject to phaseout if your income is too high.

Other Education Benefits

Find out if your employer will help you pay for school. Employer-provided educational assistance can be extremely powerful. If you have a family business, it can pay for somebody's schooling. Then the business can take up to a $5,250 deduction, which the recipient receives tax-free. Another possibility is a deduction for tuition and fees. Interest on EE U.S. Savings Bonds may be tax-free if used to pay for qualified education expenses. Student loan interest may be tax deductible as well. Each of these tax benefits is subject to phaseout if your income is too high. See IRS Publication 970 for details.

Lastly, you may be able to take a deduction against your state income taxes (if your state has a tax) by making contributions to a 529 college savings plan. In many cases, you can take the money back out shortly after making the contribution (within a few months or less).

Tax Breaks Related to Having Children

There are many tax subsidies related to having children. Here is a short list of some of the more common tax benefits:

1. The Basic Dependency Exemption—For 2012 this deduction is up to $3,800 per dependent child. To qualify, the child must live with you, be under nineteen (twenty-four if a full-time student), and not be self supporting. See IRS Publication 501.
2. The Child Tax Credit—There is a $1,000 credit available for each child under the age of seventeen. This credit is subject to a phaseout if the taxpayer has too much income. See IRS Publication 972.
3. Educational Credits and Deductions—the American Opportunity Tax Credit and the Lifetime Learning Credit benefits will apply if you are paying them on behalf of your dependent children.
4. Dependent Child Care Credit/Exclusion—A tax credit is available for a portion of your child care expenses each year if your child is under the age of thirteen. This could include payments made to summer day

camps and grandma as long as you give the IRS the identification number and address of the person or entity you are paying. Your employer may offer you the option to exclude part of your wages (up to $5,000) instead of using this credit. See IRS Publication 503 for details.

5. Earned-Income Credit—Certain lower earning taxpayers with children may qualify for this refundable tax credit, which means it would behoove you to file your tax return even if you did not have enough taxable income to incur any tax liability. See IRS Publication 596 to determine if you qualify.

CHAPTER 17

Investing: Profits and Risks

Let's dispel the two biggest myths that keep people from investing: you need to be a financial guru, and you need to have a lot of money. To be a successful investor, you need to understand the basics about stocks, bonds, mutual funds, and cash equivalents. It takes effort, but it's not voo-doo or rocket science.

The Big Picture

If you have credit card debt, get rid of it before diverting money to investments. If you don't have an emergency fund that would cover three to six months of basic expenses if you were to lose your job or become unable to work, establish one before tying up your cash in investments. In addition, if you're not taking advantage of company matching in your employer's 401(k) plan, you're ignoring a great opportunity.

If You're Ready

If you allow yourself to be intimidated by the complexities of the stock market, you'll miss out on the benefits of one of the best investments available. Forget about futures, options, puts and calls, and all those confusing terms you hear bandied about by news analysts. The average investor never deals with them.

QUESTION

Where's the best place to invest my long-term savings?
Over the last eighty years or so, the stock market has produced average returns in the double digits when you take into account growth and dividend income. You can buy individual stocks or you can diversify your risk by buying mutual funds, which invest in many different companies and feature professional management at relatively modest cost.

Your overall investment objective is to create wealth. You may want to save for a down payment on your first house, finance your kids' college educations, go on a luxury vacation, provide for a comfortable retirement, or achieve any number of other objectives.

Each of your financial goals has a time frame that will influence your decision regarding the types of investments you choose. The shorter the time frame, the more conservative the investment should be. The longer the time frame, the more aggressive the investment can be. That's why the bulk of your 401(k) plan or other retirement funds should be in stocks or mutual funds when you're young and won't need the money for several decades. If you're saving for a down payment on a house that you hope to buy in three years, your money should be in much more conservative investments, such as CDs and other places to stash your short-term cash.

Risk Tolerance and Asset Allocation

Before you can begin investing intelligently, you need to assess your risk tolerance. This is your ability to watch your investments decline in value in the short term because you believe they'll increase in the long term. The higher the risk, the greater the potential reward, and vice versa. You may risk only the impact of inflation if you put your money in an interest-bearing savings account at an FDIC-insured bank, but there's no chance that you're going to make more than the prevailing interest rate. You risk everything if you put your money into junk bonds or highly speculative stocks, but there's a small chance that you could strike it rich. The key is to strive for a balance between risk and return.

What's Your Risk Level?

If you can tolerate fluctuations in market value by focusing on the long term, consider investing in aggressive assets, such as stocks. If you become nervous and uncomfortable when your investments suffer even a small decline in value, then conservative, low-risk choices are probably more your style.

ESSENTIAL

Low-risk investors face a significant risk: not having enough money for retirement. If you don't invest in stocks, you miss out on the most financially rewarding investment. Historically, the stock market has always outperformed other investments (and the pace of inflation) over time.

High-risk investors are willing to take major risks in exchange for the possibility of substantial returns. They can still sleep at night even if they lose large amounts of money. Moderate-risk investors are willing to take low to medium risks to increase their chances of investment growth. Conservative investors are uncomfortable at the thought of losing money in their investments and will give up the chance of high returns for the stability and safety of conservative investments with more predictable income. They are more concerned about losing money than they are about the potential for higher returns.

The highest-risk investments are futures, commodities, limited partnerships, collectibles, real estate investment trusts (REITs), penny stocks (stocks that cost under $5 per share), speculative stocks (such as stock in new companies), foreign stocks from volatile nations, and high-yield (or "junk") bonds. Moderate-risk investments include growth stocks (companies that reinvest most of their profits to grow the business), corporate bonds with lower ratings, balanced mutual funds, aggressive mutual funds, rental real estate, annuities, index mutual funds, blue chip stocks, and international stocks in developed nations. Limited-risk investments are corporate and municipal bonds with high ratings. The lowest-risk investments are Treasury bills, U.S. savings bonds, bank CDs, and money market funds.

ALERT

It's not a good idea to buy bonds when interest rates are expected to rise soon, because you'll be stuck with a lower-than-market interest rate and will be earning less than you would have if you'd waited a short time. The price of a bond tends to go up when interest rates go down and vice versa.

Practicing Wise Asset Allocation

Traditional asset allocation uses a formula to divide your portfolio among the three main types of investments: stocks, bonds, and cash equivalents, such as money market accounts. An aggressive asset allocation might include 80 percent stocks, 15 percent bonds, and 5 percent cash. A conservative asset allocation might include 40 percent stocks, 40 percent bonds, and 20 percent cash. Because different types of investments grow at different rates, it's a good idea to reallocate (or "rebalance") your investments once a year. For instance, after you've been investing for a while, you might have a conservative portfolio of 40 percent stocks, 40 percent bonds, and 20 percent cash. If your stocks have a banner year and bonds are sluggish, the value of your portfolio might change to 60 percent stocks, 20 percent bonds, and 20 percent cash. This switch could cause your portfolio to change from conservative to aggressive without your even realizing it, so you may want to realign it by making some changes in your investments.

Choosing what percentage to invest in each category depends on a number of factors, including your risk tolerance, your age, or how much time you have to invest before you need the money, the current state of the market, and what direction interest rates are headed. A popular rule of thumb used by some experts is to reduce 100 by your age to figure out how much of your investment portfolio should be at risk in the stock market. For instance, a 27 year old should have 73 percent of his portfolio (100 − 27) in the market.

Diversify, Diversify, Diversify!

Diversification means not putting all your eggs in one basket. The more you spread out your investments between different kinds of securities and different sectors of the market (financial services, biomedical, technology), the lower the risk of substantial losses. Of course if all markets should sell off, as happened in 2008, diversification would not help you. Risk that threatens the entire market is called systematic risk. Diversification minimizes *unsystematic* risk.

A well-diversified portfolio includes cash or cash equivalents (Treasury bills, CDs, money markets, etc.), stocks, bonds, and mutual funds. The latter should include small-cap, mid-cap, and large-cap stocks (more on this to follow). Usually when one sector or type of investment has low returns, another has high returns, so diversifying evens out some of the ups and downs of the market.

A word about cash equivalents. All cash equivalents are not the same. Even though there is a high expectation that cash equivalents are relatively riskless, money market funds outside of FDIC-insured banks (or NCUA-insured credit unions) are not government guaranteed to retain their price. In 2008 some of these funds, which are expected to hold steady at $1 per share, actually slipped to under $1 per share, or "broke the buck" when investors withdrew their shares in droves in the wake of the financial crisis. The government did step in temporarily to guarantee these accounts but this guarantee no longer exists.

Investing in Stocks

Stocks are important investing tools. However, you don't necessarily need to invest in individual stocks. Publicly owned companies sell shares of stock to raise money for operations or business expansion, invest in new technology or equipment, or meet other financial needs. When you own stock, you actually own part of that company, and the value of your share rises and falls as the company's value changes.

When stock prices go down, you don't actually lose anything unless you sell while the price is low. A loss that is only on paper can be recouped the next time the stock rebounds, but selling locks in your loss and makes it final. It's important not to be scared out of your position prematurely. You must understand what you are investing in so that you can determine whether a decrease in stock price represents an opportunity to buy more shares "on sale" or whether something has fundamentally changed within the company that may cause you to rethink your position.

Stock Price

A stock's price has more to do with investors' perceptions than it does with the actual financial standing of the company. In the late 1990s, Yahoo!, Amazon, and other Internet stocks were inflated far beyond their real value because investors were enamored with the concept and the demand for the stocks kept pushing up the prices. When the bottom fell out of the technology market, some of these stocks lost most of their value. Yahoo!, for instance, which was once at $250 per share, traded below $5 per share in September of 2001 and September of 2002, and was valued at just $15 per share early in 2012.

When a stock price gets so high that investors are reluctant to buy, the company may declare a stock split. With a two-for-one split, you receive a free share of stock for every share you own, and the price per share is cut in half. The value of your investment doesn't change since there is twice the amount of shares in the company available for purchase, but the lower price may make it more attractive to investors and demand for the stock may actually increase the price as soon as the stock split is announced. Since you have more shares, your investment would be worth more than it would have been without the split.

Risk Level of Stocks

Stocks don't offer a guaranteed return, so don't ever invest in something you don't understand. Making an informed decision to assume risk creates an opportunity for a greater return on your investment. Jumping into investments you know nothing about, or that you hope will create a quick profit, puts your money at risk.

Stock Indexes

A stock index reports changes in prices for the market that it tracks. There are many U.S. and international stock indexes, but the best known in the world is the Dow Jones Industrial Average (DJIA), which tracks thirty U.S. blue chip stocks. Blue chips are the stocks of very large, well-established companies (in poker, the blue chips are the ones with the highest dollar value).

Other U.S. indexes include the Russell 2000, which measures the overall performance of small- to mid-cap companies; the S&P 500, an index of the 500 largest companies in America; and the Wilshire 5000, which tracks the entire stock market. It's helpful to compare the performance of your stock or mutual fund to the applicable index. If you have a small-cap mutual fund, compare its return to the Russell 2000. If the fund consistently underperforms the index, consider selling your shares and putting the money in a fund with better performance.

How to Buy Stocks

You can buy stocks through a full-service brokerage or a discount brokerage by calling a stockbroker and placing an order, or you can use a discount Internet broker such as E*TRADE (*www.etrade.com*), TDAmeritrade (*www.tdameritrade.com*), or Scottrade (*www.scottrade.com*) to execute your own orders. Make sure you understand all of the terms on the online form before finalizing your purchase. You don't need a full-service broker unless you want advice regarding which stocks you should buy. Since brokers are paid on commission, they stand to gain financially from their recommendation; you should make up your own mind about what to buy or sell. Don't buy on a broker's recommendation alone.

Another way to buy stocks is through a direct stock purchase plan (DSPP). There is little or no cost and you will have the shares registered in your name. Some of the most well-known companies such as AT&T ($500 minimum), ExxonMobil ($250 minimum), Intel ($250 minimum), Coca Cola ($500 minimum), and McDonalds ($500 minimum) can be bought this way. Purchasing shares through a broker will cause the shares to be registered in the broker's name, commonly referred to as "street name." The advantage of having shares registered with your broker is the convenience of having instant access to sell those shares, making the shares more liquid, but don't be tempted to sell those shares prematurely.

If the brokerage company has some difficulties with its finances or government regulations, those shares may be frozen for a period of time. A listing of shares that have a DSPP can be found online at *www.computershare.com*.

Many companies also offer dividend reinvestment plans (DRIPs). Corporations often pay out part of their earnings as dividends to shareholders, usually quarterly. The dividend can be paid in cash or stock. With a DRIP, you can reinvest the dividends in additional shares of stock, often without paying a commission. When the stock price goes up, so does the value of your reinvested shares. If you take your dividends in cash instead of stock, you lose the opportunity for them to increase in value as the price of the stock goes up.

The best way to invest is to do your research. Some really good investment research websites include *www.motleyfool.com*, *www.finance.yahoo.com*, and *www.smartmoney.com*. You don't need to "churn" your stocks, buying and selling constantly and trying to anticipate ups and downs in the market. You can't afford to ignore changes in the financial condition of the companies you've invested in, but you shouldn't have to review their status more than quarterly. If something fundamental about a company has changed and you believe the stock won't regain its value, think about selling it.

You should also heavily consider those companies that have a long history of paying dividends to their shareholders, and tend to increase those payouts every year. Dividends are discretionary distributions of a corporation's earnings made by its board of directors to its shareholders. A solid dividend paying history lets you know that the corporation is profitable, and there is a high degree of confidence that it will stay that way. You also have the advantage of getting paid during the time you hold the investment, frequently at rates far above the interest being offered in alternative investment vehicles such as CDs and money markets. Current income tax laws also favor dividend income received by shareholders as it is subject to a lower tax rate than other forms of income such as salaries, interest, or rents. The maximum rate of federal income tax on dividend income is currently 15 percent, while the maximum rate of taxation on those other forms of income can be as high as 35 percent. Please note that many current federal income tax laws are scheduled to expire on December 31, 2012, and if no congressional action is taken to extend the current law, dividends will lose this tax-advantaged rate.

Investing in Bonds

Bonds are known as fixed-income securities because their income is fixed at the time the issuer sells them. When you buy a bond, you're lending the bond issuer money in return for a fixed rate of return. The issuer usually pays the interest semiannually, but sometimes the issuer pays the dividend at maturity when it repays the principal it borrowed from you.

FACT

Bonds are rated for safety by bond-rating companies and given a grade between AAA (low risk) and C (high risk) to indicate the likelihood that the issuer will pay the interest and principal as promised. Look up ratings at A. M. Best (*www.ambest.com*), Moody's (*www.moodys.com*), and Standard & Poor's (*www.standardandpoors.com*).

Corporations, states, cities, and governments all issue bonds for the same reason companies issue stock: to raise money for operations, expansion, or other financial needs. Unlike a stock, where you technically own a part of the company you are invested in, by investing in a bond you become a lender to the company. Therefore, interest payments are a legal obligation of the company while the payment of a dividend, which is a distribution of a corporation's earnings to its stockholders, is a nonobligatory payment made at the discretion of the corporation's management (i.e., its board of directors).

Risk Level of Bonds

Bonds issued by the federal government are extremely safe. Some corporate bonds are safe and others are high-risk. High-yield bonds pay a higher interest rate, but their nickname of "junk bonds" should give you fair warning of their risk. One of the risks associated with bonds is related to interest rates. If you lock in your money for a number of years at a fixed-interest rate, you may not be able to sell the bond for full price if other bonds are paying higher interest rates. Many bonds trade on the open market like stocks. Generally, if market rates of interest go up, the value of bonds already issued will decline. Should market rates of interest go down, then the old bond with a higher interest rate will increase.

ESSENTIAL

At the U.S. Treasury website at *www.treasurydirect.gov* you can download the Savings Bond Wizard, a program that allows you to maintain an inventory of your U.S. savings bonds and determine the current redemption value and interest earned to date.

Municipal bonds are issued by states and cities to fund projects such as road repairs, bridge building, prison renovations, and any number of other projects requiring large amounts of money. These bonds aren't guaranteed, but defaults are rare. However you should exercise caution when considering this alternative as forty-seven out of the fifty states are currently in a deficit position. The main attraction of state and local bonds is that their earnings are exempt from federal income tax, which makes them attractive to people in a high tax bracket. Likewise, U.S. Treasury interest is exempt from state and local income taxation. Should you purchase a state or local bond of the state where you reside you will find that the interest on the bond will be exempt from federal, state, and local income taxation. That is why they are often called "triple tax-free."

How to Buy Bonds

You can buy federal government bonds, including U.S. savings bonds, directly from the U.S. Treasury, and both government and corporate bonds through a stockbroker. If you don't want to buy individual bonds, you can buy shares in a bond fund, which invests in a number of different bonds. You'll incur fund expenses that will decrease your net return, so bond funds are best if you'd rather pay a fee for broad diversification and professional management instead of choosing the bonds yourself.

Series EE U.S. Savings Bonds

U.S. savings bonds are fully backed by the U.S. government, free of state and local income taxes, and federal income tax deferred. Furthermore, if you use the bond to pay for qualified higher education costs the interest may be tax-free. You won't get rich buying U.S. savings bonds, but neither will you lose your shirt. Bonds issued by the U.S. government are considered to be the safest bonds available. The assumption is that the U.S. government will not go out of business and fail to pay as agreed. Some bonds may fluctuate in price, but principal and interest payments are guaranteed.

There are several different types of U.S. savings bonds. You purchase Series EE Bonds at face value (a $50 bond costs $50) in amounts of $25 or more, to the penny. The interest rate is fixed and is based on the yield on ten-year U.S. Treasury securities. As of January 1, 2012, Series EE U.S. Savings Bonds are only available on the Internet at *www.treasurydirect.gov*.

Series I U.S. Savings Bonds

I Bonds are similar to EE Bonds. The interest is paid when the bond is redeemed and you can purchase up to $10,000 of I Bonds in a year. Your return is based on two factors: a fixed rate (set when you purchase the bond) and an inflation rate. If inflation is high, the interest you earn during that period will be higher. Likewise, as inflation decreases the interest you earn decreases.

U.S. Treasury Securities

Unlike U.S. savings bonds, U.S. Treasury securities (bills, notes, and bonds) can be transferred from one person to another, so you can buy and sell them in the securities market. They provide steady income, flexibility, and security. Treasury bills (or T-bills) mature ninety days to one year from their issue date. You buy them for less than their face value, and you receive full face value when they mature. Treasury notes pay a fixed rate of interest every six months until maturity, which is from one to ten years.

Treasury Inflation Protected Securities (TIPS)

TIPS work like U.S. Treasury securities except that the principal amount may be adjusted every six months by any subsequent increase in the Consumer Price Index (CPI), which is the U.S. government's chief barometer of inflation. Any subsequent decrease may reduce the principal amount but not below its original face value. Since the interest rate is determined as a percentage of the principal, any increase to the principal will bring about a corresponding increase in interest. The original interest rate on a TIPS will be somewhat lower than a U.S. Treasury bond which has a fixed rate of interest throughout its term. TIPS are issued in terms of five, ten, and thirty years.

ALERT

Savings bonds are meant to be long-term investments. You can cash them in after you've owned them for one year, but you should wait at least five years. Before five years, you'll pay a penalty equal to three months of interest payments.

Don't Go Overboard

U.S. savings bonds and Treasury securities have a place in your portfolio, but are too conservative to get the lion's share of your investment money. Use them for your cash savings. You'll earn more interest than you would on savings accounts, and Series I Bonds can help protect you from inflation. You can also use them for long-term investments to balance more aggressive and riskier investments, such as stocks.

Mutual Funds

Mutual funds are a way for investors to pool their money so they can invest in many different stocks or bonds. Each investor is charged a percentage of his investment as a fee to pay for the expenses of having a professional fund. Mutual funds are the best alternative for most people for several reasons:

- They offer the average investor an opportunity to have professional management at a relatively modest cost.
- They automatically diversify your portfolio.
- Some funds invest in stocks, bonds, and cash equivalents, which give you even greater diversification.
- They require only a small amount of money to get started, sometimes as little as $25.

Like stocks, some mutual funds are riskier than others, so be sure to read the fund's objectives and know what it invests in. Will your money be buying stocks in blue chip companies or in the corporations of developing countries? Although past performance is no guarantee of the future, look at how the fund has done over the last several years and compare it to an applicable index to see if it kept pace with its competitors. Also consider the expense ratio (the costs of owning the fund). The lower it is, the more of your return you get to pocket.

Risk Level of Mutual Funds

Mutual funds tend to be less risky than individual stocks because their investment in any one stock is relatively small compared to their entire holdings. If one company takes a nosedive, the effect on the fund is usually minimal, or at least diluted. When entire sectors, such as technology stocks, head downhill, the impact can be great if the fund is heavily invested in technology stocks.

Income Versus Growth

Different funds have different investing objectives. Funds whose objective is current income invest heavily in bonds because of the steady interest income they generate. These funds appeal to retirees and those on a fixed income. Funds whose objective is long-term growth invest in stock, stock mutual funds, and real estate because those investments usually increase in value over time. Growth and income funds are a hybrid of these two types and invest in both kinds of securities.

Load and No-Load Funds

Load is a sales fee or commission charged by some mutual funds, and is usually stated as a percentage of the amount purchased or sold. Front-end loads are fees charged up front when you buy the fund so that the full purchase price will not be invested. Back-end loads are fees you pay when you sell the fund. If the load is 6 percent and you invest $2,000, the load will be $120. Funds that don't charge front-end or back-end loads are called no-load funds. When choosing a mutual fund, consider the load, if any, and the annual expense ratio. These will reduce your return. If you buy a fund with a 6 percent load and a 2 percent expense ratio, you have to earn an 8 percent return the first year before you break even. Many investment websites will provide a comparison of the average load and expense ratios of the mutual fund type you are interested in.

FACT

The best-known index is Standard & Poor's 500, which invests in the top 500 U.S. stocks. The largest and best-known index stock fund is Vanguard 500 from The Vanguard Group. Over the last decade it has outperformed 90 percent of all other mutual funds, while having one of the lowest expense ratios in the market. These funds usually are no-load and have very small expense ratios since there is no need to have the fund actively managed.

Loads typically go (in part) to an advisor or broker who sells you the fund. If you're paying a load, you're paying somebody for advice. That's fine if you are getting valuable advice—but don't pay a load unless you're getting something out of it. Also, beware of "back-end" load products. Sometimes it's hard to tell that you're paying a sales charge because you don't see it up front.

Index Funds

If you don't want to spend a lot of time keeping up with the financial status of the companies you're invested in, and you don't want to pay a manager to pick stocks, a stock index mutual fund is the best choice. An index fund's objective is to match the return of a specified index by buying shares in each stock in that index.

Market Capitalization

Mutual funds are classified based on the market capitalization of the companies they invest in because cap is one of the criteria investors look at when choosing funds. A company's cap is calculated by multiplying the current stock price times the number of outstanding shares of stock. The categories are:

- Large-cap funds: Companies with market capitalization over $5 billion.
- Mid-cap stock funds: Companies with market capitalization of $1 to $5 billion.
- Small-cap funds: Companies with market capitalization of $250 million to $1 billion.
- Micro-cap funds: Companies with market capitalization of less than $250 million.

Experts consider the large-cap funds, such as Vanguard's 500 Index, the least volatile, and the smaller company funds the most volatile.

How to Buy Mutual Funds

You can use full-service or discount brokers to buy mutual funds, or you can buy directly from a family of mutual funds, such as Vanguard (*www.vanguard.com*) or Fidelity (*www.fidelity.com*). Call the company's toll-free number or request an investor's kit online, fill out the forms, and send them in with your check. You can initiate this procedure on the mutual fund's website, but you'll still have to send in your check, unless you want to transfer the money electronically.

Exchange-Traded Funds (ETFs)

An ETF is a security that tracks an index, a commodity, or a basket of assets like an index fund, but trades like a stock on an exchange. ETFs experience price changes throughout the day and are sold on the secondary market like individual stocks, so that the purchase price might be at, above, or below its NAV (Net Asset Value) depending on the number of buyers and sellers interested in the particular ETF. Therefore, a buyer of an ETF will have to pay a commission much like the purchase of an individual stock.

Both mutual funds and ETFs give the purchaser the ability to diversify and take on additional risk with the added security of professional management.

Alternative Investments

In recent years, individual investors have gained more and more access to so-called alternative investments. Alternative investments include assets beyond traditional stocks, bonds, and cash. For example, real estate, commodities, and hedge funds might be considered alternative investments. For the most part, you can get exposure to these investments within mutual funds or ETFs. However, you may need to hunt for specialized funds.

Alternative investments can help your portfolio because they behave differently than traditional investments. They're less likely to go up and down at the same time (or in the same direction) as the other investments in your portfolio. As a result, your account balance should not react as wildly to market gyrations as a more traditional account would.

Investing experts disagree on exactly how much alternative investment you should have in your portfolio. A good place to start is with 5 to 10 percent of your portfolio—with that amount diversified among a variety of alternative strategies.

Using a Financial Planner

You may want to see a financial planner to help you chart a course for the future, or you may want to consult with a planner at a big turning point in your life. If you use a financial planner to help you choose investments, be aware that using expert advice is not a guarantee that your investments will make money. If you have the time and interest to do your own research and educate yourself, you probably don't need a financial planner for choosing investments, unless you have a complex situation. Consider developing your own written financial plans, but meet every few years with a financial planner to make sure there are no glaring issues or gaps in the course you've charted for yourself.

If you use a professional, educate yourself about the recommended investments and be involved in the buying and selling decisions she executes on your behalf. Many financial planners earn commissions from the companies they deal with, so they may not be entirely objective when making recommendations. You can avoid this problem by choosing a fee-only planner who is paid by the hour and doesn't benefit from recommending one investment over another.

To locate a fee-only financial planner near you, use an online search form provided by the National Association of Personal Financial Advisors (NAPFA) at *www.napfa.org*. There you can also learn what you need to know before hiring a financial planner, including interview questions, an overview of the industry, and how to compare planners.

Sample Investment Allocations

You should make sure that the types of investments in your accounts are reasonable for the type of investor you are. For example, if you're an aggressive investor you might ask yourself or your advisor why your account has a large portion in cash.

Conservative Investor

A conservative investor is mostly concerned with avoiding large losses, and instead, earning income. A conservative portfolio will fluctuate with the stock and bond markets, but it should be less volatile than a more aggressive portfolio.

- 8 percent—Large-cap stocks
- 2 percent—Mid-cap stocks
- 5 percent—Alternative investments

- 6 percent—International stocks
- 5 percent—High-yield bonds
- 19 percent—Intermediate-term bonds
- 40 percent—Short-term bonds
- 15 percent—Cash equivalents

Moderate Investor

A moderate investor wants a balance of long-term growth with moderate volatility. Current income is not a primary goal. The account value will most likely fluctuate more than a conservative investor's account.

- 22 percent—Large-cap stocks
- 8 percent—Mid-cap stocks
- 5 percent—Small-cap stocks
- 10 percent—Alternative investments
- 15 percent—International stocks
- 3 percent—High-yield bonds
- 13 percent—Intermediate-term bonds
- 19 percent—Short-term bonds
- 5 percent—Cash equivalents

Aggressive Investor

An aggressive investor is mostly concerned with long-term growth of capital. This investor is comfortable with dramatic account value fluctuations, and invests mostly in stocks.

- 32 percent—Large-cap stocks
- 12 percent—Mid-cap stocks
- 8 percent—Small-cap stocks
- 10 percent—Alternative investments
- 28 percent—International stocks
- 10 percent—Intermediate-term bonds

This is just a basic template that you can use to compare and contrast against your existing holdings. As you get more advanced, you'll find that the classifications can get split into more and more detail. For example, large-cap stocks can be further split into large-cap growth and large-cap value. Likewise, international stocks might include large developed countries and smaller, emerging markets.

Investing in a Low Interest Rate Environment

In February 2012, the effective federal funds interest rate was 0.25 percent. The federal funds rate is considered one of the most important interest rates in the U.S. markets. In fact, the federal funds rate has been near zero since late 2008. In this incredibly low interest rate environment, there are some investments you'll probably want to avoid, as well as some better choices for where to invest.

What to Avoid

When the average one-year CD is yielding a paltry 0.34 percent, you may be tempted to buy a longer-term CD in order to get a better yield. Currently the average rate on a five-year CD is about 1.15 percent. It is probably a bad idea to lock in for the long term at such low rates. If inflation rebounds, these low interest rates might yield little to no real return. If you do choose to go with a long-term CD, try to choose one with a low early withdrawal penalty so that if rates do rise sharply you will be able to move your funds.

Bonds have a strong inverse link to interest rates. That is, when market interest rates increase, the prices of existing bond issues decrease. In addition, the longer it is to the bond's maturity, the more sensitive its price is to changes in the market interest rate.

Due to these facts, long-term bonds are usually a bad choice in a low-interest rate environment. This is particularly true since the federal funds rate is so close to zero. There is nowhere for interest rates to go but up. As interest rates climb, long-term bond prices will fall significantly, resulting in losses on long-term bond portfolios.

Where to Invest

Unlike many other investments, low interest rates are good for stocks, at least in theory. Since companies are able to borrow money at lower rates in the market, they are able to fund more growth initiatives. If these investment programs were successful, you would generally expect stock prices to rise due to increased earnings. In addition, many great blue chip companies are offering dividend rates well in excess of the rates of return you can get in "safe" investments like bank accounts and U.S. Treasury bills. With these rates, you are getting "paid to wait" with a dividend that can match or even exceed the inflation rate!

In reality, it is much more difficult to say how stocks will behave in a low-rate environment because there are so many confounding factors such as how low interest rates often coincide with poor economic conditions. So, as we have seen over the past couple of years, it could be that the Federal Reserve Board will lower interest rates dramatically, but stocks will still fall in anticipation of a recession.

Short-term bonds can be a good choice because they are much less sensitive to changes in the market interest rate. In fact, if you are able to hold a short-term bond to maturity, you don't even have to worry about changes in a bond's price. This is because bond investors have an option that stock investors do not—rather than selling the bond, they can simply wait to get the principal amount back at maturity. Short-term bonds usually don't pay as high an interest rate, but a modest return is still a good result as you wait for more promising investment opportunities.

CHAPTER 18

Retirement: Planning for Tomorrow

You're never too young to start investing for retirement. Compounding of earnings is so powerful that if you start investing in your twenties, you can amass a large nest egg with little effort by the time you are in your sixties or seventies. All that's required is a basic understanding of retirement plans and the commitment to start now.

The Younger, the Better

The younger you are when you start investing, the less you'll need to invest, thanks to the power of compounding and the length of time until retirement. You can't rely on social security as your sole source of retirement income, but fortunately there are a growing number of alternatives. Employers sponsor some of them; others are the do-it-yourself variety. Most employer-sponsored plans fall into one of three categories: defined benefit, defined contribution, and profit sharing.

Defined-Benefit Plans

Employer-sponsored, defined-benefit plans, also known as pensions, provide a guaranteed income for the rest of your life after you retire. The amount varies depending on your years of service with the company, your salary, and your age at retirement. Your employer uses an actuarial formula to arrive at the amount to put into the fund each year to ensure there's enough to meet the future retirement needs of its employees. All funds are mingled in one account managed by your employer.

ALERT

By the time you reach retirement age, traditional pension plans may be a thing of the past. They're already being replaced or supplemented in large numbers by defined-contribution plans, which put more of the responsibility for retirement savings on you and less on your employer.

Defined-Contribution Plans

Unlike defined-benefit plans, employee-sponsored, defined-contribution plans don't guarantee a specific dollar amount at retirement. How much you receive depends on how much you and your employer contributed and how well your investments performed over the years. Your contributions, as well as your employer's (if any), are always kept in an individual account in your name.

With defined-contribution plans, you'll choose from a variety of stock or bond mutual funds, guaranteed funds, annuities, cash equivalents such as money market accounts, or your company's stock. Your plan will stipulate how frequently you can change your investment choices. Many plans allow you to manage your account online and make investment changes as often as you like.

One of the attractive features of defined-contribution plans is that they're portable. If you change jobs, you can take your money with you. The following are the most common defined-contribution plans:

- 401(k) plans, offered by private companies
- 403(b) plans, offered by nonprofit, tax-exempt employers, such as schools and colleges, hospitals, museums, and foundations
- 457 plans, offered by federal, state, and local government agencies and nonprofit organizations

Other defined-contribution plans include ESOPs, profit-sharing plans, simplified employee pension (SEP) plans, savings incentive match plans (SIMPLEs), and thrift or savings plans (TSPs). These plans all have one important thing in common: you pay no taxes on your contributions or your earnings until you withdraw the money.

401(k) Plans

A 401(k) plan is an employer-sponsored retirement plan that gives a special tax break to employees saving for retirement. Here's how the tax break works: If you contribute $2,000 a year and you're in the 28 percent federal tax bracket, you'll save $560 because the $2,000 is deducted from your pay before your taxes are calculated. If you live in one of the states where 401(k) contributions are tax deferred, and you're in a 6 percent state income tax bracket, you'll save another $120 in state taxes, for a total savings of $680.

The bottom line is that you add $2,000 to your investment account but only $1,320 comes out of your pocket ($2,000 – $680 = $1,320). You don't pay taxes on your earnings until you withdraw them, presumably at retirement, so your investments grow faster as your untaxed earnings benefit from compounding.

Employer Match

Many employers match a certain percentage of your contributions. The amounts vary but a typical match is between fifty cents and $1 for every dollar you contribute, up to 6 percent of your salary. Even if your employer doesn't contribute, 401(k) plans are great, but if a match is offered and you don't participate, it's like walking past money lying on the sidewalk and not picking it up.

Contribution Limits

The IRS sets limits, adjusted annually for inflation, on how much you can contribute to a 401(k) plan each year. For 2012, you can contribute up to $17,000 as long as it doesn't exceed 100 percent of your earnings. Once you reach age fifty, you're allowed to make additional "catch-up" contributions of up to $5,500 in 2012. The total of all contributions, including yours and your employer's, cannot exceed 100 percent of your compensation for the year, or $50,000 in 2012, whichever is less. These limits are increased periodically to adjust for inflation.

Your employer is subject to strict IRS regulations to ensure that your 401(k) plan doesn't discriminate against lower-paid employees. If you're a highly compensated employee (an employee who made $100,000 or more in the prior year or owned 5 percent or more of the company), your contributions will be limited by how much the less highly compensated employees contribute. Your employer may have adopted a safe-harbor provision that does away with the limits for highly compensated employees by making a certain level of matching contributions or nonelective employer contributions for all eligible employees.

401(k) Vesting

You're always 100 percent vested in your own contributions to the plan. The employer match is often subject to vesting, which means you earn the right to it gradually, over a number of years of employment with the company. There are two types of vesting schedules. About half of all 401(k) plans have *cliff vesting*, where you don't own any of the matching contributions until you've worked for the company for a certain amount of time. The Economic Growth and Tax Relief Reconciliation Act of 2001 shortened the maximum vesting schedule for cliff vesting to no more than three years. The other type of vesting schedule is *graded vesting*, where you own an increasing percentage of the employer match over several years. Under the 2001 law, vesting must take place in no more than six years. A typical vesting schedule will now be 20 percent after the second year, 40 percent after the third year, 60 percent after the fourth year, 80 percent after the fifth year, and 100 percent after the sixth year.

It's important to consider the impact on your 401(k) when you're thinking of changing jobs. If your plan has cliff vesting, and you leave before working the required number of years, you walk away from everything your employer has contributed as matching funds. You could possibly earn thousands of additional dollars in company matching funds by staying in your current job for a few more months or years. Let's assume you had matching contributions of $6,000 and a vesting schedule of 20 percent per year for five years. If you left for a new job after three years, you'd take $3,600 ($6,000 × 60 percent = $3,600) of matching funds with you, plus all the contributions you made from your salary and any associated earnings, but you'd forfeit $2,400 ($6,000 × 40 percent = $2,400) plus any earnings that money has accumulated.

Switching Jobs

The portability of 401(k) plans is a great feature, but what do you do with your money when you change jobs? You have three choices:

1. If you have over $5,000 in your account, you have the option of leaving your funds in your employer's plan.
2. You may be able to roll your balance over into your new employer's plan.
3. You can set up an individual IRA at a bank, through a broker, or directly with a mutual fund.

401(k) Loans

If your 401(k) plan allows loans, you can borrow up to 50 percent of your vested balance, not to exceed $50,000. Loans typically have to be repaid over no more than five years unless the funds are used to buy a first home. Interest rates are typically low—between one and three points above the prime rate. Because you pay yourself back instead of paying a creditor, 401(k) loans are touted as a great deal. Even the interest you pay goes back into your 401(k).

FACT

The limit on the amount of elective deferrals that you can contribute to your traditional or safe harbor 401(k) plan was $16,500 for 2011 and is $17,000 for 2012. If you are older than fifty, the elective deferral limit increases by $5,500 for 2011 and 2012.

Because of the tax consequences, you should avoid borrowing from your 401(k) if possible. Your repayments are not tax-sheltered. They're made with after-tax money. If your monthly payment is $200 and you're in the 28 percent federal tax bracket and a 6 percent state tax bracket, you'd have to make $303 to net enough to make the payment. Worse, when you retire and take withdrawals, you pay taxes on that money again. You should also avoid borrowing from your 401(k) because of opportunity costs. The money that you borrow could be earning interest or appreciating if left in your plan.

403(b) and 457 Plans

Defined-contribution plans or 403(b) plans are for nonprofit organizations. They work very much like 401(k) plans, and over time they have started to look more and more like 401(k) plans. Your contributions are tax deductible and your earnings are tax deferred until you take the money out at retirement. Like 401(k) plans, the amounts that you and your employer can contribute are limited by law.

Section 457 plans are defined-contribution plans established by government agencies. Like 401(k) and 403(b) plans, they allow you to make tax-deductible contributions and your earnings grow tax deferred until retirement. One important difference is that your account is funded solely by your own contributions. Your employer doesn't contribute a dime. These plans are still a great benefit because of their tax-deferred feature.

Individual Retirement Accounts

Individual retirement accounts (IRAs) have evolved in the more than twenty years since they were established and now include such variations as SEP IRAs, Roth IRAs, SIMPLE IRAs, and more. IRAs provide the same tax-deferred benefits as 401(k) and similar employer-sponsored plans and allow you to decide how your funds will be invested.

If you have employment income in any year, you can make contributions to an IRA. The annual limit was $5,000 in 2012, and you're allowed to make an additional contribution (of $1,000 in 2012) once you reach age fifty. You can set up an IRA through most banks and financial institutions, or through a mutual fund company or broker. You can start making withdrawals at age fifty-nine and a half, and, unless it is a Roth IRA, you must start doing so by age seventy and a half. As with 401(k) plans, income tax and a 10 percent penalty apply to any funds you take out early unless you qualify for a waiver of the penalty (for very high medical expenses, disability, death, higher education, as a first time home buyer up to $10,000 or to pay health insurance premiums if unemployed for more than twelve months).

Contributing to an IRA doesn't make sense unless you're maximizing the match that you can receive from your employer in your 401(k) plan. After that, you can decide where you prefer to contribute additional dollars each month. Take into account the costs, investment selection, and control over the money as you make this decision. If you don't have access to an employer-sponsored plan, then by all means, invest as much as possible in IRAs.

ALERT

Take advantage of every opportunity to plan for retirement. You'll want to know as soon as possible whether or not you're on track to retire in comfort. Try searching the web for "retirement calculator," or use one provided by your employer-sponsored plan.

Keep in mind that IRAs can be held anywhere including mutual fund companies and brokerage houses; financial advisors also offer IRAs. The IRAs in banks and credit unions typically allow you to invest only in CDs or cash equivalents, which may not be the best choice for a young person's retirement savings.

Traditional IRAs

Depending on your income, your filing status, and whether you have a qualified retirement plan at work, your IRA contributions may not be fully tax deductible. If you (and your spouse) aren't eligible for any employer-provided retirement plan, you can deduct the full contribution to an IRA. If you are married and filing jointly, and you (and your spouse) do participate in an employer's retirement plan (see if the pension box on your W-2 is checked), you'll be able to take the full deduction if your AGI is below $92,000 (for 2012; this limit increases periodically to keep up with inflation). For 2012, if your AGI is between $58,000 and $68,000 (for singles), and between $92,000 and $112,000 (for married couples), you'll only be able to take a partial deduction. You have until April 15 to make an IRA contribution for the previous year, but make sure you do it before filing your income taxes. The IRS will check to make sure your contribution was made within the deadline.

Roth IRAs

There are several important distinctions between traditional IRAs and Roth IRAs. Traditional IRA contributions are tax deductible as long as you qualify with the eligibility restrictions. Roth IRA contributions are not. Traditional IRAs grow tax deferred until you withdraw the funds at retirement, and then they're taxed at your regular income tax rate. Roth IRA contributions are never tax deductible and the growth and earnings are never taxed, as long as you follow all the rules. You're required to withdraw a minimum amount each year from your traditional IRAs once you reach the age of seventy and a half. There are no such requirements for Roth IRAs.

The income limits for Roth IRAs are much more liberal and you can contribute even if you participate in an employer-provided retirement plan. To make the full contribution in 2012, your income must be $173,000 or less if you're married and filing jointly and $110,000 or less if you're single. You can make a partial contribution if your income is between $110,000 and $125,000 if you're single and between $173,000 and $183,000 if you're married. If your income exceeds these limits, you can't contribute at all.

Choosing the Best IRA for You

It can be difficult to determine whether you'd come out ahead in the long run with a traditional or a Roth IRA. It depends on a number of factors, such as how long before you retire, when you plan to start taking money out, and your tax bracket now and at retirement. There are benefits to Roth IRAs besides tax-free earnings. You can withdraw your contributions before retirement without owing taxes or penalties, although you may have to pay taxes on the earnings. The tax law allows you to distribute the amount you contributed before the withdrawal of earnings so that the tax-free amount will be distributed first. You can withdraw up to $10,000 in earnings without penalty to buy your first home if the money has been in the Roth IRA for at least five tax years, to pay medical expenses exceeding 7.5 percent of your gross income, to pay college expenses for certain family members, to pay for health insurance if unemployed for at least twelve months, or if you're unable to work because of disability. Any other withdrawals before the age of fifty-nine and a half will be subject to the penalty.

ESSENTIAL

If your income exceeds the limits for a traditional IRA (and you are an eligible participant in a qualified plan), you can still contribute, but it won't be tax deductible. If you don't qualify for the tax deduction, then a Roth IRA is probably the best choice. However, if the Roth IRA is not an option because your AGI is too high, you should still consider making a contribution to a nondeductible traditional IRA. When distributions from this IRA commence, a portion of each distribution will be deemed a nontaxable return of your nondeductible contribution.

Diversify

Just as you diversify your investments, you should diversify your tax strategies. It's a good idea to have some money in each type of account. Since you never know what's going to happen with tax laws in the future, you should avoid having all of your eggs in one "tax basket."

As you decide how much to save in each type of account, consider your income, your prospects for the future, and your thoughts on future legislation. If you are relatively young and just starting your career, chances are that you are not earning much money (and therefore paying taxes at a relatively low rate). In that case, getting a deduction may not be worth much to you—and you might prefer the potential to take your money out tax-free in retirement. In addition, the ability to take back your contributions at any time may serve as a safety valve. You don't need to worry about taxes and penalties if you need to get that money back.

As you move up the income scale, a deductible contribution to your IRA or 401(k) can save you a bundle. Some people prefer to get something of value today instead of hoping for something of value later. They'd rather take a deduction because they are certain they can get it. They are not as certain about future tax law changes. In a worst-case scenario, Congress could decide that Roth was a bad idea—and charge everybody income tax on distributions anyway!

Roth 401(k) and Roth 403(b)

Starting in 2006, employer-sponsored retirement plans allowed Roth-type contributions. In other words, the benefits of a Roth IRA became available in some 401(k)s and 403(b)s. Previously, you could only make pretax (or deductible) contributions to these plans. For many young people, the Roth 401(k) is an attractive option.

FACT

If you're not eligible to contribute to a Roth IRA due to high income limits, you may still be able to save Roth-type money. Roth 401(k) plans allow you to save after-tax money regardless of your income. The challenge is finding an employer who offers such a plan.

How is a Roth 401(k) different from a Roth IRA? For starters, you can make a larger contribution into a Roth 401(k) account. You can allocate the maximum 401(k) contribution ($17,000 in 2012) toward Roth-type dollars without the AGI limitations of Roth IRA's. However, you can also mix and match your contributions—putting 5 percent of your pay in pretax and 5 percent of your pay in after tax, for example. In addition, you can contribute to a Roth 401(k) regardless of how high your income is.

Roth 401(k) simply adds an additional "bucket" of money to your retirement plan. Your investment mix doesn't change—it's just the tax treatment that changes. If you leave your job, your money is still portable. However, you have to keep Roth-type money separate from traditional (deductible) money. For example, you'd roll your Roth 401(k) money into a Roth IRA, and you'd roll your traditional money into a traditional IRA.

Small Business Plans

For small businesses, costs are always an issue. Small employers don't have the resources that large enterprises do. However, they have to compete against larger organizations for good employees. As a result, many small businesses will offer plans that help people save for retirement while keeping costs low. SIMPLE IRAs and SEPs allow employers to offer incentives with very little administrative cost.

SIMPLE IRAs and SEPs

The Savings Incentive Match Plan for Employees (SIMPLE) IRA is a plan offered by businesses with no other retirement plans and with fewer than 100 employees. As in 401(k) plans, your contributions and earnings are tax deferred. You can contribute up to $11,500 a year with an additional "catch up" amount of $2,500 for those fifty or over. The employer must either match 100 percent of your contributions, up to 3 percent of your salary, or contribute 2 percent of compensation for each eligible employee, even those who don't contribute to the plan.

A Simplified Employee Pension (SEP) IRA is similar to a SIMPLE IRA, except that only your employer can contribute. The disadvantage of this plan is that you have no control over how much goes into your plan because you can't contribute any of your own money, but if you're self-employed, you're the employer and the employee at the same time, so you get to control things. The limit on employer contributions is 25 percent of your compensation up to a maximum of $50,000 in 2012. With both the SIMPLE IRAs and the SEP IRAs, you can still invest in a traditional or Roth IRA.

Solo 401(k) Plans

Solo 401(k) plans are among the most powerful options available to small businesses, but they only work for a one-person (or family-only) business. They share many of the characteristics of a standard 401(k) plan, including the ability to take loans. However, they are less expensive to administer.

If you do any freelance or contract work, consider opening a Solo 401(k) plan. In addition to your "salary deferral" contributions, you can give yourself a profit-sharing contribution of up to 25 percent of compensation. In other words, you can contribute the same amount as you would to a SEP, and then some.

Other Retirement Plans

Nonqualified plans and other retirement benefit plans may be available to you if your skills are in high demand or if your employer is creative. For example, DB(k) plans provide a small pension-like guaranteed income stream, along with the ability to save money as you do in a 401(k). Other plans might promise you a lump-sum payout every ten years or so.

Choosing the Right Investments

If you have a traditional pension plan, your employer makes all the investment decisions for you. With most other retirement plans, you're in the driver's seat. By now, you should have a basic understanding of the investment options that are probably available in your retirement plan: stocks, bonds, mutual funds, cash equivalents, and maybe your employers' stock. Putting all your funds in one type of investment increases your risk of loss if that investment doesn't perform well, so spread your funds out over several types of investments.

Stocks, Bonds, and Mutual Funds

Because retirement earnings grow tax deferred and you have many years before you'll make withdrawals, retirement plans are best suited for your most aggressive investing, which means stocks and mutual funds. Don't make the mistake of putting all your money in money market funds or guaranteed investment contracts (GICs) unless you have a good reason to do so (for instance, if you know you're going to cash out and spend the money within a few years). Diversify your portfolio to balance risk and reward and you should come out far ahead in the long term. This doesn't mean you shouldn't choose your investments carefully. If 80 percent of your retirement funds are in stock mutual funds, most of it should be in well-established funds with a history of solid performance. If you want to get aggressive with some of your money, you can place a small percentage of your stock investments in higher-risk funds.

Lifestyle, Lifecycle, and Asset Allocation Funds

Most retirement accounts these days offer a prepackaged option so that you don't have to select investments and build your own portfolio. Instead, you use a model portfolio designed by an investment company. For most people, this is the way to go. These portfolios are generally diversified among large, medium, and small companies within the United States and abroad. In addition, these funds will have corporate, government, and high yield bonds, along with some cash. In this way, you get a diversified portfolio by choosing just one investment option.

In addition to diversification, many of these programs adjust themselves for you over time. So-called lifestyle or lifecycle funds use a target date to determine how much risk the portfolio should have. For example, you might have the "XYZ 2040 Fund" as an investment option in your retirement plan. The "2040" refers to the year 2040. This fund might be used by a person planning to retire in 2040 (in other words, the year 2040 is the target date for the fund). Perhaps this is a person born in 1975, so she'll be sixty-five years old in 2040.

These funds are managed based on the amount of time until the target date. If the year is 2010, the managers of the XYZ 2040 Fund will most likely have a high percentage of assets in stocks. As the years pass, the fund's managers will gradually reduce risk by adding bonds and cash. The investor (you) does not have to spend time and energy making these adjustments.

ESOPs

ESOPs give you an opportunity to own stock in the company that employs you. These plans can be a great benefit, but there's one very important caveat:

don't put all your eggs in one basket. Thousands of employees who did so have lost their entire retirement fund when their employer's stock lost value due to corruption or shaky accounting practices that hid serious financial problems. If company stock is the only option available to you in your 401(k) plan, look at other investment vehicles for some of your retirement savings.

Consider a worst-case scenario for people who invest heavily in company stock. If something bad happens to the company, it's likely that the stock price will fall. In addition, your job could be in jeopardy—if there are layoffs or if the working environment becomes unbearable. In this case you suffer a double whammy: your retirement savings take a hit at the same time as your income.

Annuities

Annuities are insurance contracts. They allow you to deposit money into the contract, and take income immediately or leave the money invested. Your grandparents may have used annuities to buy themselves a guaranteed income stream in retirement (or their employer did this to provide a pension). At your age, you would most likely put money into an annuity and leave it there.

Annuities may be fixed or variable. Fixed annuities credit your account at a fixed rate agreed to by the insurance company. Variable annuities invest your money in the financial markets, very much like mutual funds. In addition to investment options, annuities can offer a dizzying array of bells and whistles called "riders." A rider may guarantee to refund your money after ten years if you lose it in the markets, or it may offer an enhanced death benefit to your beneficiaries if you die.

Your earnings grow tax deferred, but the money you put in is not tax deductible, so this is an investment best suited to someone who has already taken full advantage of all the tax-deductible plans available and still has money left over to invest. It's unlikely that the average person in her or his twenties or thirties would choose this investment vehicle, but you should be aware of it in case an insurance agent attempts to sell you one.

Belt and Suspenders

Annuities are useful in some situations, but they are prone to abuse. They are terribly difficult to understand for consumers and even professionals. All annuities have a cost, and you have to pay extra for any riders. In many cases, you have to leave your money with the insurance company for years before you can do anything else with it. Therefore, be very careful when buying an annuity.

Be especially careful about putting retirement savings into an annuity. Don't roll a 401(k) or IRA into an annuity unless you have a very good reason. At your age, the most likely benefit you can get from an annuity is tax deferral. Retirement accounts already benefit from tax deferral, so annuities must offer you an additional benefit if you're going to pay the costs associated with them. Putting retirement savings into an annuity for the purpose of tax deferral is like wearing a belt and suspenders at the same time to keep your pants up.

A Word on Social Security

Social security is a benefit plan that's been around since 1935 for employed persons who pay into the system for the required amount of time, i.e. forty payroll quarters. In addition to retirement, social security includes several other programs, including Medicare (the health care plan for people over sixty-five), disability benefits, and survivor benefits for spouses or dependents. These programs are funded by mandatory taxes deducted from your pay and matching taxes paid by your employer. The employee's current tax rate is 5.65 percent to be deducted from the employee's pay (until January 1, 2013, when the employee amount is slated to return to 7.65 percent) up to $110,100 in 2012 and 1.45 percent of wages over that amount. Beginning in 2013, this 1.45 percent will be increased to 2.35 percent to the extent that salaries exceed $200,000 for a single individual ($250,000 if married filing jointly) as a subsidy to pay for the new Affordable Care Act.

Social Security Benefits Statement

When you reach retirement age, you'll receive benefits based on a complex calculation using the number of years you worked, the income you earned during those years, and your age at retirement. You can request a Social Security Benefits Statement that will include a record of your earnings history by year as reported on your W-2s and the amount you and your employers paid in social security taxes. It also includes an estimate of the benefits you can expect to receive at early retirement age (sixty-two), normal retirement age (sixty-seven for those born in 1960 or later) and late retirement age (seventy). However, this is just an estimate and it's subject to change.

Counting on Social Security

There was a time when many retirees relied on social security to get them through their golden years. Today social security is considered a supplement to your retirement income, not the main source.

ESSENTIAL

You can compute estimates of your future social security benefits and get information about the factors that influence your benefit amount by visiting the planner and calculator section of the Social Security Administration's website at *www.ssa.gov.*

There's been much discussion about whether social security is going broke as the baby boom generation (those born between 1946 and 1964) starts to hit normal retirement age. Sixty-five million baby boomers will put a strain on the system when they start collecting benefits, but some experts project that even then they'll be able to pay 75 percent of the benefits that workers have earned. This will probably equate to no more than 40 percent of your preretirement income and will fall far short of what you'll need for even the simplest lifestyle. Also to be taken into account is the fact that all of the social security "surplus" has been taken by the federal government to pay for other programs, including defense, and the interest on the national debt.

CHAPTER 19

Insurance and Estate Planning

The purpose of insurance is to protect your assets against catastrophic losses that could damage your financial future. Whether the asset is a house, a car, or your income-earning ability, insurance protects you from financial disaster. Decide how much risk you can assume and insure the rest.

Life Insurance

You may or may not need life insurance, depending on your personal situation. To figure out whether or not you need life insurance, consider its purpose, which is to replace income in the event of the policyholder's death. If you're single and have no dependents, nobody is relying on the income you bring in, so you don't need life insurance.

However, if you're certain that you want to have a family (and you are otherwise financially healthy—eliminating debt, saving for retirement, etc.), you might take a look at a term policy. By purchasing a policy while you're young, you lock in lower costs. Further, you can buy a policy before any health problem rears its head and you become uninsurable (or insurance becomes more expensive due to your health problems).

If your salary is important to supporting your family, paying the mortgage, or sending your kids to college, life insurance can ensure that these financial obligations are covered in the event of your death. However, just because you're not receiving a signed paycheck doesn't mean you don't contribute to your family's income. If you are a stay-at-home mom, and something happened to you, your spouse is probably going to need some outside help to cover your absence. In 2006, financial guru Dave Ramsey estimated a $300,000–$400,000 policy would be necessary to make up the costs of everything a stay-at-home mom does every day.

QUESTION

Should I buy life insurance policies on my kids?
Although insurance companies use advertising that pulls on your heartstrings to encourage parents to buy life insurance on their kids, it's unnecessary. Your kids don't produce income and therefore their lives don't need to be insured. You'd be better off putting the money you'd spend into a savings account.

How Much Insurance Do I Need?

The amount you need depends on your other sources of income, the number of dependents you have, your debts, and your lifestyle. There's no hard and fast rule of thumb, but the general guideline is between five and ten times your annual salary.

To estimate your need, list your family's annual expenses, such as the mortgage, day-care expenses, debt payments, and educational costs. Multiply the total by the number of years you need the insurance to cover. For example, if you have a child who has four years of high school ahead, you need coverage for at least four years. Add the costs of the funeral and burial of the insured person. If you can afford the premiums, consider adding in the total balance of your mortgage so your family can pay it off after your death, as well as the cost of sending your kids to college.

The cost of pure life insurance is based on actuarial tables that project your life expectancy. If you're considered a high risk—for instance, if you're overweight or a smoker, have a pre-existing health condition, or have a dangerous hobby or occupation (such as flying)—you'll pay higher rates. It's not a good idea to lie about any of these factors on your application. The insurance company could end up refusing to pay your beneficiaries if they find that you didn't tell the truth.

ESSENTIAL

Your employer may provide a basic amount of life insurance at no cost (one or two times your salary) and allow you to purchase additional coverage at group rates, which are often lower than you could find on your own.

Life insurance comes in a wide variety of flavors. In general, you can think of two major categories: term insurance and permanent insurance. Term insurance is plain-vanilla insurance, and it's adequate for most young people. Permanent policies can be further broken down.

Term Life

Term insurance is pure insurance that offers a predetermined death benefit if you die within the term covered, but doesn't build up a cash value during your lifetime. The life insurance that many employers offer to their employees is generally term insurance that is in force only during your period of employment with the company. If you die during that time, your beneficiary receives the life insurance proceeds. If you leave the company, your policy terminates, unless you convert it to an individual policy.

If your employer doesn't offer term life insurance, you can buy a policy through an insurance agent. The cost will depend in part on your age, your health, and whether you smoke. A healthy thirty-year-old man could expect to pay approximately $300 a year for $300,000 of term life insurance. To buy the same amount of whole life insurance would cost over $3,000.

Whole Life

Whole life is part life insurance and part investment. A portion of your premium goes toward the insurance coverage, a portion goes toward administrative fees, and a portion goes toward the cash value or investment. You have no control over how the insurance company invests the cash value. Unlike term insurance, whole life covers you for your entire life. The premiums remain fixed. You can borrow against the cash value or cash the policy in, but it takes a number of years to build up any real cash value because large commissions and fees eat up most of your premium in the early years. Some experts say you lose money if you cash in a whole life policy within the first twenty years.

FACT

The Wall Street Journal has reported that half of all cash value policies are surrendered or cashed in within the first seven years. This makes the coverage very expensive because it doesn't allow enough time for the cash value to build up enough to cover the initial commissions and fees.

Variable and Universal Life

Variable life policies allow you some choice in what your cash value will be invested in, though you can usually only put it in investments your insurance company manages. With variable life, the amount of your life insurance coverage (and the required premiums) fluctuates depending on how well the investment portion is doing.

Universal life insurance differs from variable life in one important aspect. In universal life policies, the pure insurance part of the policy is kept separate from the investment part of the policy. The insurance premium costs are paid out of the proceeds of the investment part of the policy. Universal life offers more flexibility in the death benefit and the annual premium. In years when the investment portion does well, you may choose to put more of the money into building up the cash value. In years when the investment doesn't do as well, you may elect to reduce premiums or let the entire premium for the year be deducted from the investment account. You pay for this flexibility in higher administrative fees.

Which Type of Insurance Is Best?

Many financial experts recommend that you keep your life insurance and your investments separate. If you need life insurance, buy term life. If you want to invest money, do it yourself. If you're convinced that you want a whole life policy, consider consulting with a fee-only insurance advisor who, for a fixed fee, will research the various policies available to you and recommend the one that best suits your needs. Make sure the advisor isn't affiliated with any particular insurance company and receives no commissions so you can be sure you're getting objective advice.

Health Insurance and COBRA

If you have health insurance, you're most likely covered under a group plan provided by your employer or your spouse's employer. Some people who don't have the benefit of a group plan through work purchase their own individual policies or are covered under COBRA. Others have no coverage at all.

No matter how old (or young) you are, you need health insurance to protect yourself against financial disaster if you become seriously ill or have an accident. If you simply can't afford the premiums, buy a policy with a very high deductible ($5,000 for example) to limit your exposure.

Indemnity or Fee-for-Service Plans

Whether you're eligible for health insurance under an employer's plan or buying your own individual policy, you'll probably be offered a number of choices, including HMOs, PPOs, and point-of-service or indemnity plans. Indemnity plans, also referred to as fee-for-service plans, are traditional plans that allow you to go to any doctor you choose. These plans provide the most flexibility, but due to spiraling health care costs and higher premiums, fewer employers are offering them. Employers are attempting to control costs by shifting more of the cost to employees who choose these plans instead of HMOs and PPOs. Often indemnity plans require you to pay up front and submit a claim to your insurance company for reimbursement.

ALERT

If your health history makes you uninsurable, you may be able to buy health insurance through your state's risk pool. Find out what your state has to offer before you go without insurance. Start your research at *www.naic.org*, and continue on to your state's insurance resource site.

The biggest advantage of indemnity plans is that you can get your medical care anywhere you want without getting referrals or approvals from your primary-care physician. You don't have to go to doctors that belong to a specific network. Because this freedom of choice results in higher costs, insurance companies shift more of the costs to you, making indemnity plans the most expensive type of coverage.

Health Maintenance Organizations (HMOs)

An HMO is an association of health care professionals and medical facilities that sell a fixed package of health care services for a fixed price. Each patient has a primary-care physician, who is often referred to as a gatekeeper because services provided by a specialist are not covered unless the gatekeeper determines that the specialist is necessary.

The advantages of HMOs are lower and more predictable out-of-pocket costs and no claim forms. The major disadvantage is that services provided by health care professionals outside the network of your HMO aren't covered. If your network is small, your choices of doctors and other health professionals will be very limited, and services provided by specialists will be dependent on a referral from your primary physician. In HMOs, it's possible that you might not receive the medical care you need because of incentives paid to HMO doctors by the insurance company that reward doctors who limit tests and referrals to specialists.

Preferred Provider Organizations (PPOs)

PPOs combine the managed-care aspects of an HMO with the flexibility of a fee-for-service plan. When you use doctors in your approved network, more of your medical costs are covered, but you can go outside the network of health care professionals and facilities to any health care provider of your choice when you feel it's necessary. The main advantage of a PPO is the flexibility and a wide choice of doctors and facilities. The only disadvantage is that it's more difficult to predict your out-of-pocket costs and you'll pay more for your health care if you go out of network.

ESSENTIAL

If group health coverage isn't available to you, buy an individual policy, but be prepared to pay dearly for it. Research your options and compare benefits and costs. If you're in good health, consider buying a policy with a higher deductible to cover you in the event of a serious illness. You'll pay less for it but you could incur out-of-pocket costs up to the deductible amount.

What about COBRA?

Under the Consolidated Omnibus Budget Reconciliation Act (COBRA) of 1986, employees who lose medical and dental insurance for certain reasons can often buy group coverage for themselves and their dependents for a specified period of time at group rates. The law applies to group health plans maintained by private sector and state and local government employers with twenty or more full- and part-time employees in the prior year. It doesn't apply to plans maintained by the federal government or church organizations.

To be eligible, you must experience a qualifying event. These events as applied to the employees, as well as their spouses and dependents, are outlined in the COBRA Insurance Continuation chart.

Qualifying Event	Beneficiary	Coverage Period
Termination of employment; reduced hours	Employee, spouse; dependent child	18 months
Employee entitled to Medicare; divorce or legal separation; death of covered employee	Spouse, dependent child	36 months
Loss of dependent child status	Dependent child	36 months

The Process of Electing COBRA

It's your responsibility to notify your employer or your spouse's employer within sixty days of a qualifying event that the plan administrator might not know about, such as legal separation, divorce, or a child reaching the maximum age to be a covered dependent. Your failure to do so can cause you to forfeit your COBRA rights. Your plan administrator has fourteen days after the qualifying event (or after being notified by you of a qualifying event) to provide you and any other covered person with written notice of your rights under COBRA. You have an election period of sixty days from the date of the qualifying event or the date the notice was sent to choose whether to continue your coverage under the employer's group health plan.

Once you elect coverage, you need to pay premiums retroactive to the date of the qualifying event, which will provide you with continuous health insurance with no lapse in coverage. Your cost for COBRA coverage is the employer's actual cost plus a 2 percent administrative fee. You have the same grace period that the employer has from the insurance company, usually thirty days. If you don't pay the premium within the grace period, your coverage terminates. Each qualified beneficiary may elect COBRA coverage independently of any other qualified beneficiary. Coverage ends at the end of the maximum coverage period (eighteen or thirty-six months) or sooner, if one of the following occurs:

- You fail to pay your premium within the grace period.
- The employer no longer maintains any group health plan.

- You obtain coverage under another employer group plan that doesn't limit coverage for any pre-existing condition.
- You become entitled to Medicare benefits.

You may be eligible to convert your group health coverage into an individual policy at the end of the maximum COBRA continuation period. Check with your plan administrator.

ALERT

It's very important for you to familiarize yourself with your rights related to health care and other benefits. Employers are required to provide a summary plan description and plan booklets that spell out the coverage, your rights, and your responsibilities. Read this material and ask questions about anything you don't understand.

Should You Elect COBRA?

If you lose coverage and are eligible to elect COBRA, you should do so unless you have other options that provide at least basic coverage at a reasonable cost. Even if you pick up coverage with a new employer, you may want to elect COBRA during the period that you'd be subject to a pre-existing condition if you've had recent serious health problems. Be aware, however, that under the Health Insurance Portability and Accountability Act of 1996 (HIPAA), if you've been continuously covered by insurance for at least twelve months, a new plan can't limit coverage for a pre-existing condition that was covered under the previous plan. When you lose coverage, your employer or spouse's employer should give you a notice stating that you were continuously covered for twelve months so you can prove this to a new insurance company if necessary.

You may want to consider COBRA if your new employer doesn't offer a health plan or you've had recent health problems, are taking expensive prescriptions, have been declined for private health insurance, have had an accident within the election period, or are pregnant.

Health Savings Accounts

A health savings account (HSA) is a tax deductible contribution that you can make to a high deductible health plan (HDHP), which is an inexpensive health insurance plan with a much higher potential for out-of-pocket costs than traditional health insurance plans. The minimum deductible on an HDHP for 2012 is $1,200 for an individual plan and $2,400 for a family plan. Premiums may be deducted up to $3,100 per year (for 2012) in an individual plan and $6,250 per year (for 2012) for a family plan. Those fifty-five or over can increase these limits by $1,000. As long as these distributions are paying for qualified medical expenses, all growth and income on the amount contributed will be tax-free. Out-of-pocket qualified expenses for the year (not including payments for premiums) may not exceed $6,050 for individual plans and $12,100 for family plans. Any amount not spent during the tax year may be carried over to future tax years. Penalties for unqualified distributions from these plans are 20 percent of the amount of the distribution, and drugs are only considered qualified expenses if prescribed, except for insulin.

Patient Protection and Affordable Care Act

This legislation, signed into law on March 23, 2010, will require U.S. citizens to maintain qualifying health coverage or pay a penalty beginning in 2014. In 2014 the penalty will be equal to $95 per family member (not to exceed three family members) or 1 percent of their taxable income, whichever is greater. The penalty then increases in 2016 to $695 per family member or 2.5 percent of taxable income. After that the penalty will be increased annually by a cost of living adjustment. Certain exemptions will be granted for economic hardship, religious objections, etc.

In order to finance this government-sponsored program, certain tax increases will be implemented starting in 2013. Among these changes will be an increase to the Medicare portion of the payroll tax, which is to be levied on wages or self-employment income that exceeds $200,000 ($250,000 if married filing jointly). This means that the Medicare payroll tax rate of 1.45 percent will be increased to 2.35 percent for wages in excess of these threshold amounts.

There will also be a 3.8 percent tax increase on unearned income (interest, dividends, and capital gains, etc.) to the extent of the lesser of the total of the unearned income or the excess of taxpayer's adjusted gross income over the $200,000/$250,000 threshold amounts. This means that if the excess amount of the taxpayers AGI is less than their unearned income only the excess will be subject to the 3.8 percent tax.

For example, an individual taxpayer who has $300,000 in wages and an AGI of $5,000 of unearned income qualifying for the new tax will pay $2,350 on the wages exceeding the threshold amount (2.35 percent × $100,000) and $190 on his unearned income (3.8 percent × $5000). If his AGI is only $202,000, then the tax on unearned income would be limited to 3.8 percent of the excess over the $200,000 threshold amount, or $76.

Disability Insurance

Short- and long-term disability insurance protects your income-producing ability when you're unable to work due to illness or injury. Many employers provide group disability insurance as a benefit at little or no cost to employees. If there's a cost for the coverage, it's usually paid with pretax dollars and is much less than you'd pay for an individual policy. Be aware that many employers only provide short-term disability coverage. When you have both coverages through your employer, the policies often dovetail so that your long-term coverage would pick up as soon as your short-term coverage expires (if your disability lasts that long).

FACT

According to the Social Security Administration, the average twenty-year-old worker has a 30 percent chance of becoming disabled before retirement. For a thirty-year-old, disability is 4.1 times more likely than death, yet many people in their twenties and thirties insure their lives but not their income-producing ability.

The Purpose of Disability Insurance

Although the likelihood of becoming disabled is greater than the likelihood of dying during any given period of time, more people buy life insurance than disability insurance. Don't make the mistake of thinking that you're too young or healthy to require disability insurance. Before purchasing an individual disability policy, be sure you understand the terms used and read the policy carefully to make sure you know what benefits you're getting. Find out what, if any, exclusions there are, what the elimination period is, what the benefit period is, and what the definition of total disability is.

Elimination and Benefit Periods

With both types of disability insurance, there's an elimination period, which is the period of time after you become unable to work before you can begin receiving benefits under the policy. A short-term disability policy may have an elimination period of one to two weeks for illness or a shorter time for accidents. Long-term disability elimination periods are typically at least thirty days and more commonly ninety days.

If you become disabled, you'll receive benefits until you recover or reach the maximum benefit provided by your policy. Short-term disability policies pay benefits for a shorter period of time, from six weeks to two years. Long-term disability policies pay benefits for several years or until the age of sixty-five (or longer). The shorter the elimination period and the longer the benefit period, the higher the premium will be. Most policies replace only 60 percent of your income, up to a maximum of $5,000 to $10,000 per month.

Definition of Disability

The best policies will have a definition of disability that includes the inability to perform the major duties of your own occupation. Under these policies, if you're unable to perform your major duties, you can go to work in a different occupation that you *are* able to perform and still collect your disability pay. Less expensive or lower-quality policies won't pay benefits unless you're unable to do any work you're reasonably suited to do, or they'll offset your monthly benefit check against any income you're earning elsewhere. There are three types of long-term disability policies:

1. Noncancelable and guaranteed renewable: The insurance company guarantees that you'll be able to renew the policy for as long as you wish at the same premium and for the same monthly benefits, regardless of any changes in your occupation or income.

2. Guaranteed renewable: The insurance company can't drop you but it can raise prices.
3. Conditionally renewable: The company can decide not to renew your policy, perhaps when you most need it, or it can raise prices and add conditions at any time.

Obviously, noncancelable and guaranteed renewable is the best type but will also be the most expensive. Avoid conditionally renewable policies. You want to have the assurance that your coverage will be there when you need it.

Buy residual disability benefits. This means if you aren't totally disabled but can't work full-time, you'll be paid partial benefits. Expect to pay between 1 and 3 percent of your annual income for a long-term disability policy, so if you're earning $30,000, a policy will probably cost you between $300 and $900 a year. Your cost will depend on your age and the policy features you choose. The average period of disability is about three years.

Homeowner's and Auto Insurance

Homeowner's insurance protects you if your home and any structures attached to it or other structures on your property are damaged or destroyed. It also covers your home's contents if they're damaged or destroyed, and it helps protect you from liability and medical costs if someone is hurt on your property.

If you own a home, you can't afford to be without this coverage. If you want to keep costs down, choose a higher deductible, but don't forgo the insurance altogether. If your house were destroyed, you'd still be responsible for paying the mortgage, and you'd have to pay for housing elsewhere.

Be Prepared

There are several basic types of homeowner's policies. They vary by the types of perils or potential damages covered and by the extent of coverage. For example, some policies reimburse you only for the depreciated value of your belongings. You'd have to come up with a chunk of change of your own to replace the items that were destroyed. Replacement coverage, on the other hand, reimburses you for the cost to replace those items at their current prices. You should always choose replacement coverage.

The part of the insurance that covers the house itself, or the dwelling, is based on what it would cost to rebuild the house if it were completely destroyed. It's important that you increase the limits as the costs of home-building increase. You can do this by buying an inflation rider, which increases your coverage annually at the rate of inflation, but you may end up overpaying if the value of your home decreases. It's best to review your policy every year and make sure you don't have more or less coverage than you need. Homeowner's insurance doesn't cover land, so when you are deciding how much insurance you need, exclude its value.

Auto Insurance

Most states require you to have bodily injury liability insurance on your vehicle, which pays your medical bills and lost wages, the medical bills of others hurt in an accident you caused, and property damage, up to the limits you've chosen. The limits are shown in thousands of dollars as bodily injury for one person, bodily injury for more than one person, and property damage. For example, 20/40/10 would mean $20,000 of coverage for one person, $40,000 of coverage for more than one person, and $10,000 of coverage for property damage. Personal injury protection or medical coverage pays your own medical costs if you're injured in an accident. It's required in approximately one-third of all states. Some states also require you to buy additional coverage that will cover your medical costs and lost wages if you're injured in an accident caused by an uninsured motorist.

The legally required minimums for liability coverage are so low that they're not adequate if you own a house or other assets that an injured person could come after if your insurance wasn't enough to cover his or her medical expenses. Unless you have no assets to speak of, you should elect limits of at least 100/300 for bodily injury.

Collision coverage pays for repairing your car if you hit something, whether it's another car, a building, or any other object. Comprehensive coverage covers other types of damage such as theft, broken windshield, fire, flood, falling objects, and so on. Cars with a Blue Book value of $2,000 or less are probably not worth insuring for collision coverage, and you'll save a lot of money by dropping it. If you have a good driving record, consider raising your deductible to $500 or $1,000 to significantly lower your collision premiums.

Many insurance companies offer reduced premiums if you have more than one car insured with them, if you also have your homeowner's insurance with the same company, if your car has certain safety features such as antilock brakes or air bags, or you have a good driving record. If your car is expensive to repair or is a favorite with thieves, be prepared to pay higher insurance rates.

Other Types of Insurance

Do you need contact lens insurance? Air travel insurance? Rental car insurance? No, no, and probably not. Trip insurance may be worthwhile if you're going out of the country and you've prepaid large amounts, but it doesn't come cheap. Expect to pay between 3 and 7 percent of your costs in premium. For example, if your trip costs $6,000, you'll pay between $180 and $420 for trip insurance. Be sure to read the fine print very carefully.

ESSENTIAL

Don't buy travel insurance from your tour operator. If they go out of business, the insurance will do you no good. If you feel you need trip insurance, buy it from an independent company. You can get quotes on trip and other types of insurance online at Insure.com (*www.insure.com*).

Umbrella Insurance

Umbrella insurance limits your liability against a wide variety of events. Think of it as extra coverage on your homeowner's and automobile policies. Umbrella insurance covers behavior that may not be covered under those policies, and it can pay for damages above and beyond the dollar limits on those policies.

For example, you may cause an auto accident and be liable for $900,000 of medical expenses. If your auto insurance policy only covers $300,000, you're on the hook for the next $600,000. If you can't write a check for

$600,000, the person you owe can go after your home and other personal assets. Of course, the legal fees involved would be significant as well.

Umbrella insurance may protect you in the scenario above. If you have a $1 million umbrella policy, you would most likely be covered. Your auto insurance would pay the first $300,000 of damages, and the umbrella policy would pay the next $600,000. In addition, many umbrella policies will pay for your legal defense.

Umbrella insurance (or excess liability insurance) is extremely inexpensive. For $300 a year or less you can usually purchase $1 million of umbrella coverage. However, you have to maintain minimum required coverage limits on your homeowner's and auto insurance policies.

Group or Individual?

If your employer offers insurance benefits, you should take advantage of the low-cost coverage available in group insurance plans. However, remember that your insurance coverage is tied to your job. If you change jobs or quit working, your insurance coverage may go away.

Most people should investigate individual life and disability policies. If your employer offers these benefits, you may find that it's not enough to meet your needs. While you can often purchase more through your job, you should compare the costs with an individual policy. An individual policy can stay with you for multiple jobs—and cover you when you're self-employed.

What Is Estate Planning?

In your twenties and thirties estate planning may seem like a low priority, but don't believe the misconception that it's only for the elderly or the wealthy. Tragedy can strike at any age. Planning for the unexpected is best done today, especially if you have a family.

Estate-planning attorneys refer to their craft as managing your "social capital." If you (or your parents) pass away with too much in assets, a portion of your estate will be heavily taxed. The government will use those funds to pay for its foreign and domestic programs, not to mention its humongous national debt. Because your money goes to society, you can call it social capital. However, you may have your own programs that you'd like to support.

Am I Too Young for Estate Planning?

If you own anything, are married, or have kids, for example, you need a will to disclose how you would like your property to be left if you become incapacitated or die. If you have minor children, you would also need to leave your property in trust for their care, and name both a trustee over the property and a guardian to physically care for the children. A durable power of attorney for health care, a living will, and durable power of attorney for finances are important to ensure that your wishes are carried out if you become incapacitated by accident or illness and are unable to make your own health care and financial decisions.

Reviewing Your Plans

Regardless of how simple your estate plan is at this point in your life, review it whenever significant events take place. If you marry, divorce, remarry, or have a child, you may want to make changes to your will. If you move to another state, make sure your will complies with the laws in that state and is still valid. If the value of your assets changes significantly, you may want to review the terms of your will and decide if any changes are in order. If one of your heirs dies, you should change your will to remove that person. If the executor of your will, administrator of your trust, or the guardian you appointed for your kids dies or becomes incapacitated, make changes immediately.

Where There's a Will, There's a Way

A will is a legal document that's used to transfer assets you own to the people or organizations you want to leave them to after your death. In it, you name an executor (or personal representative), who is the person you choose to carry out your wishes, and an alternate in case your first choice is unable to serve. If you have minor children, you use the will to name a guardian to care for them.

Who Needs a Will?

As soon as you acquire your first assets as an adult (car, stocks, bonds, stereo equipment, savings accounts), get married, or have a baby, you should make a will. If you die intestate (without a will) the state will determine who gets what. More importantly, the state will decide who will gain guardianship over your minor children, regardless of what your wishes were and who you expressed them to. Don't operate under the common misconception that if you die intestate, your spouse will inherit all your property. In fact, if you have kids, in most states your spouse will receive between one-third and one-half of your assets and the rest will be split among your kids, no matter how young they are.

FACT

You may not feel that the person you appoint as guardian to raise your kids is the best person to manage their financial affairs. If this is the case, you can use your will to name a trustee, who will work with the guardian in your kids' best financial interest.

If you're married with no kids, in most states your spouse will get all of your assets. This might be particularly troublesome if you have children from a prior relationship. If you're unmarried and childless, the state will divide your estate among your relatives as it sees fit.

If you're in your twenties, single, and don't own much, you may feel that a will is unnecessary. Still, you probably own things that don't have any great monetary value but do have sentimental value and that you'd like a particular person to have.

What to Include in Your Will

The first step in estate planning is getting a handle on what you own so you can decide whom to leave it to. If you've followed earlier advice, you've already prepared a net worth statement and have a good idea of the value of your assets and belongings. To this list, add those items that have meaning to you but may not have a significant monetary value, such as family photo albums, personal journals, book or record collections, and pets.

Decide how you want your assets distributed if you die. For your primary beneficiaries, use percentages, not fixed dollar amounts, so that your will remains up-to-date as your assets increase or decrease. You can use fixed dollar amounts for secondary beneficiaries, for instance, if you want to leave money to a niece or nephew whom you dote on. However, you must always remember never to leave any property directly to a minor child. A trust will need to be set up so that a caretaker (called a trustee) can manage the assets for the children, make distributions for the children's benefit, and take care of trust administration.

Issues that you might want to address in your will include:

- Whether you want equal or unequal shares to go to your heirs
- What age you want your kids to be when they inherit
- How you want to distribute property that can't be divided without being liquidated or sold, such as a house
- What special arrangements you want made for kids from a previous marriage
- Whether you should make special provisions for one of your heirs who doesn't handle money wisely
- What arrangements you want made for a special-needs child who requires special care

One of the most important functions of your will is to identify whom you'd like to have raise your kids in the unlikely event that you can't. Name one person to act as guardian for each of your kids and one alternate guardian in case the first choice can't serve. If you name coguardians, such as your sister and her husband, and they split up, they could fight for guardianship. If it's your intention that your sister act as guardian, name her alone. You can name different guardians for each of your kids. For instance, if you have kids by two different spouses, you may want them to be taken care of by two different guardians. Talk to the person you want to name as guardian and make sure he or she is willing and able to do the job.

Is It Necessary to Use a Lawyer?

Although there are many software programs available for do-it-yourself wills, you must bear in mind that a last will and testament is a very formal legal document that must be drafted and executed in accordance with strict legal requirements if the will is to be declared valid by the state upon probate. Probate is the legal process of proving that the will is truly the last wishes of someone who is no longer living. Not using someone who is knowledgeable in this area could prove to be penny-wise and dollar-foolish in the long run.

ALERT

Should you be the adventurous type, Quicken WillMaker replaces the popular WillMaker software program created by Nolo, and adds the ability to generate living wills, financial powers of attorney, and many other legal documents. The software is available at office supply stores or from Nolo.com (*www.nolo.com*) for around $50.

The Legal Requirements for Signing a Will

For a will to become legal, it should be typed or computer-generated. Handwritten wills are legally binding in only twenty-five states and those states have different requirements about signing the pages and other issues. Your will must state that it's your will and it must be signed and dated. At least two (in some states three) people who won't inherit anything under the will must witness your signature and sign their names to the will. The witnesses must watch you sign and you must watch them sign. They don't need to read the will or know what's in it.

Durable Power of Attorney for Finances

A durable power of attorney (a form that must be signed in front of a notary public) allows you to appoint a trusted agent to manage your financial affairs if you become unable to do so yourself due to physical disability or mental incapacity. The power of attorney lasts until your death, unless you revoke it. The person you give power of attorney to can enter into contracts, negotiate, pay bills, buy and sell property, and handle your other financial affairs on your behalf if you're not able to. These documents are important for elderly people who may suffer from Alzheimer's disease or senile dementia, but they have to be created and signed while the person still has his mental faculties.

Keep in mind that every institution may not honor your power of attorney. Some banks or brokerage houses may require you to use one of their forms. Even if you have a legitimate legal document, they may refuse to honor your instructions. It would be wise to check with every institution that you'll need to deal with and find out if you need to use a specific form. You also must be very careful whom you choose as your agent as there are many instances of agent's abusing their position by entering into transactions for their own benefit rather than for the benefit of the person they are representing (known as the principal).

Medical Health Care Proxy and Living Will

This document, also known as a Durable Power of Attorney for Health Care, names a designated health care agent to make health care decisions for another if the person executing the document is not fit to make health care decisions for themselves. These decisions can range from signing the hospital admittance papers to making life and death decisions for certain medical procedures. Most states will only allow one person to be a designated health care agent, although you could appoint a backup in case the primary agent cannot, or will not serve in that capacity.

FACT

Make sure the insurance company you purchase a policy from has the financial strength to pay your claims. Check the company's rating at *www.moodys.com*, *www.standardandpoors.com*, or *www.ambest.com*. You should stick to insurance companies that are rated A by one or more of these rating companies.

A living will provides that in certain specified circumstances the person executing the instrument directs that all life-sustaining equipment be disconnected and life-prolonging drugs stopped. The goal of this directive is to prevent one from living a life in a permanently vegetative state with no prospect for recovery.

Probate and Trusts

Probate is the legal process that validates your will and oversees the transfer of assets from your estate to your beneficiaries after your death. Probate takes place in the probate court of the city or county where the legal residence of the deceased was located. Wills must go through probate in order to be legally validated, a process that can take anywhere from a couple of weeks to several years to complete. Attorney and court costs usually range between 3 and 5 percent, so if the estate is worth $100,000, the probate process costs between $3,000 and $5,000. The caretaker of the estate designated in the will, known as the executor, is also entitled a commission for the administration of the estate. The commission is based on the value of the probate estate and is usually determined by state statute.

Alternatives to Probate

One simple way to avoid probate is to transfer your assets to your loved ones during your life. Since the decedent will no longer own the property gifted away, this might be undesirable for a couple of reasons:

1. Once the donor relinquishes dominion and control to the donee, the donor will no longer have the right to use the asset, thus making them dependent on the whims of the donee.
2. Once the donor has transferred ownership, the donee can use the property to satisfy his creditors. In addition, the donee's future ex-spouse, in the event of separation or divorce, may have claims to the property.
3. For income tax purposes, the donee will assume the same cost as the donor. This means that if the property has significantly appreciated in value, the donee would be stuck with the donor's tax bill. If the donee had inherited the property at donor's death the tax gain would disappear.

Joint accounts with rights of survivorship is a form of co-ownership that says the title will automatically pass to the surviving owner should the other owner die. This will happen by operation of law no matter what the decedent's last will and testament provides. Again, some potential negative consequences of this form of ownership could be:

1. Either co-owner has immediate access to the whole account, which means they can spend it without the other owner's consent.
2. The property will be exposed to the creditors of both co-owners, not to mention both co-owner's future ex-spouses.
3. If either owner is in need of long-term care, the government can require that the owner spend all of the assets out of that account before qualifying for government assistance.

Using transfer-on-death accounts and designated beneficiary accounts (i.e., retirement plans and life insurance policies) will take care of the problems associated with relinquishing ownership during an owner's lifetime, but it still will expose these assets to the beneficiary's creditors and potential ex-spouse's upon death.

Trusts

A trust is a legal arrangement allowing for the transfer of property to a trustee who holds it for the benefit of another person, the beneficiary. You can be the trustee of your own trust and maintain total control, or you can indicate one or more trustees to administer your trust. After you set up a trust, you have to fund it by transferring property from your name to the trust. Since the trust is a separate legal entity, once the property is transferred, it no longer belongs to you. There are legal fees associated with setting up a trust and your situation may not warrant the expense. If you do decide to set one up, find a reputable lawyer who specializes in estate planning.

One who sets up the trust is known as a grantor. Trusts set up during the grantor's lifetime can be revocable or irrevocable. A revocable trust allows the grantor to take the property back at any time. For that reason, a revocable trust is not considered transferred for tax purposes, and the grantor must continue to pay taxes on trust income. Similarly, the government would compel the grantor to take out the property before it would give government aid for long-term care purposes.

An irrevocable trust prevents the grantor from taking back the assets once transferred into the trust. This is a recognized gift for tax purposes and long-term care purposes, although the transfer would have to be made well before applying for government assistance (generally five years) in order to qualify for Medicaid.

A well-drafted trust should protect the assets transferred into it from the named beneficiary's creditors and potential future ex-spouse, in addition to bypassing the legal process of probate. It might also come in handy if the grantor designates a successor trustee in the event that the grantor loses his or her mental capacity.

Estate Taxes

Your estate consists of everything you own, from real estate to jewelry, stocks and bonds, life insurance policies, bank accounts, a business, 401(k) funds, and other items of value. When you die, everything you leave to your surviving spouse is transferred tax-free. You're allowed to transfer a certain amount as gifts to others tax-free during your lifetime and let your estate use the balance of the credit after your death.

ALERT

The beneficiaries that you list on your retirement accounts and other assets supersede the instructions in your will. Your will only applies to assets left over after beneficiary designations are processed. If there happens to be a conflict between your beneficiary forms and your will, the beneficiary designations will overpower the will.

The amount you can transfer without incurring a tax liability is determined by the applicable exclusion amount, which in 2012, allows you to transfer $5 million tax-free in addition to the unlimited amount you could leave your spouse or to qualified charities. Furthermore, any of the $5 million unused by one spouse could be added to the surviving spouse's $5 million. This concept is known as portability. For instance, if you leave your entire estate to your spouse, you did not use any of your $5 million. Therefore your spouse can leave up to $10 million free of federal estate tax. However, most states have their own estate tax system that exempts much lower amounts and has no portability feature. Please note that federal estate tax laws currently in place are due to expire at the end of 2012.

CHAPTER 20

Living in a Postrecession World

Now that the "Great Recession" is behind us, should we return to business as usual from the prerecession days or should we allow the recession experience to influence our financial habits in the future? There are some things you need to consider when managing your finances in a post-recession world. Let's use the "wake up call" many of us received through recent hard times to forge a new way of thinking about our relationship with money.

Be a More Savvy Consumer

Unemployment remains stubbornly high, and even higher for those just starting out in the professional world. The number of real estate foreclosures remains high as well, and although we have resumed saving, debt is still at or near historic highs. Now is the time to scrutinize your spending habits. Perhaps you were forced to cut back or give up certain things during the recession that you thought you couldn't live without. Keep living without them! Try avoiding credit purchases unless you know you have the cash to pay for them. This will help you avoid taking drastic measures the next time the economy retrenches.

ESSENTIAL

Remember, attitude matters. Even in the postrecession period, think of budgeting as eating right rather than being on a diet. You eat what you want in moderate amounts, you don't binge, you don't deprive yourself, and yet you end up better off.

Institute a Savings Program

Now that more Americans are saving, make sure that you maintain a reserve account just in case a short-term emergency, such as a layoff or temporary disability, forces you to rely on savings for a stretch of time. This will also help give you peace of mind if another recession ever occurs. Most experts say that at a *minimum* you should have enough cash to meet three to six months of unavoidable living expenses.

Save for the Future

If you are fortunate enough to have a job that offers you the ability to contribute to a retirement plan with pretax dollars, then you must make every attempt to take advantage of this opportunity, especially in this postrecession time. This type of saving is the primary way to accumulate significant wealth in today's society, and ensure financial stability in the future. Always remember to pay yourself first!

In the past, you could count on the government or your employer to pony up a larger portion of your retirement income. Nowadays, very few employers provide pensions or defined benefit plans, and nobody knows what social security will look like in twenty years.

Investing in a Postrecession World

Despite the prevailing sentiment in the investment community that our economy is poised for growth, many investors remain sensitive to the previous threats to the investment market's stability. In fact, some have reduced their equity exposure to levels that will produce negative returns after inflation, and have withdrawn from publicly traded markets entirely. The CPI is measuring inflation at about a 3 percent annual rate in early 2012, while a one-year CD is yielding about 0.34 percent. A one-year Treasury bill is yielding a minuscule 0.17 percent.

If you are planning to retire on your accumulated assets (or assets you are still accumulating), you should consider getting involved in the equities market, and doing so soon. The global equities markets work and you have every right to reap the positive returns they produce. Remember, as someone in your twenties and thirties, time is on your side.

Motivated by fear and greed, the typical investor always seems to buy when prices are too high and sell when prices are too low. When you go to the supermarket and see a bottle of soda that usually sells for $2.99 on sale for $1.99, you know that that is the time to buy. Yet, when investments are "marked down" or are "on sale" the typical investor runs away. According to research reports, over the past twenty years, the average equity investor has earned about 2.5 percent annually, while the S&P 500 Index has posted a gain in the double digits. This study shows the reactive nature of current investors and exactly how much their emotions cost them in the long run.

As investors slowly emerge from the fear-induced behavior of the Great Recession, it is important to revisit the principles that have produced excellent risk and inflation-adjusted returns in the past, such as practicing wise asset allocation and portfolio diversity. When investors start following these important principles once again, they will be ready to re-enter the global capital markets.

Keep Your Investment Decisions Simple

Index mutual funds and exchange-traded funds reduce costs and provide broad exposure to specific asset classes. Generally, no one has been able to beat the market year in and year out, so active investment management is not a reasonable option. Keep costs low and stay invested. Remember, you already have the most powerful asset: time.

The most important question you should ask yourself is, "How should I gain market exposure?" You have two primary options: put your money in the market all at once, or funnel it in gradually over time.

Averaging Into the Market over Time

If you know that you want to get involved in the equity markets, but have no idea when the best time to buy is, you should definitely consider averaging into the market rather than making a lump sum investment. Determining the best way to average into the market depends on your current financial situation, such as how much cash you presently need and whether you have outstanding debts. Once you feel comfortable with your financial situation, your investment options include contributing a set amount, a fixed dollar amount, a set percentage of the remaining balance, a variable amount on a random schedule, a variable amount based on fluctuations in the market, and so on. Here are a few points to remember as you consider your strategy:

1. Put your plan in writing.
2. Be careful not to execute too many trades. If you do make too many trades, you can incur very high transaction costs. You may want to consider no-transaction-fee mutual funds as well.
3. Avoid the inclination to chase investments by making subsequent purchases at higher and higher levels. Keep in mind that many investment professionals believe that the market will continue to see positive results as global economies continue to climb. If you break your investment

up into too many pieces, you are just investing the money over a longer period of time.

It is best to try to divide the investments among the least interconnected assets. For example, if you are going to invest $10,000 into five different investments, try to choose U.S. large cap, commodities, international large cap, real estate, and maybe fixed income. Get paid while you wait to realize appreciation on your investments by investing in those companies that reward you with dividends, frequently at a tax-advantaged rate.

FACT

Dollar cost averaging (DCA) is a technique that includes buying a fixed dollar amount of an investment on a habitual basis, regardless of the share price. In general, fewer shares are bought when prices are high and more shares are bought when prices are low.

No one really knows if or when it is safe to jump back into the market. No one is going to call you and say, "Now is the right time!" You have to be confident in your investments. If you don't follow at least some of this advice, and instead, depend solely on your emotions to determine when it is right to make an investment, it is likely that by the time you start feeling safe about getting back in the game, you won't be able to keep pace with the market. For your own benefit, try to keep emotions out of your investments, and stick to a well-disciplined strategy.

Glossary of Financial Terms

Personal finance has a language all its own, but it doesn't have to be intimidating. The average person only needs to know the basics, so if you have an understanding of the terms in this glossary, you're off to a good start.

APR: Annual percentage rate; a way of expressing the interest rate on a loan. Because it includes fees that are paid up front, it gives the borrower a more accurate picture of the true cost of borrowing.

asset: Anything you own that is of monetary value, including cash, stocks, bonds, mutual funds, cars, real estate, and other items.

bankruptcy: A court process in which you acknowledge that you are unable to pay your debts and you allow your assets to be sold to repay creditors to the extent possible (Chapter 7 or liquidation bankruptcy); or, you work with the court to set up a plan to pay all or some of your debt over a period of several years (Chapter 13 or reorganization bankruptcy).

Blue Book value: The market value of a car after an allowance for depreciation is deducted. This is an estimate of what a seller can expect to receive for the vehicle upon resale, as posted in the Kelley Blue Book.

bonds: Loans from investors to corporations and governments given in exchange for interest payments and timely repayment of the debt. Interest rates are usually fixed.

budget: A forecast of income and expenses by category. Actual expenses and income are compared to the forecast and a plan is developed to reduce or control expenses to provide for savings to meet financial goals.

CD: Certificate of deposit; money lent to banks for a set period of time, usually between one month and five years, in exchange for compound interest, usually at a fixed rate.

COBRA: Consolidated Omnibus Budget Reconciliation Act; a federal law that requires most employers to allow terminating employees to continue their health insurance coverage at the employee's expense, for a limited time.

compound interest: A method of accruing interest. If interest earned on an investment is calculated only on the original amount invested, it's known as simple interest. If interest earned is calculated on the original amount plus any previously earned interest, it's known as compound interest, which makes the investment grow more quickly.

defined-contribution retirement plan: A retirement plan offered by employers that allows employees to contribute to the plan but does not guarantee a predetermined benefit at retirement. 401(k), 403(b), 457, and profit-sharing plans are examples.

DRIP: Dividend reinvestment plan. DRIPs allow investors to automatically reinvest their dividends in the company's stock rather than receive them in cash. Many companies waive the sales charges for stock purchased under the DRIP.

escrow: Money or other assets held by an agent until the terms of a contract or agreement are fulfilled. Many mortgage companies require borrowers to pay prorated property taxes monthly with their mortgage payment. These funds are held in an escrow account until payment is due to the local government.

foreclosure: A legal process that terminates an owner's right to a property, usually because the borrower defaults on payments. Home foreclosures usually result in a forced sale of the property to pay off the mortgage.

head of household: A tax-filing status that provides tax breaks to single parents who maintain a home for one or more eligible dependents.

intestate: Dying without a will that specifies who should receive the property and personal belongings of the deceased.

IRA: Individual retirement account; a retirement account that anyone who has earned income can contribute to. Amounts contributed to traditional IRAs are usually tax-deferred. Amounts contributed to Roth IRAs are not deductible but taxes are not due on the earnings at retirement.

joint tenancy with right of survivorship: Shared ownership of property by two or more people, giving the surviving owner(s) rights to a deceased owner's share. See also tenancy in common.

liability: An amount owed to creditors or others. Common liabilities include mortgage, car payments, student loans, and credit card debt.

lien: A legal claim against an asset, usually used to secure a loan.

lifestyle fund: A diversified mutual fund that adjusts itself to slowly reduce risk over time.

living will: A legal document used to specify what, if any, life-prolonging measures a person wants if he or she becomes terminally ill or incapacitated.

load: A sales charge or commission paid to a broker or other third party when mutual funds are bought or sold. Front-end loads are sometimes incurred when an investor purchases the shares and back-end loads are sometimes incurred when investors sell the shares.

marriage tax penalty: A feature of the U.S. tax system that results in married couples paying more in taxes than they would if they were single.

mutual fund: An investment that allows thousands of investors to pool their money to purchase stocks, bonds, or other types of investments, depending on the objectives of the fund.

negative amortization: The process of a loan balance growing over time, as opposed to having principal and interest payments reduce the loan.

net worth: The value of all of a person's assets (anything owned that has a monetary value) minus all of the person's liabilities (amounts owed to others).

nonmarital agreement: A written agreement between two unmarried people living together, spelling out how their finances will be handled.

PMI: Private mortgage insurance; insurance that protects a lender if a borrower defaults on a mortgage. Lenders require PMI if the mortgage exceeds 80 percent of the appraised value of the home.

points: Finance charges paid by a borrower when a loan is initiated. One point is worth 1 percent of the loan amount. Borrowers can "buy down" an interest rate to get a lower rate by paying points up front.

probate: A court process to determine the validity of a will and oversee the distribution of property upon the owner's death.

risk tolerance: An investor's ability to tolerate fluctuations in the value of an investment in the expectation of receiving a higher return.

rollover: Reinvestment of a distribution from a qualified retirement plan into an IRA or another qualified plan in order to retain its tax-deferred status and avoid taxes and penalties for early withdrawal.

Rule of 72: A method of estimating the time it will take for a certain amount of money to double at a given interest rate (72 divided by the interest rate equals roughly the number of years it will take for the money to double).

standard deduction: The fixed amount deducted from adjusted gross income allowed taxpayers who don't itemize deductions.

stock: An ownership share in a corporation, entitling the investor to a pro rata share of the corporation's earnings and assets.

tenancy in common: Shared ownership of property by two or more people, giving each owner the legal right to pass on his or her share of the property to any other person in a written will. See also joint tenancy with right of survivorship.

term life insurance: Life insurance that pays the beneficiary a predetermined amount of money as long as the covered individual dies within a specified period of time (the term of the policy).

whole life insurance: Insurance that covers an individual for his or her whole life rather than a specified term. Whole life policies contain a savings component that allows cash to accumulate over time.

will: A legal document that specifies how a person's belongings will be disposed of upon his or her death. It can also identify a legal guardian for children.

401(k): A defined-contribution retirement plan that allows participants to contribute pretax dollars to various investments.

APPENDIX B

Internet Resources

In this day and age, one of the greatest resources available to us is the Internet. There are an astounding number of websites out there. Some are very helpful, but others may have a hidden agenda or be a scam. The websites listed in this appendix are reputable sources of information. Although many of them are there mainly to offer paid services, there are plenty of useful insights that you can get for free.

Banking

Bankrate.com
www.bankrate.com

Federal Trade Commission
www.ftc.gov

Federal Deposit Insurance
Corporation
www.fdic.gov

National Credit Union
Administration
www.ncua.gov

BankDeals Blog
www.bankdealsblog.com

About.com Banking
www.banking.about.com

Budgeting and Saving Money

Financial Planning at About.com
http://financialplan.about.com

Personal Budgeting and Money
Saving Tips
www.personal-budget-planning-saving-money.com

The Dollar Stretcher
www.stretcher.com

Frugal Living at About.com
www.frugalliving.about.com

Pear Budget Spreadsheet
http://pearbudget.com

Cars

Autos at MSN
http://autos.msn.com

Autobytel
www.autobytel.com

CarBuyingTips.com
www.carbuyingtips.com

CarInfo.com
www.carinfo.com

Consumer Reports
www.consumerreports.org

Edmunds
www.edmunds.com

IntelliChoice
www.intellichoice.com

Kelley Blue Book
www.kbb.com

AutoTrader.com
www.autotrader.com

LeaseGuide.com
www.leaseguide.com

Warranty Direct
www.warrantydirect.com

Consumer Information

Consumer World
www.consumerworld.org

ConsumerREVIEW
www.consumerreview.com

Better Business Bureau
www.bbb.org

Credit and Debt

National Foundation for Credit
Counseling
www.nfcc.org

Consumer Credit Counseling
Service
www.cccsintl.org

Bankrate.com
www.bankrate.com

Myvesta Foundation
www.myvesta.org

Credit Reporting

Equifax
www.equifax.com

Experian
www.experian.com

TransUnion
www.transunion.com

Free Credit Reports
www.annualcreditreport.com

FICO
www.myfico.com

Employee Ownership

National Center for Employee
Ownership
www.nceo.org

Financial Advice

The Motley Fool
www.fool.com

CNNMoney
http://money.cnn.com

Financial Planning at About.com
http://financialplan.about.com

MSN Money
http://money.msn.com

Quicken
www.quicken.com

MsMoney.com
www.msmoney.com

SmartMoney.com
www.smartmoney.com

NewlywedFinances.com
www.newlywedfinances.com

Financial Calculators

Java Financial Calculators
www.dinkytown.net

Kiplinger.com
www.kiplinger.com/tools

Fraud

The National Fraud Information
Center
www.fraud.org

The Federal Trade Commission
www.ftc.gov

National Association of Attorneys
General
www.naag.org

Contractor Fraud
www.contractorfraud.net

Home Buying

National Association of Realtors
www.realtor.com

For Sale by Owner
www.forsalebyowner.com

Zillow
www.zillow.com

Insurance

Northwestern Mutual Financial
Network
www.nmfn.com

Insure.com
www.insure.com

Insurance Information Institute
www.iii.org

Health Insurance Association of
America
www.hiaa.org

Investing

Morningstar.com
www.morningstar.com

Investing Online Resource Center
www.investingonline.org

Savings Bonds from the Treasury
Department
www.treasurydirect.gov

Job/Occupational Information

U.S. Bureau of Labor Statistics
www.bls.gov

Monster.com
www.monster.com

Job Search at About.com
www.jobsearch.about.com

Vault
www.vault.com

Salary.com
www.salary.com

Legal Advice

Nolo
www.nolo.com

Loans and Mortgages

Federal Trade Commission on
Credit
www.ftc.gov/credit

Advice from the Mortgage
Professor
http://mtgprofessor.com

E-Loan
www.eloan.com

HSH Associates
www.hsh.com

Mortgage101.com
www.mortgage101.com

Money and Young People

Kids' Money
www.kidsmoney.org

Young Money
www.youngmoney.com

Jump$tart Coalition for Personal
Financial Literacy
http://jumpstart.org

Moving

National Association of Realtors
www.move.com

Fannie Mae
www.fanniemae.com

Moving Center
www.movingcenter.com

Podcasts and Audio Programming

Marketplace & Marketplace Money
www.marketplace.org

Wall Street Journal: Your Money Matters
http://feeds.wsjonline.com/wsj/podcast_your_money_matters

Terry Savage: The Savage Money
www.nbc5.com/money/6371520/detail.html

TaxMama's Tax Quips
http://taxquips.com/?cat=TaxQuips

On the Money
www.onthemoneyradio.org

Renting

Rentlaw.com
www.rentlaw.com

ApartmentGuide.com
www.apartmentguide.com

Craigslist
www.craigslist.org

Retirement

RetirementPlanner.org
www.retirementplanner.org

Social Security Administration
www.ssa.gov

American Association of Retired Persons
www.aarp.org

Profit Sharing Council of America
www.401k.org

Roth IRA
www.rothira.com

401(k) Help Center
www.401khelpcenter.com

Student Loans

U.S. Department of Education
http://studentaid.ed.gov

FinAid
www.finaid.com

Northwest Education Loan
Association
www.nela.net

Sallie Mae
www.salliemae.com

Taxes

H&R Block
www.hrblock.com

WorldWideWeb Tax
www.wwwebtax.com

Internal Revenue Service (IRS)
www.irs.gov

TurboTax software
www.turbotax.com

National Association of Tax
Professionals
www.taxprofessionals.com

About.com Taxes
www.taxes.about.com

We Have EVERYTHING on Anything!

With more than 19 million copies sold, the Everything® series has become one of America's favorite resources for solving problems, learning new skills, and organizing lives. Our brand is not only recognizable—it's also welcomed.

The series is a hand-in-hand partner for people who are ready to tackle new subjects—like you!

For more information on the Everything® series, please visit *www.adamsmedia.com*

The Everything® list spans a wide range of subjects, with more than 500 titles covering 25 different categories:

Business	History	Reference
Careers	Home Improvement	Religion
Children's Storybooks	Everything Kids	Self-Help
Computers	Languages	Sports & Fitness
Cooking	Music	Travel
Crafts and Hobbies	New Age	Wedding
Education/Schools	Parenting	Writing
Games and Puzzles	Personal Finance	
Health	Pets	